Felix Wiedemann
The Modern Hammurapi

CHRONOI
Zeit, Zeitempfinden, Zeitordnungen
Time, Time Awareness, Time Management

Edited by
Eva Cancik-Kirschbaum, Christoph Markschies and
Hermann Parzinger

on behalf of the Einstein Center Chronoi

Volume 20

Felix Wiedemann

The Modern Hammurapi

An Old Babylonian King in Imperial Germany

DE GRUYTER

ISBN 978-3-11-914202-1
e-ISBN (PDF) 978-3-11-222335-2
e-ISBN (EPUB) 978-3-11-222374-1
ISSN 2701-1453
DOI https://doi.org/10.1515/9783112223352

This work is licensed under the Creative Commons Attribution-NonCommercial-NoDerivatives 4.0 International License. For details go to https://creativecommons.org/licenses/by-nc-nd/4.0.

Creative Commons license terms for re-use do not apply to any content that is not part of the Open Access publication (such as graphs, figures, photos, excerpts, etc.). These may require obtaining further permission from the rights holder. The obligation to research and clear permission lies solely with the party re-using the material.

Library of Congress Control Number: 2025946803

Bibliographic information published by the Deutsche Nationalbibliothek
The Deutsche Nationalbibliothek lists this publication in the Deutsche Nationalbibliografie; detailed bibliographic data are available on the internet at http://dnb.dnb.de.

© 2026 with the author(s), published by Walter de Gruyter GmbH, Berlin/Boston, Genthiner Straße 13, 10785 Berlin. This book is published with open access at www.degruyterbrill.com.

www.degruyterbrill.com
Questions about General Product Safety Regulation:
productsafety@degruyterbrill.com

Acknowledgements

What might pique the interest of a modern historian when it comes to Hammurapi? Old Babylonia is, of course, far outside my area of expertise. From this project however, as well as from previous ones, I have learned that the exploration of ancient pasts and the ways that societies engage with previously unknown periods of human history can be highly revealing from the perspective of modern history. The idea of delving deeper into the German fascination with an ancient Babylonian king originated from a friendly invitation by Paul Michael Kurtz to present a paper at a wonderful workshop on German constructions of biblical law since the late eighteenth century, which he organised at the University of Cambridge during the hot summer of 2019. Having completed another project that led me away from the history of Ancient Near Eastern Studies to the history of Egyptology and art history, my position at the Einstein Center Chronoi allowed me to revisit and further develop the ideas I had outlined in Cambridge.

Understanding the intensive scholarly and public debates in Germany that followed the 1902 discovery of the famous stele inscribed with the Code of Hammurapi requires a consistent interdisciplinary perspective. Discursive explosions such as this cannot be reduced to developments within the field of Ancient Near Eastern Studies alone, nor can they be explained solely by their cultural or political context in the sense of a vague zeitgeist. At Chronoi, I was fortunate to be able to discuss my ideas with friends and colleagues in the field of Assyriology and to undertake the present project as part of a wider Chronoi exploration entitled "The Multiple Lives of Hammurabi", which investigates the perception of Hammurapi and his era at various later points in history and within different cultural contexts. In December 2024, we presented our ideas at an international conference organised by my Chronoi colleague Cinzia Pappi and Nicola Laneri (University of Catania), held on the occasion of the opening of the exhibition *Da Babilonia a Baghdad: Sulle tracce di Hammurabi* at the University of Catania. The 16th Melammu Symposium, organised by the DFG-Kollegforschungsgruppe "Rethinking – Governance in the Ancient Near East" in July 2023, had also provided me the opportunity to discuss my ideas surrounding the concept of "enlightened absolutism" as regards modern representations of ancient Near Eastern rulers.

I am grateful to the Executive Board of the Einstein Center Chronoi for including this monograph in the Chronoi book series. Furthermore, I would like to express my sincere thanks to all of my colleagues from Ancient Near Eastern Studies who have brought me closer to a field that seems so far removed from my own. In this respect, I am especially grateful to Cinzia Pappi and Eva Cancik-Kirschbaum, with whom I worked on "The Multiple Lives of Hammurabi". Dominique Charpin, Sophie Cluzon, Paul Delnero, and Sue Marchand also contributed helpful information and insights to this book. I fondly remember the lively conversations I had with Christian W. Hess about German ancient Near Eastern scholars at the turn of the twentieth century and the strange quirks they sometimes displayed. I clearly recall him encouraging me to choose the debate about Moses and Hammurapi as the topic for the Cambridge workshop. Sadly, he is no longer with us to witness the outcome. Finally, I would like to thank the entire Chronoi team for the inspiring time we spent together, as well as the fellows of the Center whom I had the pleasure of getting to know during my time at Chronoi.

Felix Wiedemann, July 2025

Contents

List of Illustrations — IX

Introduction — 1

1 Time and History — 14
1.1   *Ex oriente lux* in the Age of Historicism — 17
1.2   The Great Men of History — 27
1.3   Babylonian Modernity — 33

2 State and Law — 39
2.1   Enlighted Absolutism — 40
2.2   The Monarch — 47
2.3   The *Rechtsstaat* — 61

3 Religion and Ethics — 68
3.1   Hammurapi and Moses — 69
3.2   Law, Morality and *Sittlichkeit* — 77
3.3   Babylonian Secularism — 87

Summary and Outlook — 94

References — 101

Author Index — 127

List of Illustrations

Fig. 1: Eine Babel-Bibel-Allee. *Jugend. Münchner illustrierte Wochenschrift für Kunst und Leben* 8:1903 (No.13). Available from https://digi.ub.uni-heidelberg.de/diglit/jugend1903_1/0231/image,in fo,thumbs, accessed 31 May 2025. —— 2

Fig. 2: Hammurapi-Stele: © 2009 GrandPalaisRmn (Musée du Louvre) / Franck Raux, Numéro principal: SB 8, Autre numéro d'inventaire. Available from https://collections.louvre.fr/en/ark:/53355/cl010174436, accessed 31 May 2025. —— 5

Fig. 3: "Det is det persönliche Rejiment!". Pp. 6786. *Der Wahre Jacob. illustrierte Zeitschrift für Satire, Humor und Unterhaltung* 27:1910 (No. 631). Available from https://digi.ub.uni-heidelberg.de/diglit/wj1910/0319/image,info, accessed 31 May 2025. —— 52

Fig. 4: Hammurapi-Stele_Relief [dark]: © 1999 GrandPalaisRmn (musée du Louvre) / Christian Larrieu, Numéro principal : SB 8, Autre numéro d'inventaire. Available from https://collections.louvre.fr/en/ark:/53355/cl010174436, accessed 31 May 2025. —— 80

Introduction

In the spring of 1903, the popular Munich magazine *Jugend*, which gave its name to an entire artistic movement that dominated the decorative arts at the turn of the century – *Jugendstil* (Art Nouveau) – published a highly complex cartoon entitled *Eine Babel-Bibel-Allee* (fig. 1).[1] The title alluded to the so-called Babel-Bible controversy, which engrossed the German public during those months. A year earlier, the Berlin Assyriologist Friedrich Delitzsch (1850–1922) had given a public lecture on the question of how much the Bible owed to ancient Mesopotamia, which many Christians and Jews perceived as an open attack on the Old Testament respectively the Hebrew Bible. In a second lecture in January 1903, the Assyriologist sharpened his thesis, while his antisemitic motives, already present in his first lecture, became increasingly apparent.[2] What made the lectures a true scandal was the presence of an illustrious audience of cultural and political celebrities, including Kaiser Wilhelm II (1859–1941).[3] The cartoon features the most prominent names present in the debate, without distinguishing between mythical and historical figures and the actual protagonists involved. It ironically suggests placing stelae for each of them along Berlin's significant east-west axis (today Straße des 17. Juni), another contentious topic in contemporary discussions. Thus, we find Delitzsch himself, the theologian Adolf von Harnack (1851–1930) and the German-British antisemitic ideologue Houston Stewart Chamberlain (1855–1927) alongside Abraham, Moses (both of whom are portrayed in a clearly antisemitic manner), Homer, and Kaiser Wilhelm I (1797–1888), the grandfather of the Kaiser and the first ruler of the newly founded Reich.[4]

Against the backdrop of the contemporary debate, the appearance of most of these figures in a cartoon is not surprising. However, the figure on the first stele in the row is particularly significant: it is King Hammurapi of Babylon, ruler of the Old Babylonian Kingdom from c. 1792 to c. 1750 BC.[5] While the other characters were likely recognisable from the historical canon or everyday politics, Hammu-

---

[1] See on the influence of the magazine Spielmann 1988; Danguy 2009; Pearce 2024.
[2] See his lectures devoted to the subject: Delitzsch 1902, 1903, 1904, 1905.
[3] See on the debate Johanning 1988; Lehmann 1994; Sweek 1995; Arnold and Weisberg 2002; Cancik-Kirschbaum and Gertzen 2021.
[4] Space does not allow for a detailed description of the cartoon here. It also features the court chaplain of Wilhelm I Adolf Stoecker (1835–1909, well-known for his antisemitism), the Bishop of Trier, Felix Michael Korum (1840–1921), Chancellor Otto von Bismarck (1815–1898), and the Prussian field Marshall Helmuth von Moltke (1800–1891).
[5] The date of his reign is given according to the so-called middle chronology. On the life of Hammurapi see the two most recent biographies by Van de Mieroop 2005 and Charpin 2021.

Figure 1: The cartoon "Eine Babel-Bibel-Allee" was published in 1903 by the journal *Jugend*.

rapi was almost entirely unknown beyond the niche field of Assyriology before 1900. Unlike other rulers from the ancient Near East, such as the Neo-Babylonian king Nebuchadnezzar or the Assyrian ruler Sargon II, he was not mentioned in the Bible or by the ancient Greek writers; even Assyriologists had only come across his name a few decades before. The Old Testament scholar Rudolf Kittel (1853–1929) may have exaggerated when he claimed that the Babylonian king was discussed "in trains and cafés" during the late Wilhelmine era, but there can be no doubt that Hammurapi emerged as an important historical reference in the first decade of the twentieth century, with his fame seemingly taken for granted even by cartoonists.[6]

Hammurapi's comet-like rise to modern fame can be traced back to one of the great moments in the history of archaeology and Ancient Near Eastern Studies, which took place in December 1901: Three weeks before Delitzsch gave his controversial first lecture on Babylon and the Bible French archaeologists excavating the ancient site of Susa in southern Iran came across a remarkable object, a fragment of a black basalt stone covered with text in small cuneiform signs rendering the Akkadian (Babylonian) language. One month later in January 1902, two more fragments were found, thereby completing one of the most important archaeological discoveries from the ancient Near East, the Stela of Hammurapi, now housed in the Louvre in Paris. Originally erected in the southern Babylonian city of Sippar, it was probably taken by the Elamites to their capital, Susa, when these arch-enemies of the Babylonians sacked the region in the twelfth century BC.[7] The stele is probably a replica of an original that was likely erected in the Great Temple of Marduk in Babylon, and fragments from other stelae suggest that there were additional replicas in other locations.[8] The cuneiform inscriptions covering the entire object soon revealed a table of around one hundred laws and regulations, framed by a prologue and epilogue in which the king addresses the reader directly.[9] Until that moment, the only evidence for Old Babylonian law were fragments of later copies.[10] In contrast, the law collection that had now come to light, probably issued near the end of Hammurapi's reign, was almost completely intact. For

---

[6] Quote taken from Lehmann 2018, 56.
[7] See on the history of this object André-Salvini 2003; Charpin 2023, 1–2. Due to errors in early literature, the material of the stele is often referred to as diorite instead of basalt. See on the background of this error Charpin 2023, 1–2 (note 1).
[8] On the other fragments, see Nougayrol 1957; Nougayrol 1958; furthermore Charpin 2023, 16–17.
[9] In this work I will use the translation into modern English by Roth 1995a, 71–142. The individual Laws of Hammurapi (LH) are referred to as paragraphs (§).
[10] Fragments of the Laws of Hammurapi had previously been published by Felix Peiser and Bruno Meissner in the 1890s. See Peiser 1890; Meissner 1898. On the transmission and tradition of the Laws of Hammurapi in later periods of Mesopotamian history, see Oelsner 2022, 39–70, 98–105.

this reason, the text became known as the 'Code of Hammurapi', widely considered at the time to be the oldest written law in human history (fig. 2).[11]

Vincent Scheil (1858–1940), a French Assyriologist and member of the Susa expedition, immediately recognised the importance of the find and began translating the cuneiform text at a breathtaking pace. His French translation was published in summer 1902, only a few months after the object was excavated.[12] Translations into other modern languages followed apace: the Berlin Assyriologist Hugo Winckler (1863–1913) published a German version in his journal *Der Alte Orient* that very same year, and the first English translation, by Robert Francis Harper (1864–1914), followed in 1904.[13] Two years later, the Orientalist Felix Peiser (1862–1921) and the legal historian Josef Kohler (1849–1919) issued the first of a series of volumes on the Laws of Hammurapi – including a new critical edition, transcription and translation of the famous code and other Old Babylonian legal documents.[14] With the second volume, Peiser was replaced as editor by Arthur Ungnad (1879–1945); after Kohler's death in 1919, the final volume was co-edited by Paul Koschaker (1879–1951) the leading historian of ancient Babylonian law in the inter-war period.[15] While this became the standard scholarly reference edition, Scheil and Winckler also published the first popular – French and German – versions of the Laws of Hammurapi for what was commonly called the educated public.[16]

The rapid dissemination of the text of the Code of Hammurapi was accompanied by an extensive scholarly and public debate on the significance of this new find, particularly for the history of civilisation, the history of law, and the history of religion. Looking at this debate, to which the present monograph is devoted, one is immediately struck by the deep fascination of contemporary Germans for the Old Babylonian king. Hardly any author portrayed Hammurapi in a negative light, and no one employed the stereotype of 'oriental despotism' to characterise his reign.[17] Instead, he was typically depicted as a modern ruler, often compared to other admired leaders in German and European history, such as

---

[11] The Laws of Hammurapi remain a central object of scholarly interest in various fields, including Assyriology, archaeology, Biblical Studies, and Legal History. For further references, see the most recent monograph by Barmash 2020.
[12] Scheil 1902. On Scheil, see Charpin 2020.
[13] Winckler 1902; Harper 1904.
[14] Kohler and Peiser 1904.
[15] Kohler and Ungnad 1909a, 1909b, 1910, 1911; Koschaker and Ungnad 1923; see also Koschaker 1917.
[16] Scheil 1904; Winckler 1904.
[17] On the concept of 'oriental despotism', see with further references chapter 2.1 below.

Figure 2: The Stele of Hammurabi, which features the famous 'Code', was discovered by French archaeologists in the winter of 1901/1902. It is currently on display at the Louvre Museum in Paris.

Charlemagne or Frederick II (1712–1786) of Prussia (Frederick the Great). One of Hammurapi's greatest admirers was the Kaiser himself, as evidenced by a small book on kingship in ancient Mesopotamia that he wrote towards the end of his life during his Dutch exile.[18] But already shortly after the discovery of the stela, he had expressed his enthusiasm for Hammurapi in his correspondence with Chamberlain. Certainly not least to flatter the emperor, the ideologue joined the chorus, lamenting "every page of paper that is not devoted" to the "sympathetic monarch" of ancient Babylonia.[19]

In other countries too, the sensational discovery of the stele attracted considerable attention and debate. However, as I aim to demonstrate in this work, the German discourse on Hammurapi had some peculiarities. While British, American and French scholars were concerned with similar issues – notably the relationship between Babylonian and biblical law – there was neither comparable public attention nor such a political dimension to the debate. Above all, the German romance with Hammurapi was characterised by an admiration and sympathy for the Old Babylonian king that had no parallel in Britain, the USA or France (even though the stele was excavated by French archaeologists and transported to the Louvre).[20] Major discursive events, such as the Babel-Bible controversy, which had no counterpart in other countries, certainly contributed to – or even triggered – the Hammurapi hype and can hardly be separated from it. The same applies to the great German excavation in Babylon, which had begun only a few years earlier. (It should be noted that, the fact that twelve hundred years separate the Old Babylonian and Neo-Babylonian periods, the latter of which was then coming to light through excavation, was not widely registered in public perception). However, as I hope to demonstrate, the debate surrounding Hammurapi had several specific features and cannot be reduced to either the Babel-Bible controversy or the broader German 'Babelomania' of the early twentieth century. It should instead be analysed against the backdrop of the specific discourses prevalent during the Wilhelmine era.[21]

In the heyday of nationalism and race theory, positive references and identifications with particular historical figures were often based on imagined common descent or supposed direct historical connections. It is all the more surprising that

---

18 Wilhelm II 1938.
19 Chamberlain 1928, 197 (letter to William II dated 27 March 1903).
20 Due to my personal knowledge of particular languages, I only mention Britain, the USA and France here. However, I would venture to say that in no other country did the discovery of the Code of Hammurapi spark a response comparable with that it did in Wilhemine Germany.
21 For an overview of German 'Babelomania' see Polaschegg and Weichenhan 2017. Unfortunately, the book contains some misinformation about the intellectual background.

such claims did not play a central role in the admiration of Hammurapi; even racial ideologues like Chamberlain did not care that the Babylonian king was not of Indo-Germanic or Aryan origin, but rather Semitic, according to contemporary racial categories.[22] Much more crucial to the German romanticised view of Hammurapi than race were contemporary conceptions of history, law, and religion, which stood to be either confirmed or challenged by the discovery of the Old Babylonian law collections. Late nineteenth and early twentieth century Germany witnessed significant discursive shifts and transformations in all of these subject areas. The modern "regime of historicity" described by the French historian François Hartog some years ago has always been less dominant than this phrase suggests.[23] Already during the so-called "crisis of historicism" at the turn of the century, ideas of historical continuity, progress, development, or evolution – usually considered constitutive of modernity – became increasingly implausible and were partly replaced by alternative conceptions.[24] The discovery of an almost unknown period of civilisation, which embodied less of 'eternity' (a trope commonly applied to ancient Egypt) than 'modernity,' contributed to these debates and even accelerated the dissolution of older concepts.

The fact that Hammurapi was a historically attested ruler, whose deeds could be narrated like those of other so-called 'great men' was crucial in this respect and had obvious political implications. As we shall see, the debate about the Old Babylonian king in many ways reflected the political and legal discourse about the (unclear) constitutional position of the German emperor, triggered not least by the autocratic behaviour of a monarch who positioned himself within a tradition of divine rulers that he traced back to none other than Hammurapi. A similar idea was the linking of Hammurapi and selected rulers of other epochs under the conceptual framework of 'enlightened absolutism', initially introduced to characterise the reigns of Prussian and Austrian kings in the eighteenth century. Although the enlightened kings were seen as initiators of progress and modernisation for their countries, crucially they ruled without constitutional constraints. The question of governmental constitutions however, was linked to the broader concept of the rule of law, or *Rechtsstaatlichkeit*, in imperial Germany. The leading schools in the philosophy and history of law, such as natural law theory, Kantian rational law, neo-Hegelianism, and legal positivism, all attempted to claim the stele of Hammurapi for their own approach. In this context, the ancient

---

[22] This is not to say, of course, that racial theories were absent from Ancient Near Eastern Studies, quite the opposite, as I have shown elsewhere. See with further references Wiedemann 2020, 2024b.
[23] Hartog 2015. See the critique of his ideas by Lorenz 2019 and Hölscher 2020, 55–58.
[24] See with further references Oexle 2007b.

law code played a central role, as it challenged assumptions about the history of law and the relationship between positive (written) law and customary (unwritten) law. This also raised the question of the general relationship between law and morality (or *Sittlichkeit*), a central issue in modern legal philosophy since the eighteenth century, marked in the German tradition by the opposing positions of Immanuel Kant (1724–1804) and Georg Wilhelm Friedrich Hegel (1770–1831).

As we shall see, the Code of Hammurapi was employed as a historical reference for various, even contradictory, arguments in this regard. The ethical aspect was, of course, closely linked to the question of the religious basis of law. However, in the case of the Code of Hammurapi, the historical-religious question of the relationship between Old Babylonian and biblical law was far more significant. This issue became particularly contentious during the Babel-Bible controversy, as the apparent parallels between the two seemed to support Delitzsch's arguments and were thus perceived by conservative Christian and Jewish scholars as a threat to the belief in the revelation of biblical law. As a consequence, an intense debate ensued on the relationship between Hammurapi and Moses. This is usually treated by modern scholars such as Klaus Johanning, Yaakov Shavit and Mordechai Eran as a subchapter of the Babel-Bible controversy.[25] However, despite the obvious parallels, 'Moses vs. Hammurapi' became a debate in its own right, rather than just an offshoot of the discourse surrounding 'Babel and Bible'.[26]

In contemporary Germany, all debates about the relationship between Babylonia and the Bible involved the purported heirs of the ancient Israelites, the modern Jews, as is evidenced by the clearly antisemitic stereotypes in the cartoon. As a result, antisemitic motifs and prejudices played an important role in the Babel-Bible controversy and became even more strongly pronounced over the course of the debate, ultimately leading Delitzsch to become a fierce advocate of *völkisch* antisemitism in his later years.[27] The same reasoning applied to discussions of the Code of Hammurapi. The triumphant tone of certain archaeologists and Assyriologists who argued that biblical law might be a copy of older Babylonian sources, an argument that could be seen as attempting to render Moses an impostor, was motivated in large part by their personal antisemitism. Biblical law, now seemingly disenchanted by Babylonian law, had been a bone of contention for Christians since antiquity and continued to haunt modern atheists and agnostics. Against this

---

25 Johanning 1988, 291–316; Shavit and Eran 2007, 342–48.
26 Discussions about Moses and Hammurapi also took place in the Anglo-Saxon world. However, these were usually less heated than those in the German-speaking world and lacked the escalations associated with the Babel-Bible controversy. See, among others, Cook 1903; Duncan 1904; Davies 1905.
27 See especially his last book, Delitzsch 1920; on Delitzsch's antisemitism see Arnold 2021.

background, "ideas of Judaism" have always been present in fundamental critiques of law, in the sense, as David Nirenberg has argued, that anti-Judaism served as a negative foil to Western thought against which "new ways of thinking about the world" were developed.[28] As we shall see, this mechanism was also at work in the discourse surrounding the complex relationship between law, morality and constitutional rights within the German Reich. Given these implications, it is not surprising that antisemitic ideologues such as Chamberlain followed the scholarly debate on biblical law with great interest.

The intersections between Biblical Studies, Orientalism, Assyriology, and antisemitism since the late eighteenth century have rightly attracted attention in recent scholarship.[29] While it is present in all the branches of discourse that I will explore in this book, it would be a mistake to overemphasise this point and to reduce public and scholarly enthusiasm for Hammurapi and ancient Babylonia to mere antisemitism. Some of the scholars who championed Hammurapi, so to speak, were themselves Jews or of Jewish background, such as Peiser or Lehmann-Haupt, while most of the Christian defenders of Moses and the Bible were by no means defenders of the Jews. Finally, important factions of contemporary antisemitism simply did not care about the debate, as they were entirely focused on the alleged Germanic or Aryan roots of particular European peoples and thus rejected early twentieth century 'Babelomania'.

There can be no doubt that all contemporary references to and interpretations of the Code of Hammurapi were shaped by the political, cultural, and epistemological contexts of the nations that were engaging with it. As a result, these interpretations may reveal more about the discourses of history, law and religion in imperial Germany than about Old Babylonia and certain of them may seem outdated or even anachronistic. As we shall see however, this was not a unidirectional process and the reverse was also true: the famous object itself influenced discourses on history, law and religion at this time and helped contemporaries to understand their own present. Certainly, the parallels between the two worlds that seemed so striking to early twentieth century German society are no longer as convincing to us. But it is precisely this temporal entanglement between ancient Babylonia and modern Germany that makes the debate about Hammurapi highly relevant from a 'Chronoi' perspective. What I am particularly interested in is how the temporal distance between ancient Babylonia and modern Germany was bridged by overlooking the gaps. I am also intrigued by the conceptual frame-

---

28 Nirenberg 2013, 5.
29 See among others Hoheisel 1978; Kusche 1991; Cooper 1993; Pasto 1998; Hess 2000; Wiese 1999; Beckmann 2002; Heschel 2005, 2008; Rohde 2009; Gerdmar 2009; Wiedemann 2023.

work that enabled contemporary scholars to draw direct connections between different historical contexts without being accused of unhistorical or anachronistic thinking. As I will argue, this frank use of different pasts not only illuminates contemporary historiographical practice but also offers significant insights into the historical consciousness *(Geschichtsbewusstsein)* in Germany at the turn of the twentieth century. Scholars were, of course, acutely aware of the considerable differences between the societies of ancient Babylonia and modern Germany. However, a decontextualised perspective on the so called great historical men (such as Hammurapi and other rulers considered exceptional), along with the systematic and synchronic approaches to the history of law and religion that were gaining traction, allowed them to set aside traditional historiographical notions such as continuity, development, and progress.

The present work focuses on the relatively short period between 1902, the year of the discovery of Hammurapi's stele and the beginning of the Babel-Bible controversy, and the fall of the German Reich at the end of the First World War. However, to understand the complex debates surrounding conceptions of history, German constitutionalism, and the relationship between law, morality, and religion, it is necessary to trace the relevant discourses back to the early nineteenth century, or even the late eighteenth century. Later developments and texts published after 1918 are only occasionally considered. For Germany, the end of the First World War brought not only profound political changes but also a discursive rupture in most of the fields discussed here. Therefore, it is reasonable to assume that if the Code of Hammurapi had been discovered twenty years later, the entire discussion would have been different.

As a historian of modern history, my general aim is to contextualise the scholarly and public debates regarding Hammurapi in Wilhelmine Germany. Therefore, I will not attempt to relate contemporary views on the ancient Near East to recent scholarship and so 'correct' them; such an endeavour that would be presumptuous anyway, given my lack of expertise in the complex fields of Ancient Near Eastern and Biblical Studies.[30] This is not to say that the questions raised by early twentieth century scholars or the answers they found are generally obsolete today (while in many cases they are, in others quite the opposite is true). My argument is, however, that both their questions and their answers existed in a complex relationship within the political, cultural, and epistemological contexts of their time, from which they cannot be extracted. This, of course, also applies to the scholarship of today, including my own. The present short study is situated at the intersection of the history of ideas, the history of historiography, and the

---

[30] On the history of research, see Oelsner 2022, 34–38; Barmash 2020, 6–11.

political history of the German Reich during the Wilhemine era. It addresses a range of general questions that are raised and intensively discussed in these disciplines, including the formation and transformation of conceptions of time and history at the turn of the twentieth century, the contributions of Oriental Studies and Biblical Studies to contemporary antisemitism, racism, and nationalism, as well as the actual or perceived peculiarities of German historical thinking and German (constitutional) law. While the present work draws significantly on recent scholarship in these fields, it cannot explore each these issues in depth. Above all, this book is concerned with the question of German Orientalism. However, as I have argued elsewhere, I propose a different understanding of the term 'Orientalism' than that presented in postcolonial theory, which often follows Edward Said's misleading approach. Nevertheless, I do not wish to condemn such perspectives, as has become common in recent 'anti-woke' discourse from the political right, which I consider far more dangerous to academic freedom. At this point, I will only refer to my earlier remarks on the subject.[31]

Outline of the Present Work

I have chosen not to present my material in biographical or chronological order, but to follow a topical approach, dividing this monograph into three chapters that do not necessarily build on each other and can be read independently. The first chapter is of a general introductory nature and attempts to explain the German Babelomania of the turn of the twentieth century in order to understand the positive cultural references to Hammurapi. This chapter is devoted in particular to the conceptions of history that were commonly applied in the nineteenth and twentieth centuries to the presentation and writing of the history of the ancient Near East. It discusses the impact of the exploration of ancient Babylonia, specifically the discovery of Hammurapi and his code, on these conceptions, focusing on the idea of great men as almost transhistorical entities existing in a historical universe of their own. In the case of Hammurapi, it is particularly striking that he was portrayed as the ruler of an ostensibly modern society. In the second chapter, I place the discourse surrounding Hammurapi and his rule in the context of the ongoing discussions regarding the constitutional position of the monarch and the meaning of the rule of law in the newly founded German nation-state. This examination includes the classification of Hammurapi as an enlightened ruler in con-

---

[31] See Wiedemann 2020, 393–411; 2021. On German Orientalism and its peculiarities, see among others Marchand 2009.

temporary scholarly and public discourse, as well as the direct and indirect analogies that this concept evokes. The third chapter discusses the relationship between law, ethics, and religion with reference to the Code of Hammurapi. It begins with the debate within Assyriology and Biblical Studies regarding the impact of Old Babylonian law on the laws recorded in the Bible, then moves on to the philosophical discussions regarding law and morality that were prompted by the new discovery. Finally, it outlines contemporary portrayals of Hammurapi as a secular ruler, which often aligned with anti-clerical and, in many cases, antisemitic views.

A Note on Translation and Spelling

One of the major problems in writing this book was the issue of translation. German discourses on law, politics, and religion at the turn of the twentieth century feature a distinctive language that is difficult to understand, even for modern native speakers. This difficulty arises less from outdated wording and formulations and more from the use of certain key concepts that once played a significant role in such discourse, but which are either no longer in use (e.g., *Sittlichkeit*) or have changed their meaning in contemporary German. Furthermore, corresponding to different legal traditions, national peculiarities are particularly noticeable in the language of law. For instance, there are important German concepts that generally have no equivalents in other languages, such as *Rechtsstaat* (which does not only mean 'the rule of law'). Against this backdrop, providing adequate translations into modern English proved challenging. For classical philosophical or historiographical texts by authors such as Kant, Hegel, Nietzsche, and Burckhardt, I could draw on contemporary or modern translations, although I have highlighted some problematic translations where appropriate. As few translations were available for most of the German texts, in the case of longer quotations I have provided both the German original and an English translation.

Modern scholars agree that the traditional designation 'Code' or 'Codex' of Hammurapi, coined by Scheil in the early twentieth century, is highly misleading, as it originates from the European legal tradition and evokes comparisons with the Code of Justinian and the Code of Napoleon. While the actual status the Laws of Hammurapi held within the legal system of ancient Babylonia is still debated, it is clear that they were not a code in the modern sense.[32] Aware of this discussion, I will nevertheless refer to the 'Code' of Hammurapi, as this was the

---

[32] See among others Renger 1994; Westbrook 2009a [1989]; Charpin 2010, 71–82; Barmash 2020, 15–17.

term used by the participants of the debate and it deeply shaped their perceptions of Babylonian law through the conceptual analogies it provides. Concerning the spelling of the name of the Old Babylonian king, Hammurabi or Hammurapi, a definitive solution was not possible, as both variants, alongside others, appear in contemporary texts. For the sake of consistency, I have chosen a coherent spelling that follows the suggestion of my Assyriological colleagues and use 'Hammurapi' (except in direct quotes).[33]

---

[33] Transliterating the proper name from the Akkadian cuneiform script allows for both readings, Hammu-rāpi and Hammu-rabî. See on this issue Streck 1999.

1 Time and History

When reviewing the remarkable progress of their field, scholars of Ancient Near Eastern Studies in the late nineteenth century were justifiably proud of their achievements. Ancient civilisations such as that of Babylonia and Assyria, once lost and forgotten, seemed to come alive again through the discoveries made by modern archaeology and philology. Even colleagues from neighbouring fields, such as the Heidelberg historian Wilhelm Wattenbach (1819–1897), were deeply impressed:

> So viel aber war sicher, daß Ninive von der Erde verschwunden war; man kannte seine Stätte nicht mehr. Von den Einzelheiten der assyrischen Geschichte, von den Zuständen und Einrichtungen des Reiches, von den Sitten, der Cultur, der ganzen Art und Weise des Volkes wußte man gar nichts. Wie anders ist das alles jetzt![34]
>
> [But one thing was certain: Nineveh had disappeared from the face of the earth; its location was no longer known. Nothing was known about the details of Assyrian history, the conditions and institutions of the empire, the customs, culture, or the entire way of life of the people. How different everything is now!]

However, the excitement surrounding these developments can only be understood in the context of the significant role that the ancient Near East has always occupied in European cultural memory. In fact, the Babylonians and Assyrians have never been forgotten, and the Middle East has never been a blank spot on European maps or a chapter missing from European history books. Nevertheless, both maps and history books had to undergo major revisions in the nineteenth century. While colonial expansion led to a more detailed understanding of geography, archaeological discoveries unearthed valuable material and textual evidence which revealed previously unknown historical actors.

The archaeological exploration of the Middle East by Europeans varied across different regions. Already in the eighteenth century, scholars embarked on expeditions to Egypt, Palestine, and Persia to uncover the rich ancient histories of these regions.[35] Since the turn of the nineteenth century, the combination of imperial and scholarly influence that emerged with Napoleon's expedition into Egypt altered the circumstances for European scholars. In Egypt particularly, archaeological exploration often devolved into exploitation.[36] The situation in Mesopotamia was different, as the entire region remained under the control of the

---

34 Wattenbach 1868, 3.
35 See the overview by Harbsmeier 2002.
36 See among many others Jasanoff 2006, 211–306.

Ottoman Empire until the First World War. It was not until the mid-nineteenth century that systematic exploration of this latter area began. The most significant contributions were made by two diplomats, Paul-Emile Botta (1802–1870) and Austin Henry Layard (1817–1894), who excavated ancient Assyrian sites in the 1840s in what is now northern Iraq on behalf of the French and British Empires, respectively. The late nineteenth century witnessed further significant excavations at major archaeological sites spanning from the Levantine coast to northern Syria and from Turkey to southern Iraq.[37]

German scholars, fascinated by these developments but for a long time confined to their armchairs, could only enter this race later, after the establishment of the new German Empire in 1871.[38] The first German excavations at the site of Zincirli, in what is now southern Turkey, attracted relatively little public attention.[39] However, the situation changed suddenly with the great Babylon excavation, which was crucial to understanding the German fascination with all things Babylonian at the turn of the twentieth century. Commencing in 1899, a team of German excavators led by the architect Robert Koldewey (1855–1925) unearthed the vibrant remains of the capital of the Neo-Babylonian king Nebuchadnezzar (reigned 605–562 BC), well-known from the Bible and ancient Greek writers. Of particular note was the discovery of the Ishtar Gate, which was subsequently reconstructed in the Berlin Pergamon Museum.[40] Despite the fact that Hammurapi's reign predates that of Nebuchadnezzar by over a millennium, the public's fascination with the Old Babylonian and the Neo-Babylonian periods amalgamated, so that colourful objects from the first millennium BC increased general interest in a law code from the second millennium BC, and vice versa. In reality, the historical distance is akin to conflating Imperial Rome and Renaissance Rome.[41]

These "blessings of the spade," as the Assyriologist Carl Bezold (1859–1922) called them, included not only buildings and works of art but also the most valuable treasures for reassembling the history of the ancient Near East: objects containing texts.[42] The archaeological exploration of ancient Near Eastern sites was only the initial phase in studying the civilisations of the ancient Near East. The second phase involved deciphering writing systems. Only through the interplay

---

37 On the history of these discoveries, see among others Larsen 1996; Bohrer 2003; McGeough 2015.
38 On German Orientalism in this period, see Marchand 2009; additionally Mangold 2004; Wokoeck 2009.
39 See Dörner and Dörner 1989, 293–301; Wartke 2005.
40 On the palace and its reconstruction, see Fügert and Gries 2020.
41 See among others Fischer 1985, 154–300; Crüsemann 2001; Seymour 2014, 185–216.
42 Bezold 1903, 3.

of material and textual sources was it possible to adopt a historiographical approach that, in principle, was no different from that used in studying classical antiquity. Of course, even before the rise of Ancient Near Eastern Studies, it was widely recognized that Babylonia, Assyria, and Egypt were scriptural cultures. However, these scripts were neither understandable to Europeans nor to the people of the modern Middle East. While hieroglyphics were not the first ancient writing system to be decoded, their decipherment by Jean-François Champollion (1790–1832), the French founder of modern Egyptology, was the most sensational event of its kind.[43] The decipherment of cuneiform script, which had been used in the ancient Near East from the fourth to first millenniums BC, proved to be a more complex task. One of the main challenges was the fact that cuneiform was used for various languages including Sumerian, Akkadian (Babylonian and Assyrian), Hittite, and Persian, some of which were previously totally unknown. In fact, it was not until the second half of the nineteenth century that texts from the Old Babylonian period could be read by modern scholars, including the Code of Hammurapi.[44] As with archaeological exploration, philological exploration was predominantly led by the British and French in the first half of the nineteenth century. This was mainly due to the fact that accessing new materials and textual discoveries was much more convenient in London and Paris, the metropolises of the two leading colonial powers, compared to other European countries. This situation began to change during the second half of the nineteenth century, and by around 1900, German Orientalists had taken the lead in this field. There were two reasons for this shift. Firstly, the longstanding tradition and prominent status of philological, historical, and theological disciplines at German universities had led to an early and comprehensive institutionalisation of Ancient Near Eastern Studies.[45] Secondly, Germany itself had become an imperial power capable of conducting expeditions and excavations by the end of the nineteenth century, which freed scholars from relying solely on French and British materials.[46]

These archaeological and philological discoveries significantly reshaped the European understanding of the history of the ancient Near East. It is important to note however, that ancient Near Eastern history did not need to be newly written but rather *rewritten*. As the Near East had long occupied a prominent place in European conceptions of history, scholars attempted to reconcile the new findings with traditional historical narratives, but this was only possible to a certain extent. On the one hand, the discovery of Hammurapi and the Old Babylonian peri-

---

[43] On Champollion, see among others Robinson 2012; Messling 2012.
[44] See among others Pallis 1956, 132–87; Daniels 1995; Doblhofer 2008, 144–83.
[45] See Mangold 2004.
[46] See Marchand 2009.

od, dating more than a thousand years before biblical and Greek sources, appeared to confirm the traditional narrative of *ex oriente lux*, which posits that the ancient Near East was the cradle of civilisation. However, these discoveries also challenged the biblical and Greek narratives by revealing the existence of historical periods not mentioned in these sources. Furthermore, they called into question conventional chronologies and assumptions about historical continuity, progress, and evolution, including the theory of *ex oriente lux*. As we will see, the discovery of the Code of Hammurapi coincided with the 'crisis of historicism' at the turn of the twentieth century, leading to new conceptions of history. One of these was the idea of 'great men' as the central actors of history, not arranged in a temporal order but presented as contemporaries. As a result, it became possible to extract not only these heroic individuals but entire historical epochs from the course of history and arrange them in parallel. Against this background, Hammurapi's Babylonia appeared as an 'archaic modernity', so to speak, with the Kaiser's empire as its revenant.

1.1 *Ex oriente lux* in the Age of Historicism

Following Reinhart Koselleck, the idea of a homogeneous and linear human history – history in the singular, in contrast to manifold histories in the plural – only emerged in the eighteenth century and served as both a conceptual and narrative framework to make sense of the past.[47] This new idea raised the question of the specific position of different historical phenomena and entities, such as epochs, regions, peoples, empires, and nations on the timeline, as well as their relation to one another. It is not a coincidence that European universal historiography emerged in the mid-eighteenth century with a specific dedication to addressing these questions.[48] For historians of the Enlightenment, it was highly important to synchronise various data from different periods and cultural traditions in order to create a comprehensive narrative of historical events and the course of history.[49] The history of the ancient civilisations of Asia; including China, Japan, and India, with their own chronological systems and historiographical traditions

---

47 See Koselleck 1975a; Koselleck 1975b; Koselleck 2018 [1959]. Recent scholarship has rightly questioned this general claim, placing greater emphasis on the ambivalences and coexistence of contradictory temporal conceptions in the eighteenth and nineteenth centuries. See among others Seifert 1983; Sawilla 2004; Sawilla 2011; Stockhorst 2011; Jordan 2012; Décultot and Fulda 2016.
48 On the genesis of this historiographical genre, see Muhlack 1991, 97–143; for a short review see Osterhammel 1994.
49 See Jordheim 2017.

played a crucial role in this endeavour.[50] During the nineteenth century however, European historiography became increasingly exclusionary. Although Enlightenment scholars had developed comprehensive narratives that at least theoretically encompassed the history of the entire human race, the turn of the nineteenth century saw the concept of history become more limited in both space and time: *Geschichtlichkeit* was tied to certain conditions that not every actor in the past and not everywhere seemed to have fulfilled. Entire continents such as (sub-Saharan) Africa or pre-Columbian America were excluded because they were considered unhistorical, as Hegel infamously wrote: "What we properly understand by Africa, is the Unhistorical, Undeveloped Spirit, still involved in the conditions of mere nature, and which had to be presented here only as on the threshold of the World's History."[51] Although less harsh than the philosopher, Leopold von Ranke (1795–1886), the so-called founding father of modern historiography as an academic discipline, also excluded from the scope of historiographical interest all "peoples who are still in a kind of natural state."[52]

However, this exclusionary practice was not applied the Orient, a concept with no clear boundaries that encompassed Japan, China and India as well as the Middle East and North Africa, becoming restricted to the area of the modern Middle East only in the late nineteenth century.[53] The Orient was never considered *geschichtslos* (ahistorical) by German writers, which means that it was not seen as lacking in history at all. According to Andrea Polaschegg's meaningful distinction, the Orient was always seen as "another culture," but not as "the *Other* of culture".[54] The same applies to the inhabitants of the region who did not assume the same position in the writings of the nineteenth and early twentieth centuries as other non-European peoples. Instead, 'the Orientals' were assigned to a specific order, which was evident both conceptually and disciplinarily. While most non-European peoples were classified as *Naturvölker* (natural peoples) and studied within the field of ethnology, those from the Orient were categorized as *Kul-*

---

50 On the position of Asia and the Middle East in eighteenth century historiography, see Osterhammel 2018.
51 Hegel 1914, 103 (capitalisation in the original); German original Hegel 1970, 129. On the exclusion of Africa from nineteenth century historiography see among others Marx 1988. Hegel's racism and eurocentrism have been widely discussed in recent research. See among others Bernasconi 2000; Purtschert 2010; Tibebu 2011.
52 Ranke 1975b [1831/32], 85.
53 On the concept of the Orient in nineteenth century German geography, see among others Wardenga 1992; Nissel 2006; Bauriedl 2007; Escher 2011.
54 Polaschegg 2005, 135–42. For this reason alone, the concept of Orientalism, as developed by Edward Said, is not very appropriate as a general term to describe European representations of the non-European (and colonized) world. See Said 2003 [1978].

turvölker (cultural peoples) and studied by philologists and historians.⁵⁵ In fact, the concept of *Kulturvölker* was specifically aimed at placing both Orientals and Europeans within the same conceptual framework, and it is no coincidence that it emerged in the mid-nineteenth century, around the same time as the decipherment of ancient Near Eastern languages and scripts. It was the ability to write that posed as entry ticket into the realm of culture and history. Thus, for Ranke, the existence of written documents were the decisive criteria for distinguishing between natural and cultural peoples, between prehistory and history: "History only begins when the monuments are understandable and credible written records are available."⁵⁶

To understand the unique position of the ancient Near East in European conceptions of history, it is necessary to acknowledge the enduring influence of and reliance on the traditional narratives that had circulated long before the emergence of modern archaeology and historiography. By far the most influential source in this respect was the Old Testament, a text (or a collection of texts) that derived itself from the ancient Near East. The biblical books cover two areas of history that have become relevant to the historiography of the ancient Near East; the very early history of humankind, which the Bible says began in the Near East, and the history of ancient Israel and its interactions with Egypt, Babylonia, Assyria and Persia in the first millennium BC. The Book of Genesis deals with the early history of humankind, including the stories of the Flood, the Sons of Noah, and the dispersion of peoples after the destruction of the Tower of Babel. These narratives remained important in debates about the origin and diversity of humans until the early twentieth century and continue to shape popular conceptions today.⁵⁷ Compared to the stories found in Genesis, the biblical accounts of Israel's interactions with the surrounding great powers in the later books of the Old Testament, especially the Prophets and the Writings, seemed more historically accurate and thus more promising as sources for writing the history of the ancient Near East. However, the Bible has almost nothing to say about earlier periods of Babylonian history and so makes no mention of Hammurapi.⁵⁸

The second most important set of sources that greatly influenced European perspectives on the history of the ancient Near East were the writings of Greek

---

55 On the history of these concepts see Grotsch 1984.
56 Ranke 1881, 6.
57 See Wiedemann 2014; Wiedemann 2020, 437–50.
58 See among others Kratz 1999; Frahm 2007; Seymour 2014, 36–51. Some biblical scholars have, however, attempted to identify Hammurapi with figures mentioned in the Bible. See chapter 1.2 below.

and Roman historians and ethnographers.[59] Among these, the most influential was undoubtedly Herodotus, who wrote during the late fifth century BC. Herodotus' focus was primarily on the history of the Persian wars, but he also provided brief accounts of the various peoples involved in these conflicts, both historically and ethnographically.[60] However, like the Bible, Herodotus only covered the Neo-Babylonian period and thus also omits Hammurapi. The Bible and Greek historiography influenced European ideas about the ancient Near East in ways that went beyond factual history but strongly shaped European conceptions of history. According to both sources, there was no question that Egypt and Babylonia were very old and that modern societies owed a great deal to them. The two origins of mankind mentioned in the Bible, the Garden of Eden (Gen 2–3) and Mt. Ararat, where Noah's Ark rested (Gen 8:4), were located in the Middle East and Mesopotamia clearly appears as the cradle of human civilisation, symbolized by the Tower of Babel and the dispersion of humanity (Gen 11:1–9). The Bible also presents a fundamental narrative of history that has significantly influenced the European exegetical tradition since the Middle Ages: the concept of four consecutive kingdoms or world empires, as outlined in the Book of Daniel, which also indicates a geographical shift of history from east to west.[61]

It seemed clear, then, that the first chapters of human history were written in this area, and that any book on the history of humanity must begin with the history of the ancient Near East. With reference to the classical Latin phrase *ex oriente lux*, philosophers and historians at the turn of the nineteenth centuries condensed these ideas into a geo-historical narrative, claiming that not only did all cultural achievements originate in the ancient Near East, but that history itself followed the course of the sun from its eastern origins westwards. Highly influential in this respect was the essay *Auch eine Philosophie der Geschichte zur Bildung der Menschheit* ("This Too a Philosophy of History for the Formation of Humanity", 1774) by Johann Gottfried Herder (1744–1803). The philosopher, theologian and writer described the course of history by using an "analogy taken from human

---

[59] On the perspective of the classical writers on the ancient Near East, see among others Kuhrt 1995; Rollinger 2008; Seymour 2014, 51–78.

[60] However, the credibility of his work has been a subject of much debate. While Herodotus claimed to have personally travelled to Babylonia and Egypt, the question of whether or not he actually did so has been fiercely disputed since the nineteenth century. Despite this ongoing debate, it is undeniable that his work had a profound impact on the writing of ancient Near Eastern history. See Henkelmann et al. 2011; on the general importance of Herodotus in the historiographical discourse of the nineteenth century, see Marchand 2020.

[61] On the reception of the Book of Daniel, see among others Delgado, Koch and Marsch 2003; on the idea of the successive empires and the concept of *translation imperii*, see the classic study by Goez 1958; on the origins of this topos, see Oellig 2023.

ages in life", which had been introduced into the historiographical discourse by the Italian philosopher Giambattista Vico (1668–1744).[62] In Herder's view, the Orient symbolized "the Golden Age of humanity in its childhood," which he romantically portrayed as a positive alternative to his own ossified European present:[63]

> *Morgenland*, du hiezu recht auserwählter Boden Gottes! Die *zarte Empfindlichkeit* dieser Gegenden, mit der raschen, fliegenden Einbildung, die so gern alles in göttlichen Glanz kleidet: *Ehrfurcht* vor allem, was Macht, Ansehn, Weisheit, Kraft, Fußstapfe Gottes ist, und sodann gleich kindliche Ergebung, die sich ihnen natürlich, uns Europäern unbegreiflich, mit dem Gefühl von Ehrfurcht mischet. [...]. Anfangs unter der *milden Vaterregierung* war nicht eben der Morgenländer mit seinem *Zarten Kindessinne* der *glücklichste und folgsamste Lehrling?* Alles ward als Muttermilch und väterlicher Wein gekostet! Alles in Kindesherzen aufbewahrt und da mit dem Siegel *göttlicher Autorität* versiegelt! der menschliche Geist bekam die erste Formen von Weisheit und Tugend mit einer *Einfalt, Stärke* und *Hoheit*, die nun – gerade herausgesagt in unsrer philosophischen, kalten europäischen Welt wohl nichts, gar nichts ihresgleichen hat.[64]
>
> [*Orient*, you land of God truly chosen for this! The *delicate sensitivity* of these regions, with the quick, flying imagination that so likes to clothe everything in a divine radiance; *reverence* for everything that is might, respect, wisdom, force, footstep of God, and hence immediately childlike *submission*, which for them naturally, for us Europeans incomprehensibly, mixes with the feeling of reverence. [...]. [A]t the beginning, under gentle *paternal government*, was not precisely the Oriental with his *sensitive child's sense* the *happiest* and *most obedient student?* Everything was tasted as mother's milk and father's wine! Everything preserved in children's hearts and sealed there with the seal of *divine authority!* The human spirit received the first forms of wisdom and virtue with a *simplicity, strength*, and *loftiness* that now – speaking frankly – in our philosophical, cold, European world surely has nothing, nothing at all, like it.[65]]

It was Hegel who articulated the narrative scheme of *ex oriente lux* in its most complex form. Although he rejected the romantic search for origins, the Orient played an essential role in his reflections on the history of the world, appearing as the space where the history of human civilisation (not necessarily the history of humanity) began: "Asia is, characteristically, the Orient quarter of the globe, – the region of origination. [...]. In Asia arose the Light of Spirit, and therefore the history of the World."[66] Drawing upon Herder's analogy between history and the

---

62 Herder 2002 [1774], 281 (German original Herder 1994 [1774], 20). See also Vico 1744.
63 Herder 2002 [1774], 276 (German original Herder 1994 [1774], 15).
64 Herder 1994 [1774], 16–17 (emphasis in the original).
65 Herder 2002 [1774], 277–78 (emphasis in the original). On Herder's concept of the Orient, see among others Marchand 2014; Münster 2021.
66 Hegel 1914, 104 (Original German Hegel 1970, 130). On Hegel's perspective on Oriental history, see the still ground-breaking work of Ernst Schulin 1958, 13–125.

stages of human life, he presents the Orient as the "childhood of history," followed by the adolescent and adult stages represented by Greek and Roman antiquity.[67] Hegel's perspective was distinctly teleological: He viewed history as a dialectical process in which the *Weltgeist* (world spirit) unfolds, driving societal progress and shaping historical development. Furthermore, he expanded this teleological narrative to include a geographical dimension. According to this perspective, human civilisation emerged in the ancient Near East and gradually moved westward over time, ultimately reaching modern Europe:

> In der geographischen Übersicht ist im allgemeinen der Zug der Weltgeschichte angegeben worden. Die Sonne, das Licht geht im Morgenlande auf. [...] Die Weltgeschichte geht von Osten nach Westen, denn Europa ist schlechthin das Ende der Weltgeschichte, Asien der Anfang.[68]
>
> [In the geographical survey, the course of the World's History has been marked out in its general features. The Sun – the Light – rises in the East. [...] The history of the world travels from East to West, for Europe is absolutely the end of History, Asia the beginning.[69]]

Thus, in his highly influential lectures on the history of religion, philosophy, art and above all, world history, the first sections were devoted to Asia, making it clear that history began in the East.[70] Consequently, all of Hegel's lectures began by discussing China and India, followed by Persia and Egypt and largely overlooked Assyria and Babylonia. This is not only due to the fact that he wrote before the important archaeological and philological discoveries of the mid-nineteenth century, but also because Egypt and Persia played crucial roles in his geohistorical narrative that neither Assyria nor Babylon could assume.[71]

However, while the teleological view of world history continued to be influential throughout the nineteenth century, it was never an uncontroversial one. Already by the late eighteenth century, the concept of historical progress was causing contradictions. In fact, Herder's main goal in his 1774 essay was to critique the belief in progress (this was also the reason why he titled it "This *Too* a Philosophy

---

67 Hegel 1914, 111–13 (original German Hegel 1970, 135–38).
68 Hegel 1970, 133–34.
69 Hegel 1914, 109. The literature on Hegel's philosophy of history is unmanageable, but see with further references Rojek 2017.
70 The controversial editorial history of Hegel's lectures should be briefly addressed here. Although there are significant doubts regarding their authenticity, their considerable importance for the history of historical and philosophical thought in the nineteenth century is evident in the form in which they were edited. See Rojek 2017, 10–43.
71 See on Egypt Hegel 2018, 100–124 (German original). On Hegel's perspective on ancient Egypt, see Eschweiler 2022; on Persia Hegel 1914 [1831], 180–232 (original German Hegel 1970, 215–74).

of History"). Herder was not the first to be troubled by the reduction of the past to its presumed contribution to the present, which he saw as a central ethical dilemma, but he expressed his objection with the greatest verve and emotion.[72] He opposed turning ancestors into mere precursors, which he believed was the logical outcome of the concept of progress. Instead, each historical "individuality" (e.g., a people or a civilisation) should be evaluated based on its own standards: "Each nation has its center of happiness in itself, like every sphere its center of gravity!"[73] This idea, later called the 'principle of individuality' *(Individualitätsprinzip)*, became the founding concept of German historicism as it emerged in the early nineteenth century. It was most notably articulated by Ranke in his critique of Hegel's philosophy of history: "[E]very epoch is immediate to God, and its worth is not at all based on what derives from it but rests in its own existence, in its own self."[74]

Historicism certainly contributed a great deal to general German reservations about the ideas of evolution and progress and to the initially hesitant reception of Darwinism in German science.[75] However, the ethical demand of historicism to treat different cultures, epochs or nations equally did not lead to the dissolution of the concept of a singular and linear history into a plurality of unconnected histories. Like Herder, Hegel, and the historians of the Enlightenment, Ranke held to the idea of a homogeneous, linear and continuous world history. Furthermore, he was one of the last academic scholars who alone wrote a world history that claims to cover the subject in its entirety. Following the concept of *ex oriente lux*, Ranke also agreed with his predecessors that true history had begun in the East. But while eighteenth century universal historians like August Ludwig von Schlözer (1735–1809) and Johann Christoph Gatterer (1727–1799) attributed a significant role to China, India, and Persia (as did Hegel), Ranke focused on the ancient Near East as the initial area of historical origin: "The Near East, from the Euphrates to the Nile, is the cradle of civilisation."[76] Although he did not complete the first volume of his *History of the World* until 1881, the chapters on the ancient Near East were based mainly on the Bible and Greek historians, despite the fact

---

72 See for instance, Kant's remarks: Kant 1912 [1784], 20 (German original).
73 Herder 2002 [1774], 297 (German original Herder 1994 [1774], 39).
74 Ranke 2011 [1854], 21 (German original Ranke 1971 [1854], 59–60). On the principles and the critique of German historicism, see the classical study by Georg Iggers 1983. On the influence and the philosophical problems of historicism, see among others Schnädelbach 1974.
75 See among others Engels 2009.
76 Ranke 1975a [1833], 99. On the exclusion of Eastern Asia from history in nineteenth-century historiography, see Osterhammel 2018, 480–517.

that original written sources had become available.[77] As a consequence, Ranke's account focuses on Egypt, ancient Israel, Assyria, and Persia, whereas Babylonia (even the neo-Babylonian period) is essentially absent.

The practice of omitting Babylonian history only changed after numerous clay tablets had revealed more ancient periods of Mesopotamian history, including the era of Hammurapi, whose name had been recognized on various artefacts unearthed from the mid-nineteenth century onward. The most important source for Hammurapi before the discovery of his large stele was the correspondence between this ruler and his local administration, edited in 1898 by the British Assyriologist Leonard William King (1869–1919).[78] Naturally, it took some years for new information regarding the Old Babylonian period to be synthesized and inserted before what was known about Assyria in the first millennium BC. While British and French historiographical writings from the second half of the nineteenth century tended to focus on periods that readers were already familiar with from the Bible, German scholars took the initiative to include second and even third millennium BC history into their historiographical accounts.[79]

One of the first to write a comprehensive chapter on Old Babylonian history, including a discussion of Hammurapi's role, was not an academic historian or an Assyriologist but rather a Swabian teacher, Friedrich Mürdter. His popular *Kurzgefasste Geschichte Babyloniens und Assyriens* (1882) received input and corrections from no other than Friedrich Delitzsch, who would later become the most prominent German Assyriologist.[80] Four years later, further information about the Old Babylonian period was available as the *Babylonisch-Assyrische Geschichte* (1886) by the Dutch Theologian Cornelis Petrus Tiele (1830–1902) demonstrates.[81] However, the most important historiographical account of the history of the ancient Near East to be published during this period was undoubtedly Fritz Hommel's (1854–1936) *Geschichte Babyloniens und Assyriens*, released in 1885. The Munich Assyriologist stressed the extraordinary importance of Old Babylonia, believing that the entire culture of the Ancient Near East was founded during

---

[77] Ranke 1881, 3–154. This led Eduard Meyer (1855–1930), probably the most renowned scholar of ancient history at the turn of the twentieth century, to comment that the pioneer of German historiography obviously "felt entitled to disregard the valuable insights gained from fifty years of scholarly research" (Meyer 1910, 250–51). On Ranke's concept of Near Eastern history, see Schulin 1958, 147–288.
[78] King 1898; King 1900a; King 1900b.
[79] See Wiedemann 2020, 76–78.
[80] Mürdter 1882 (on Hammurapi pp. 66–67). The second edition of this small book, published after Mürdter's death in 1891, was completely revised and partly rewritten by Delitzsch. See Delitzsch and Mürdter 1891.
[81] Tiele 1886, 124–27.

this period.[82] Hammurapi plays a special role in Hommel's account because he believed that the "culmination point" of Babylonian culture occurred during his reign in the early second millennium BC.[83] Given the competition between the various fields of ancient studies, it was particularly important for Hommel to emphasize the idea that Babylonia was older than Egypt, thus highlighting the importance of the Old Babylonian period as the cradle of human civilisation:

> Die Weltgeschichte, soweit wir sie zurückverfolgen können, beginnt in Babylonien. [...] So bestätigen also Kultur-, Religions- und Kunstgeschichte in gleicher Weise, dass Babylonien und nicht Ägypten die meisten Steine zu jenem gewaltigen Bau, den wir Zivilisation nennen, beigetragen, und dass von Babylonien aus der Strom der Kultur theils zur See durch Vermittlung der Phöniker, theils auf dem Landweg über Kleinasien zu Griechen und Römern und damit später auch ins romanisch-germanische Europa gegangen ist.[84]
>
> [World history, as far back as we can trace it, begins in Babylonia. [...] Cultural, religious and art history thus confirm in the same way that Babylonia, and not Egypt, contributed most of the stones to that mighty construction which we call civilisation, and that from Babylonia the stream of culture went partly by sea through the mediation of the Phoenicians, partly by land via Asia Minor to the Greeks and Romans and thus later also to Romano-Germanic Europe.]

A few years later, Hugo Winckler, another protagonist of German Assyriology at the turn of the twentieth century, contributed a monograph to the historiography of ancient Mesopotamia, one with a differing political agenda to that of Hommel. While Hommel was a highly conservative Lutheran Protestant and Winckler a devoted atheist, they were both committed to a particularly radical version of *ex oriente lux*, which came to be called Pan-Babylonism. Scholars adhering to this school of thought claimed that ancient Babylonia was the homeland of nearly all of the cultural, religious, and technical achievements of human civilisation and emphasised the alleged ongoing influence from Babylonia, through Assyria, Palestine, Greece, and Rome, to contemporary European civilisation.[85] Suzanne Marchand rightly coined the term *furor orientalis* for the movement within German Orientalism that challenged the long-standing tradition of philhellenism and sought to break free from the "tyranny of Greece over Germany" as the British philologist Eliza May Butler (1885–1959) later famously wrote.[86] The subsequent fever of Orientalism, as exemplified by Pan-Babylonism, clearly indicates that

---

82 Hommel 1885, V. On Hommel, see Wiedemann 2023.
83 Hommel 1885, 380.
84 Hommel 1885, 3–5.
85 See Weichenhan 2016.
86 Marchand 2004; Butler 1935.

the narrative of *ex oriente lux* experienced a revival in the late nineteenth and early twentieth centuries. However, this particular narrative was distinct from that initiated by Herder, Hegel, and Ranke, and had to compete with various versions of world history. For example, nationalist and *völkisch* writers challenged the notion of *ex oriente lux* and attempted to replace it with the opposing narrative of *ex septentrione lux* ("light comes from the north") which asserts that the origin of all culture was to be found in northern Europe.[87]

These shifts can largely be attributed to the waning influence of the historical approaches that had dominated the humanities throughout the nineteenth century – a process that the theologian Ernst Troeltsch (1865–1923) later termed the "crisis of historicism."[88] In this context, Nietzsche's famous polemic against history in his second *Unzeitgemäße Betrachtungen* ("Untimely Meditations") published in 1874, was particularly influential for its description of the consequences of an all-encompassing historicisation of culture: "When the historical sense reigns without restraint, and all its consequences are realised, it uproots the future because it destroys illusions and robs existing things of the atmosphere in which alone they can survive."[89] As we will see later, this critique appeared particularly relevant to theology and legal theory, where the historical sense seemed to lead to relativism and the dissolution of traditional dogmas and norms, ultimately provoking an "anti-historicist revolution" in these fields during the 1920s.[90] By the turn of the twentieth century, the crisis of historicism, accompanied by a general decline in beliefs of continuity, progress, and development, had permeated all areas of cultural and political life, provoking various narratives of cultural despair or redemption.[91] However, it also spurred a search for new ways to connect the past with the present. One of these new approaches was the concept of 'world-historical individuals' – almost exclusively male – who kept the wheel of history turning.

---

87 See on these ideas Wiwjorra 2002.
88 Troeltsch 2002. There is a huge body of literature on the crisis of historicism at the turn of the twentieth century and its consequences. See among others Wittkau 1992; Rüsen 1993; Heinßen 2003; Oexle 2007a.
89 Nietzsche 1991 [1874], 95 (German original Nietzsche 1988 [1884], 295).
90 Nowak 1987. See also Graf 1997.
91 See the classical study by Stern 1974.

1.2 The Great Men of History

Extraordinary individuals and their deeds have always played a crucial role in the writing of history. In pre-modern historiography, there was a tendency to focus on a few influential and powerful individuals as the main protagonists, creating the illusion that a particular course of events had been shaped by their deliberate actions. This does not mean that these individuals appeared as autonomous subjects in the modern sense of the term, rather, the actions of great men were often viewed as being influenced by fate or the will of the gods. It was the larger historical narrative that conferred significance upon them and their actions.

This is also true of the modern philosophy of history as exemplified by Hegel, for whom these "world-historical individuals" were crucial: "At the forefront of all actions, including world-historical actions, are individuals as the subjectivities by which the substantial is actualized." As he went on to clarify, these individuals were merely "expressions of the substantial deed of the world spirit and therefore immediately identical with it," – a fact of which they themselves were unaware.[92] As "executors" of the world spirit *(Geschäftsführer des Weltgeistes)* the world historical individuals represented for him not only themselves but something general and universal: "The great individuals of world history, therefore, are those who seize upon this higher universal and make it their own end. It is they who realise the end appropriate to the higher concept of the spirit."[93] Although they faced different challenges in different eras, Hegel referred to these individuals as "heroes", who usually experienced a tragic fate, drawing upon the traditional metaphor of world history as a grand drama.[94]

Without making it explicit, it is clear that for Hegel, all heroic individuals were all male. Female heroism and a leading role for women were not envisioned in his philosophy of world history. The culture and politics of the nineteenth century were dominated by an extreme gender separation that excluded women from public affairs and from the writing of history. Given the masculine character of nineteenth-century historiography, it is not surprising that the concept of world-historical men remained stable even after Hegelian philosophy had lost its persuasive power.[95] In fact, without the overarching narrative that places individual lives as subordinate to a more or less teleological course of history, the significance of great men in the shaping of history becomes even more pronounced.

---

92 Hegel 1991 [1820], § 348 German original: Hegel 1986 [1820], 506.
93 Hegel 1975, 82–83. German original: Hegel 1970, 45–46.
94 Hegel 1975, 83–85. German original: Hegel 1970, 45–47.
95 On the masculine character of nineteenth-century German historiography, see Schnicke 2014.

Popular books that achieved international bestseller status, such as *On Heroes* (1841) by Scottish writer and historian Thomas Carlyle (1875–1881) and *Representative Men* (1850) by American essayist Ralph Waldo Emerson (1803–1882) demonstrate that the concept of great men was far from being a solely German obsession.[96]

When historians today wish to discuss the problematic reduction of history to the actions of certain heroic individuals during the age of historicism, and often when highlighting the gendered aspect of German historiography, they usually refer to the phrase "men make history," commonly associated with the nationalist and antisemitic historian Heinrich von Treitschke (1834–1896).[97] However, Treitschke never delved further into this topic. The historian who provided the most detailed insights on the role of great men in history after Hegel was the much less controversial Swiss historian Jacob Burckhardt (1818–1897).[98] Burckhardt's famous work, *Weltgeschichtliche Betrachtungen* ("Reflections on History"), based on lectures given at the University of Basel between 1868 to 1872, includes a chapter on "historical greatness," by which he meant the uniqueness and irreplaceability of certain great men: "The great man is a man [...] without the world would seem to us incomplete because certain great achievements only became possible through him in his time and place and are otherwise unimaginable."[99] Although Burkhardt still followed Hegel in insisting on the over-individualised and generalised character of the great men, he did so without any overarching idea of historical continuity and progression, let alone a systematic philosophy of history, writing: "These great individuals represent the coincidence of the general and the particular, of the static and the dynamic, in one personality."[100] It could be argued therefore, that the decline of the world spirit during the nineteenth century led to the emergence of the great man as the solitary protagonist of history, shouldering the weight of innovation and historical

---

96 Carlyle 1897 [1841]; Emerson 1850.
97 Treitschke 1879, 28. See the biography by Langer 1998; on his antisemitism and nationalism, see among others Holz 2001, 165–247; Kohler 2010. Treischke triggered the Berlin 'antisemitism dispute,' a key moment in the history of German antisemitism. See among others Stoetzler 2008; Berg 2023.
98 See on Burckhardt among others Gossman 2000.
99 Burckhardt 1943 [1905], 305. German original: Burckhardt 1978 [1905], 211. The complete title of the chapter used by the German editors is *Das Individuum und das Allgemeine (die historische Größe)* (Burckhardt 1978 [1905], 207–48). However, the English translation 'The Great Men of History' seems to be more accurate.
100 Burckhardt 1943 [1905], 325 (German original: Burckhardt 1978 [1905], 229). On his critique of the Hegelian philosophy of history, see Burckhardt 1943, 77–90. On Burckhardt's own philosophical approach to history, see the excellent analysis by Schnädelbach 1974, 48–75.

transformation alone. He was considered the only one capable of breaking the chains of the present with his visions and deeds and thereby paving the way for the future. As Burckhardt wrote: "For great men are necessary to our life in order that the movement of history may periodically wrest itself free from antiquated forms of life and empty argument."[101] The dominance of this idea, which is difficult for us to comprehend today, helps to explain the significant concern among many European intellectuals about the decline and cultural despair resulting from the lack of individuality in modern civilisation.

The concept of 'personality' *(Persönlichkeit)*, which Burckhardt attributed to all great men, became central and partially replaced the idea of 'individuality' at the turn of the twentieth century. It gained importance due to its psychological dimension, which allowed it to be connected to contemporary discourse across various fields regarding the inner lives of certain extraordinary individuals. There was a surge of literature discussing individuals referred to as geniuses, that explored their mental abilities, psychological traits, the purported reliance of genius on heredity, as well as their supposed racial background. In contrast to the idealistic and romantic notions of genius that prevailed in the late eighteenth and early nineteenth centuries, this renewed interest was characterised by a more scientific approach.[102] The discursive shift was primarily driven by psychological, medical, and biological studies, which aimed to unravel the mysteries of genius while still preserving its aura of mystique and integrity.[103] Usually, these works focused on poets, artists, philosophers, scientists, or other so-called *Geisteshelden* (intellectual heroes) as exemplary geniuses. However, they sometimes focused on particular kings, statesmen, or conquerors. As a result, the discussion of geniuses and world-historical individuals became intertwined. Although Burckhardt prioritised the "representatives of the mind," he discussed them together with "the great men of [...] world movement."[104] Of course, the psychology of rulers appeared to differ from that of poets: while poets were characterised by sensitivity and creativity, rulers possessed ruthlessness, decisiveness, and strength. Other mental traits, including megalomania, were found to be common to both groups, implying that the line between genius and insanity, as famously described by the Italian anthropologist Cesare Lombroso (1935–1909), was always a narrow

---

101 Burckhardt 1943 [1905], 345 (German original: Burckhardt 1978 [1905], 248).
102 See Köhne 2014. For a comprehensive exploration of the romantic and idealistic conceptions of genius, see Schmidt 1985a, 1985b.
103 See among others Galton 1875. On these approaches in general, see Hagner 2004.
104 Burckhardt 1943, 308, 324 (German original: Burckhardt 1978 [1905], 213, 229).

one.[105] Another idea shared by both types of great men was the concept of the charismatic leader *(Führer)*, prominently articulated by the sociologist Max Weber (1864–1920). However, Weber had merely adopted and transformed an idea that was already circulating among German writers of various political backgrounds in the early twentieth century.[106]

When it comes to the great men of political history – typically rulers, conquerors, and others regarded as *Tatmenschen* (men of deed)[107] – it is quite revealing to see which historical figures were deemed worthy of inclusion in this illustrious circle and which were not. There were, of course, national differences: almost all German writers put the Prussian king Frederick II, who established Prussia as one of Europe's leading powers in the eighteenth century (or was thought to have done so), at the top of their lists of great men, while abroad he was generally not considered extraordinary. Beyond certain national biases however, there was a surprising degree of consensus regarding great historical rulers. Notably, not only French but also British and German writers included Napoleon Bonaparte in their lists, even though their nations had been at war with him. Deeply impressed by a fleeting sight of the French emperor on horseback in Jena, Hegel famously regarded Napoleon as the "soul of the world" *(Weltseele)* and so included him within his list of "world-historical individuals".[108] The other two figures he mentioned in this context were Alexander the Great and Julius Caesar, who, like Napoleon, were included on almost every list of great men in the nineteenth and early twentieth centuries. Charlemagne, Genghis Khan, and Tsar Peter I of Russia were also considered prominent figures, though not all writers rated them highly. What all these rulers seemed to have in common was their ability to bring about lasting transformations in their societies and alter the power relations between their states and others. They achieved this by establishing institutions and ultimately guiding their people "from a more primitive condi-

---

[105] Lombroso 1872. The overlap between genius, insanity and degeneration fascinated various writers of the time. See among others Hirsch 1894.
[106] Weber 2019, 338–447. There is a vast literature on Weber's concept and its background. See among others Mommsen 1974 [1963]; Käsler 1990. On conceptions of charismatic leadership, see Schmidt 1985b, 194–212; Breuer 2001, 105–46.
[107] Kretschmer 1929, 158.
[108] In a letter to his friend Friedrich Niethammer in October 1806, Hegel recounted his brief encounter with Napoleon as follows: "[D]en Kaiser – diese Weltseele – sah ich durch die Stadt zum Rekognoszieren hinausreiten; es ist in der Tat eine wunderbare Empfindung, ein solches Individuum zu sehen, das hier auf einen Punkt konzentriert, auf einem Pferde sitzend, über die Welt übergreift und sie beherrscht" (Hoffmeister 1970, 120). This passage was later unjustly derided as Hegel's vision of the 'world-soul on horseback', *(Weltgeist zu Pferde)*. On the importance of Napoleon for Hegel's conception of world-historical individuals, see Schild 2018.

tion to a more advanced one" as Burckhardt wrote.[109] Most important in this context was the supposed power of the great men to create new political entities, especially states and empires, what Hegel already described in his Philosophy of Right as "the right of heroes to establish states."[110]

Although a newcomer to this gallery, Hammurapi seemed to perfectly fit the profile of history's great men. Credited with revolutionising the ancient Babylonian state and transforming it into an empire, he deserved to be mentioned in the same breath as Alexander and Napoleon, according to the Assyriologist Hugo Winckler: "What Hammurapi places alongside the great personalities of world history is what he did for his country, for Babylonia."[111] Not only did colleagues such as Bruno Meissner (1868–1947) agree, ranking Hammurapi among the "greatest historical figures" but scholars from other fields also praised the Babylonian king. The theologian and essayist Paul Rohrbach (1869–1956) referred to him as the "first clearly outlined person" in history.[112] In a similar vein, the Orientalist Hubert Grimme (1864–1942) proudly asserted just one year after the discovery of the stele that the "Hammurapi of Assyriology" had become the "Hammurapi of general world history" and had entered into "the pantheon of the leading spirits' of humanity."[113] Delitzsch went even further when he claimed that the establishment of the Babylonian state was "the personal and exclusive work" of Hammurapi. His entire conception of its development deserves our attention:

> Was aber unsere höchste Bewunderung erweckt, ist nicht sowohl, daß Hammurabi den Norden und den Süden des Landes unter seinem Zepter vereinte, sondern vielmehr, daß es ihm gelang, das neue Reich auf so fester Grundlage aufzuführen [sic], daß es bald zwei Jahrtausende unerschütterlichen Bestand hatte, daß er das ganze politische wie religiöse Leben durch Erhöhung Babylons zur Metropole des Landes in neue Bahnen lenkte und daß keine einzige der in alter Zeit hochberühmten und mächtigen Städte des Landes jemals den Versuch machte, an Hammurabis Werk zu rütteln. Das altbabylonische wie das neubabylonische Reich mit der Hauptstadt Babylons ist das persönliche und ausschließliche Werk Hammurabis, welchem eben dadurch der Ruhm eines der größten und edelsten Herrscher des alten Vorderasiens für alle Zeiten gewahrt bleibt.[114]

> [But what arouses our greatest admiration is not that Hammurapi united the north and the south of the country under his sceptre, but rather that he succeeded in establishing the new empire on such a firm foundation that it lasted unshakeably for two millennia, that he

---

109 Burckhardt 1943 [1905], 325 (German original Burckhardt 1978 [1905], 229.
110 Hegel 1991 [1820], § 350.
111 Winckler 1913, 14.
112 Rohrbach 1914, 37; Meissner 1926, 53.
113 Grimme 1903, 6.
114 Delitzsch and Mürdter 1891, 86.

steered the whole of political and religious life in new directions by raising Babylon to the status of the country's metropolis and that not a single one of the country's highly famous and powerful cities in ancient times ever attempted to shake Hammurapi's work. The Old Babylonian as well as the Neo-Babylonian empire with the capital of Babylon is the personal and exclusive work of Hammurapi, for whom the fame of one of the greatest and noblest rulers of the ancient Near East is preserved for all time.]

Given this admiration, it was not surprising that Hammurapi featured prominently in Delitzsch's first lecture on *Babel und Bibel*, delivered concurrently with the excavation of the Hammurapi stele. He portrayed the Babylonian king as a contemporary of Abraham, adopting a theory developed by French Assyriologists in the late nineteenth century. According to these scholars, Hammurapi was identical to the biblical king Amraphael, who, as stated in the Book of Genesis, was involved in a war against the city of Sodom during Abraham's time (Gen 14).[115] In his second lecture, delivered exactly one year later when the code had already become the talk of the Reich, Hammurapi assumed an even more central role, serving as the main historical figure in Babylonian history.[116] The German Kaiser, in attendance at Delitzsch's lecture, appeared to be very impressed by these remarks and afterward sent a letter to Admiral Friedrich Hollmann (1842–1913), the vice-president of the *Deutsche Orient-Gesellschaft* (German Oriental Society), that declared not only his position on the controversy but also his personal religious beliefs.[117] In the so-called Hollmann letter, written in February 1903 and published a few weeks later in a popular journal with his approval, the emperor outlined his idea of a twofold revelation: the first religious, centred on the appearance of Jesus as the Messiah, and the second historical, strongly influenced by the concept of a sequence of great men, as was discussed above:

> Es ist für mich keinem, auch nicht dem leisesten Zweifel unterworfen, daß Gott sich immerdar in Seinem von Ihm geschaffenen Menschengeschlecht andauernd offenbart. Er hat dem Menschen "Seinen Odem eingeblasen", d. h. ein Stück von sich selbst, eine Seele gegeben. Mit Vaterliebe und Interesse verfolgt er die Entwickelung des Menschengeschlechts; um es weiter zu führen und zu fördern, "offenbart" er sich bald in diesem oder jenem großen Weisen oder Priester oder König, sei es bei den Heiden, Juden oder Christen.[118]

> [It is not subject to the slightest doubt in my mind that God continually reveals Himself in the human race He has created. He has "breathed His breath" into man, that is, He has given him a piece of Himself, a soul. With fatherly love and interest, He follows the development

---

115 Delitzsch 1902, 8.
116 Delitzsch 1903, 21–25.
117 On the Hollmann letter, see with further references Markschies 2021; on Hollmann, see Matthes 1999.
118 Wilhelm II 1903, 495.

of the human race; in order to guide and promote it, He soon "reveals" Himself in this or that great sage, priest or king, whether among the pagans, Jews or Christians.]

Wilhelm's list of great men comprised a mixture of heroes from various fields, including the usual characters such as Moses, Abraham, Charlemagne, Luther, Goethe, Kant, and his own grandfather Wilhelm I. The first name he mentioned was that of Hammurapi however, thus ennobling the Old Babylonian king as the first world-historical figure in whom God had revealed Himself.[119] In his letters to Houston Stewart Chamberlain, written around the same time, the Kaiser justified this choice by referring to the supposedly close connection between Hammurapi and Abraham, even claiming, at one point, that they had been friends, and enthusiastically explained Babylonian Law to the apparently sceptical Anglo-German ideologue.[120] Due to the admirable work of Assyriologists, Wilhelm continued, a legendary figure had been transformed" into a bold man of flesh and blood" who now "stands before us in the brightest light of his achievements as the founder of an empire, as a man to whom God also revealed himself historically."[121]

In summary, Hammurapi's placement as the first in the series of great historical figures resulted in his removal from his own historical context, his parallelisation with other extraordinary rulers, and his transformation into a timeless figure. Furthermore, Hammurapi came to be depicted as an almost modern ruler and his kingdom as an almost modern state.

1.3 Babylonian Modernity

According to the Bible, the central source of the *ex-oriente-lux* narrative, Babylon did not represent the primitive origins of human civilisation but rather its first historical peak. For this reason, the ancient Mesopotamian metropolis became a quasi-transhistorical symbol of the condition of civilisation. This symbolic imprint had a lasting effect and continued to shape the public's perception of the information disseminated regarding ancient Babylonia by archaeologists and Assyriologists during the nineteenth and twentieth centuries. Against this backdrop, the past and the present became increasingly intertwined, with 'modernity' emerging

---

[119] Wilhelm II 1903, 495. On this idea, see also Cancik-Kirschbaum 2007, 181–83; Cancik-Kirschbaum 2008.
[120] Chamberlain 1928, 189–90 (letter from Wilhelm II to Chamberlain, 16 February 1903).
[121] Chamberlain 1928, 190 (letter from Wilhelm II to Chamberlain, 16 February 1903).

as the dominant trope in German writings on ancient Babylonia. Everything considered Babylonian began to be viewed as a symbol of modernity, and references to ancient Mesopotamia within the context of modern culture, art, and architecture became abundant.[122] An example of German Babelomania from this time is Berlin's Klosterstrasse underground station which opened in 1913 and is still in use today. Its walls are decorated with stylised palm trees, a motif borrowed from the façade of the throne room in King Nebuchadnezzar's palace, excavated by Robert Koldewey just a few years earlier.[123]

While artists and architects drew inspiration from Babylonian material remains to create a distinctly modern form of art and architecture, others were particularly fascinated by the character of the Babylonian state which seemed to embody the 'archaic modernity' that Babylonia represented to many. This fascination with the Babylonian state was particularly central to Wilhelm II. In his defence of the Babylonians written to Chamberlain, the Kaiser emphasised what were in his view the genuinely modern character of Babylonian political institutions:

> Die Babylonier waren unzweifelhaft ein so fabelhaft hochentwickeltes Volk und mit so vollkommen modernen Staatseinrichtungen und Anschauungen auf dem Gebiet der Politik, Kriegsführung usw., wie wir es uns gar nicht haben träumen lassen; das tritt alle Tage klarer hervor. Sie waren die Franzosen der damaligen Zeit, denn ihre Sprache war die Verkehrssprache aller damaligen zivilisierten Völker, die zu der Zeit das Mittelmeer befuhren.[124]
>
> [The Babylonians were undoubtedly a fabulously advanced people with such perfectly modern state institutions and views in the fields of politics, warfare, etc., as we could never have imagined; this becomes clearer every day. They were the French of that time, because their language was the lingua franca of all civilised peoples who then sailed the Mediterranean.]

The Code of Hammurapi seemed to provide the best evidence of the modernity of Babylonian society. Although most scholars did not forget to mention its "strange archaic features"[125] present in certain areas, such as criminal law, they generally agreed on the astonishingly advanced society the code seemed to reflect. In particular, scholars emphasised the supposedly progressive and modern character of Babylonian law in comparison with other ancient legal traditions, especially biblical law. As an example, many pointed to Hammurapi's abolishment of blood vengeance, commonly regarded as a major problem of oriental and especially so-called Semitic societies in the nineteenth and early twentieth cen-

---

122 For examples, see Polaschegg and Weichenhan 2017.
123 See Scheel 2023. On Babylonian glazed brick decoration and its modern reconstructions see Fügert and Gries 2020.
124 Chamberlain 1928, 191–92 (letter from Wilhelm II to Chamberlain, 16 February 1903).
125 Kohler 1904b [1903], 59.

turies.¹²⁶ Unfavourable comparisons with biblical law, with its laxer regulation of blood vengeance began to be made, with the legal historian Kohler writing: "In this respect, Babylonian civilisation is superior to Israelite civilisation."¹²⁷ Summarising penal law in the Code of Hammurapi, Kohler explicitly emphasised its modernity, – not only relative to biblical law but also in comparison to any of the legal traditions that superseded it in the Middle East, especially Islamic law.¹²⁸ In addition, he claimed that Babylonian judicial and political life as a whole was also modern in many respects, concluding that "Babylonia developed a legal culture" that had much more in common "with our culture than with the biblical traditions."¹²⁹ When reviewing the historical significance of the Code of Hammurapi the historian Lehmann-Haupt came to a similar conclusion:

> In der sittlichen Höhe des Rechtsbewusstseins, die sich in vielen Bestimmungen ausspricht, der hohen und damals schon alten Entwickelung des Geschäftsverkehrs, die sie voraussetzen, der zum Teil äußerst feinen Kasuistik übertreffen diese Gesetze weitaus alles, was uns von antiken Gesetzsammlungen aus den Anfängen der jedesmaligen Geschichte eines Volkes erhalten ist.¹³⁰

> [In the high ethical consciousness of what is right expressed in many provisions, the high and then already long-established level of commerce and business that they imply; the, at times, extremely fine casuistry, these laws far surpass anything that we can find in ancient collections of statutes from the beginnings of the history of any people.]

What fascinated scholars at the beginning of the twentieth century most was the detailed regulation of the economic sphere in the Code of Hammurapi. This is why the focus of Koschaker's work was on private sector arrangements such as the rules regarding debt and property or buying and selling.¹³¹ The way the Babylonians managed trade and commerce was studied intensively and seemed to testify to a "high level of commercial development" in that early period.¹³² As these rules had no parallels in biblical law they were believed to be evidence that Babylonia had reached a level of civilisation much higher than that of ancient Israel, and much earlier. It is clear that, from this point onward, German scholars began to merge their own experiences of economic transformation with the newly available information regarding the ancient Near East. At the turn of the twentieth

---

126 See for instance the references to Semitic peoples in Post 1894, 226–61.
127 Kohler 1904b [1903], 59. See also Kohler and Peiser 1904, 126, 139; Kohler 1914, 57, 62.
128 Kohler and Peiser 1904, 139.
129 Kohler and Peiser 1904, 142–43.
130 Lehmann-Haupt 1905, 6.
131 Koschaker 1917, 7–110.
132 Lehmann-Haupt 1905, 6.

century, Germany had experienced economic growth that overtook that of the United Kingdom, the birthplace of industrialisation, and so became Europe's largest industrial nation. Describing the Babylonian economy using the same language usually reserved for the contemporary German economy resulted in Babylonia appearing as an almost modern capitalist society. This is particularly evident in the works of Kohler:

> Ein blühender Landbau, ein ziemlich ungebundenes Privateigentum an Grund und Boden ist bereits zu erkennen: die Bevölkerung kauft und verkauft, mietet und vermietet frei; auf dem Euphrat wird ein eifriger Stromhandel betrieben, Compagniegeschäfte werden gemacht, Darlehen und andere Geldgeschäfte sind an der Tagesordnung, und so bereitet sich schon der ungeheure Geldverkehr vor, der das spätere babylonische Leben kennzeichnete.[133]

> [Flourishing agriculture, fairly unrestrained private ownership of land and soil can already be seen: the population buys and sells, rents and lets freely; there is a bustling river trade on the Euphrates, business is done between companies, loans and other monetary transactions are the order of the day; and so the enormous monetary transactions that characterised later Babylonian life began to take shape.]

Kohler was particularly interested in the Babylonian financial system, which he believed to be a fully developed banking system in the modern sense.[134] His fascination with ancient economics clearly corresponded to his fascination with modern economics, as evidenced by the striking parallels between his descriptions of ancient Babylonia and the modern economy that appeared to epitomize of the future, that of the United States of America. In 1904 while working on his research involving the Code of Hammurapi, Kohler embarked on a trip to the USA in order to receive an honorary doctorate from the University of Chicago; during a stopover in Washington D.C., he even had a private audience with President Theodore Roosevelt.[135] The German legal historian experienced the USA as a country of "exuberant vitality"[136] and was deeply fascinated by the emerging economic power of this former European colony. In his later writings, Kohler returned again and again to his memories of America, describing it as a land of an eternal future:

> Nie in meinem Leben sind so mächtige und tiefgehende Eindrücke auf mich eingestürmt wie in den 3 ½ Wochen, in denen mir ein Blick in die neue Welt vergönnt war. Und nun stand diese neue Welt vor uns, in wunderbarer Größe und Kraft und Herrlichkeit, daß wir, wie

---

133 Kohler and Ungnad 1909b, 1.
134 Kohler and Wenger 1914, 57.
135 On Kohler's trip to the USA, see Spendel 1983, 36–37.
136 Kohler 1906, XI.

ergriffen von einem neuen Zeichen, gleich jenen Conquistadoren, den Boden küssen mochten – das Land der kurzen Vergangenheit und der ewigen Zukunft!¹³⁷

[Never in my life have I been so overwhelmed by powerful and profound impressions as in the three and a half weeks during which I was granted a glimpse of the New World. And now this New World stood before us, in wonderful grandeur and power and glory, so that, as if seized by a new sign, we wanted to kiss the ground like those conquistadors – the land of the short past and eternal future!]

There are striking similarities between Kohler's visions of Babylonia and America, which become evident when considering the role each plays in his historical imagination. Contrary to the notion of *ex oriente lux*, Hammurapi's Babylonia did not represent for him the dawn or primitive origin of civilisation as a historical process culminating in the Americas. Instead, both areas are portrayed as lands without a past, focused solely on the future, and thus removed from the course of history: Babylonia symbolised past modernity, while the USA embodied future modernity.

Such historical decontextualisation, even to the point of extraction from the chronological timeline, was a common feature of German representations of Hammurapi's Babylonia in the early twentieth century and aligned well with the search for anti-historicist narratives for presentation of the past. This phenomenon is also evident in the popular conceptions of the great men of history previously described. While Hegel's world-historical individuals each occupied a specific place in history, the great men of later writers appeared to transcend time, existing outside of their temporal setting. As 'super-historical' actors, they were not compared with their contemporaries, but only with the great men of other great eras. This tendency was illustrated by the cartoon discussed in the introduction of the present work, which mockingly addresses the idea (fig. 1). Although the order of the stelae in that depiction, beginning with that of Hammurapi, implies a certain chronological sequence, there is no clear hierarchy among the great men: none of them stand upon the shoulders of another and no man represents the primitive beginnings upon which the others built. Rather, the placement of the stelae along an imagined great avenue in Berlin suggests that these persons coexisted. In this way, history was compressed into a non-temporal juxtaposition of exceptional eras, linked together in a chain.

Though it was not always made explicit, it is important to recognize the significant shift in the general understanding of history that occurred at the turn of the twentieth century during the 'crisis of historicism'. The idea of continuous history gradually gave way to the belief in certain exceptional periods such as Old

---

137 Kohler 1908, 100–101.

Babylonia and Classical Greece or Rome, each of which were supposedly shaped and led by heroic individuals. In comparison to these great epochs, other periods came to be seen as insignificant. In this context, the tables of geniuses and great men that listed Hammurapi alongside Alexander, Napoleon, or Frederick II were not as out of place as they may initially seem. They were simply based on different, non-chronological, and non-linear conceptions of history that had gained popularity long before the emergence of *Posthistoire* in the late twentieth century. As we will now see however, these conceptions were not developed in a vacuum, but rather corresponded with certain developments in the political and juridical sphere.

2 State and Law

As we have seen, German scholars placed Hammurapi alongside other historical figures considered great, such as Moses, Alexander, Charlemagne, and Frederick II of Prussia. All of these men were removed from their historical contexts and presented as timeless heroes and almost as contemporaries due to the universal achievements they seemed to embody. In national historiography, Frederick II of Prussia was considered by far the most significant epigone of Hammurapi, as he was the most revered ruler in German history, admired by both conservatives and liberals, the nobility and the middle classes. Furthermore, there appeared to be a deeper typological connection between ancient Babylon and modern Prussia (or Germany), what could be termed a true 'elective affinity'. In nineteenth and twentieth-century German historiography and political theory, Frederick II's reign came to represent a specific type of government that was increasingly attributed to rulers of very different eras: enlightened absolutism *(aufgeklärter Absolutismus)*. Subsequently, the term quickly became an established characterisation of Hammurapi's reign, although some avoided the German term *aufgeklärt* in favour of *erleuchtet* (illuminated or enlightened), or described the Babylonian king's rule as 'despotism' rather than 'absolutism'.[138] These concepts implied certain ideas about the nature of a state, the form of its government, and its laws, which, when transferred to different historical periods appeared to link them all the more closely. Behind these ideas, there existed a specific monarchical ideal: a strong and unfettered king who ruled like a strict yet just father, always personally concerned for the welfare of his state and his subjects. However, the scholarly and public representations of historical rulers deemed 'enlightened', including Hammurapi, during the Wilhelmine period also mirrored the contemporary controversies surrounding the constitutional role of the German Kaiser, particularly regarding the so-called 'personal rule' of Wilhelm II. Closely linked to the perception of Hammurapi as an enlightened ruler was the association of his famous code with the rule of law, or more precisely, with the German concept of the *Rechtsstaat*, which in this period became an object of national pride.

---

138 For Old Babylonia as an "enlightened despotism" see Kohler 1904b [1903], 64; for the use of the term "enlightened absolutism" *(erleuchteter Absolutismus)* see Lehmann-Haupt 1905, 45. But even without explicit reference to these phrases, comparisons of Hammurapi's rule to that of Frederick II of Prussia was quite common. See for instance Kohler and Peiser 1904, 2; Meissner 1926, 53; Wilhelm II 1938, 27.

2.1 Enlighted Absolutism

The concept of 'enlightened absolutism' or 'enlightened despotism' – the two terms have usually been used interchangeably – has been increasingly questioned in modern historiography.[139] The extent to which we can genuinely assert that the governance of certain eighteenth-century rulers was actually "influenced by the political theory of Enlightenment philosophy", as claimed in a famous definition by the German historian Fritz Hartung, appears as questionable as whether the combination of opposing terms such as 'enlightenment' and 'absolutism' truly constitutes a coherent historical concept.[140] In recent decades, even the suitability of the term 'absolutism' as a historiographical concept has come under scrutiny.[141] As a result, historians have either sought to avoid using the term 'enlightened absolutism' altogether or have chosen to use it only in quotation marks. Instead, alternative, though also contested, terms such as 'reform absolutism' *(Reformabsolutismus)* have emerged to characterise the style of government of eighteenth-century European rulers.[142]

In French, British, and American historiography, the concept of enlightened despotism is usually associated with the work of the French historian Michel Lhéritier (1889–1951) who chaired the International Commission of Historical Sciences in the 1920s and 1930s, which aimed to provide a working definition of the concept.[143] In German historiography and political theory however, the idea of enlightened absolutism had a longer history, appearing as early as the middle of the nineteenth century but remaining controversial. That this idea as a whole appealed to scholars until the end of the twentieth century can only be understood by reviewing the history of its two component concepts. Though the term *Aufklärung* did not come to denote an entire epoch until the mid-nineteenth century, it had already been established as a philosophical, educational, and political program in the second half of the eighteenth century.[144] Kant's famous essay *Beantwortung der Frage: Was ist Aufklärung?* ("An Answer to the Question: What is Enlightenment?"), written in 1784, was particularly influential in popularising the

---

139 On this debate, see among others Hartung 1955; Aretin 1974; Krieger 1975; Niedhart 1979; Ingrao 1986; Aretin 1988; Scott 1983; Scott 1990a; Baumgart 2000; Birtsch 1996; Reinalter 2002; Reinalter and Klueting 2002; Graber 2006; Sellin 2011, 156–64; Demel 2010, 61–92; Demel 2015.
140 Hartung 1955, 20.
141 See among others Henshall 1992; Schilling 2008.
142 See Demel 2019.
143 See Scott 1990b, 7–9.
144 See Stuke 1972.

term.¹⁴⁵ In contrast, the term 'absolutism' in its current sense did not emerge until the first half of the nineteenth century, after the era it is used to describe, had ended (particularly in northern and western Europe).¹⁴⁶ Combining the two concepts to create the idea of 'enlightened absolutism' occurred even later, as we will see. It already had, however, a precursor in the French terms *despotisme éclairé* and *despotisme légal* which were coined in the late eighteenth century.

The political concept of despotism can be traced back to Aristotle, but it has undergone major transformations and changes in meaning in later reception.¹⁴⁷ In modern political thought, the term gained new currency through the writings of the French philosopher Charles de Montesquieu (1689–1755). As early as 1721 in his *Lettres Persanes* ("Persian Letters"), he used 'despotism' to describe the supposedly typical style of government in the Middle East, not so much to denounce 'the Orient' as to hold up a mirror to French absolutism.¹⁴⁸ He revived the concept in a more systematic manner in his work *De l'esprit des lois* ("The Spirit of Laws"), published in 1748.¹⁴⁹ In this significant contribution to modern political theory, Montesquieu argued that the presence of "subordinate intermediate powers" between the ruler and his subjects was essential to the nature of any true and legitimate monarchy. In contrast, he portrayed despotism as a degenerate form of monarchy, within which kings ruled without institutional constraints, another clear critique of the French political system. Montesquieu's despot thus acts not according to the law, but solely based on personal desires and passions, resulting in an autocratic and arbitrary form of governance that amounts to tyranny.¹⁵⁰

However, not all of his contemporaries shared this highly negative view of autocratic rule or despotism. In a notable departure from Montesquieu, the Physiocrats, a group of French economic theorists who held significant positions in the absolutist state, sought to differentiate between despotism and tyranny. They advocated for a legal and just form of autocratic rule – the *despotisme légal* – in which the ruler develops the country in accordance with the goals of the Enlightenment.¹⁵¹ In contrast, the philosopher Denis Diderot (1713–1784) and others opposed this reappraisal of despotism and introduced the term *despo-*

---

[145] Kant 1923 [1784].
[146] Blänkler 2011, 34–46.
[147] See the classical account by Koebner 1951. On the transformations of this concept, see Kogge and Wilhelmi 2019.
[148] Montesquieu 1721a, 1721b. On the emergence of the idea of 'oriental despotism' in the eighteenth century, see among others Figueira 1995; Kaiser 2000; Rubiés 2005; Nippel 2013.
[149] Montesquieu 1748a, 1748b.
[150] Montesquieu 1748a, 24 (book II, chap. 4).
[151] See Holldack 1974; futhermore Krieger 1975, 20–25.

tisme éclairé with polemical intent: a deliberately contradictory formulation, this term suggested that despotism and enlightenment were mutually exclusive. These thinkers aimed to express that autocratic rulers always remain despots, even if they pretend to embrace the ideals of the Enlightenment.[152] Similar debates took place on the other side of the Rhine.[153] In the German-speaking world, it seemed particularly controversial whether the term 'despotism' could be applied to Frederick's Prussia. Kant was inconsistent in his statements: on the one hand, he strictly adhered to Montesquieu's theory of the separation of powers; following which, Frededrick's absolutist Prussia was clearly a despotic state. On the other hand, Kant referred to "the age of Enlightenment" in his famous article *Was ist Aufklärung* as the "century of Frederick."[154] Other scholars were similarly ambivalent. The historian Ludwig Schlözer, for example, praised Prussia's contributions to the Enlightenment while also acknowledging the dangers of autocratic rule, thereby coining the term "wise despotism".[155] In the early nineteenth century, expressions such as 'enlightened despotism' and 'enlightened absolutism' appeared quite frequently in political discourse and were used more or less as synonyms, usually in a polemical manner, to denounce certain regimes that presented themselves with an enlightened veneer. For example, the liberal historian and jurist Karl von Rotteck (1775–1840), in his influential *Staatslexikon*, referred to the rule of Ferdinand VII (1784–1833) of Spain, who abolished the first Spanish constitution in 1813, as "enlightened" or "liberal absolutism" (in quotation marks), while declaring that this type of absolutism was the most reprehensible of all.[156]

Contrary to what is often claimed, the term 'enlightened absolutism' was therefore not coined by the historian and economist Wilhelm Roscher (1818–1894), but it was undoubtedly he who systematised the concept and introduced it into political theory in his influential article *Umrisse zur Naturlehre der drei Staatsformen* ("Outline of the Natural History of the Three Forms of Government"), published in 1847.[157] Herein, Roscher distinguished three main stages in the development of absolutism in Europe. The first was the "confessional absolutism" of the sixteenth and seventeenth centuries, which was expressed in its Catholic variant under Philip II of Spain (1527–1598) and in its Protestant variant under Elizabeth I of England (1533–1603). This stage was then replaced in the sec-

---

152 On this development, see Sellin 1976, 90–92.
153 See Blänkler 2011, 30–34.
154 Kant 1923 [1784], 40.
155 Schlözer 1785, 292.
156 Rotteck 1840, 662. For further examples, see Blänkler 2011, 50–54.
157 The article was published in three parts: Roscher 1847a, 1847b, 1847c. See also Roscher 1874, 380–81; Roscher 1889.

ond half of the seventeenth century by "courtly absolutism," a type of governance which Roscher saw as epitomised by the rule of Louis XIV in France. The third and most advanced stage in his scheme was "enlightened absolutism," which he believed had only been fully developed in Prussia under Frederick II and in Austria under Joseph II (1741–1790). In fact, Roscher's distinction was not actually based on comparative historical analysis, but on the way these rulers had presented themselves during their reigns; in other words, it was based on monarchical propaganda. The mottoes he associated with the three types of rule were "cuius regio, eius religio" for confessional absolutism, "l'état, c'est moi" (as attributed to Loius XIV) for courtly absolutism, and "Le roi, c'est le premier serviteur de l'état" (as attributed to Frederick II) for enlightened absolutism.[158] The national bias of Roscher's three-stage model is obvious: although he maintained a liberal perspective and was by no means seeking to rehabilitate absolutism (whether enlightened or not) as a general form of government, he clearly preferred the 'evolutionary' path via which Germany had developed into a modern state, characterised by the top-down social reforms introduced by an 'enlightened absolutism', to the irreformable courtly absolutism of the French which led to revolution.

Roscher's model was quickly adopted by German scholars although some still preferred the term 'enlightened despotism' because it had the advantage of having been used already in the eighteenth century. For example, the historian Heinrich von Treitschke praised Frederick II in the first volume of his popular work *Deutsche Geschichte im Neunzehnten Jahrhundert* ("German History in the Nineteenth Century'", published 1879) for introducing "enlightened despotism" as a "new principle of the state", based on the idea of fulfilling one's duties to one's state and nation.[159] Treitschke contrasted Frederick, the Prussian "despot", positively with other German princes who had ruled Germany like "little sultans."[160] This in itself suggests that the term 'despot' did not necessarily carry a distinctly Oriental connotation in the nineteenth century and could be viewed positively in comparison with examples from the Orient (i.e., the 'sultans'). However, as a specialist in nineteenth-century history, Treitschke did not elaborate much on this conception. It was a different story with Reinhold Koser (1852–1914), an archivist and author of a prominent biography of Frederick II, who critically adopted Roscher's approach.[161] Whereas Roscher had presented enlightened absolutism

---

[158] Roscher 1847c, 450–51.
[159] Treitschke 1879, 96.
[160] Treitschke 1879, 98.
[161] See Koser 1893, 1903.

as the most advanced form of absolutist rule, Koser argued that Frederick's "enlightened despotism" represented an absolutist rule already in decline, a form that would mark the end of this type of government in European history.[162] While Roscher's typology had been based on the rulers' own self-descriptions and mottoes, Koser sought to substantiate the distinction between the despotism of Louis XIV and that of Frederick II by pointing to their different philosophical and legal legitimations:

> Das Eigenthümliche und Neue in dem "aufgeklärten" Despotismus ist also [...] auf der einen Seite: seine Berufung auf das Naturrecht, seine Anerkennung der Vertragstheorie, sein Bewußtsein von den daraus sich ergebenden Verpflichtungen; auf der anderen Seite: die Vorstellung von der Unwiderruflichkeit, Unbedingtheit der dem Staatsoberhaupt durch den Staatsvertrag zugestandenen Vollgewalt. In der eifersüchtigen und mißtrauischen Wahrung der Vollgewalt gegen jede Mitwirkung der Unterthanen bei der Entscheidung ist der Absolutismus Friedrich II. in nichts von dem Ludwig's XIV, der aufgeklärte Despotismus in nichts von dem unaufgeklärtem unterschieden.[163]

> [The peculiar and new thing in "enlightened" despotism is, therefore [...] on the one hand: its appeal to natural law, its recognition of the contract theory, its awareness of the obligations arising from it; on the other hand: the idea of the irrevocability, the unconditionality of the supreme power granted to the head of state by the state contract. In the jealous and mistrustful safeguarding of the full power against any participation of the subjects in the decision, the absolutism of Frederick II did not differ in any way from that of Louis XIV, the enlightened despotism in any way from the unenlightened.]

For both Roscher and Koser, enlightened absolutism and enlightened despotism together represented a more advanced and modern form of rule than classical French absolutism. However, these scholars' descriptions of the aforementioned type of rule were ambivalent, as they also pointed out certain negative and truly despotic characteristics of supposedly enlightened rulers. Nevertheless, in the following decades positive images of eighteenth-century rulers prevailed, particularly in the case of Frederick II, who came to be regarded as one of the great men of German history, with his darker side generally overlooked. The resulting works were highly nationalistic portrayals, such as those found in *Die Hohenzollern und ihr Werk* ("The House of Hohenzollern and its Deeds") published in the middle of the First World War by the historian Otto Hintze (1861–1940). Hintze praised Frederick's "truly Prussian sense of duty" and defended him against accusations of despotic rule:

---

[162] Koser 1889, 248.
[163] Koser 1889, 279.

> Es handelte sich aber bei ihm nicht um die Verwirklichung doktrinärer Ideale der Aufklärung, sondern um rein praktische Ziele, vor allem um die Macht und Größe seines Staates und die Wohlfahrt seiner Untertanen, die er nicht bloß im materiellen Sinne faßte.[164]
>
> [[F]or him it was not about realising the doctrinaire ideals of the Enlightenment, but rather about purely practical goals, especially the power and greatness of his state and the welfare of his subjects, which he understood not only in a material sense.]

All of these writers emphasised the importance of the ruler's personal commitment and his almost pedagogical understanding of the theory of enlightened absolutism (or despotism). Scholars agreed that the primary concern of the enlightened monarch was "to make of his subjects as many wealthy and enlightened instruments of his will as possible, according to the wisest rules of theory."[165] At the same time, the dependence of the entire system on the personal character of the ruler proved to be the weak point of enlightened absolutism, as especially Roscher argued, pointing out that if an "inferior successor" were to inherit from an enlightened ruler the artfully created "state machinery" of the predecessor threatened to fall apart and disintegrate.[166] This focus on character, personal skills, and assertiveness of the ruler also facilitated the removal of the concept from the specific political and cultural context of eighteenth-century European societies to which it had originally been applied. Subsequently, scholars extended the temporal limitation of the concept, identifying enlightened rulers in almost every historical epoch, although Frederick II of Prussian continued to pose as a role model.

Before turning back to Hammurapi, I would like to demonstrate how this extension of the concept of enlightened absolutism functioned, by looking at nineteenth century representations of another Frederick II (1194–1250), the medieval Holy Roman Emperor of the House of Staufen, also known as Frederick of Sicily. Like his grandfather, Emperor Frederick I (commonly known as Barbarossa), he occupied a central position in the German imagination of the Middle Ages, although the two Staufer emperors played different roles. Barbarossa was a key figure in German nationalism, according to the popular Kyffhäuser legend he slept in the Thuringian mountains and would one day awaken to redeem and unite the nation.[167] By the end of the nineteenth century however, critical philologists had demonstrated that the Kyffhäuser legend was a modern invention, as the earliest

---

164 Hintze 1915, 400.
165 Roscher 1847c, 450–51.
166 Roscher 1847c, 452.
167 On the adaptation and transformation of this legend in the nineteenth century, see Kaul 2007; additionally Weigend, Baumunk and Brune 1978.

versions of the story positioned Frederick II and not Barbarossa as the saviour of Germany.[168] The substitution of the later emperor with his predecessor made some sense. From a German nationalist perspective, the Sicilian Frederick II, whose politics had focused on Italy, was of little value as a figure of identification.[169] However, due to his strong position as a (Sicilian) king, his extensive legal and economic reforms, his conflict with the Church and the Pope, and his seemingly tolerant policy towards his Muslim subjects, he was perfectly suited to pose as both an enlightened ruler and the forerunner of his Prussian namesake.[170] In his famous book on the Italian Renaissance (published 1860) Jacob Burckhardt, albeit with a critical intent, described Frederick as "the first ruler of the modern type who sat upon a throne."[171] Similar to Hammurapi, scholars and popular writers characterised Frederick II as a timeless ruler, far ahead of his own era. Given that comparisons with Frederick II of Prussia were very common in German scholarly literature, it is not surprising that late nineteenth-century historians adopted the concept of enlightened absolutism (respectively enlightened despotism) to describe the new "state principle" and "style of governance" that he allegedly established.[172] In this vein, Karl Hampe (1869–1936) provided the following enthusiastic description of Frederick II of Sicily in his popular *Deutsche Kaisergeschichte* ("History of the German Emperors") published in 1909:

> Und es war eben keine launische Tyrannei, sondern ein aufgeklärter Absolutismus, der allein die Vernunft zum Maßstab nahm. In seiner allseitigen Fürsorge, in seiner Freiheit von Dogmatismus und Mystizismus, in seiner Beeinflussung durch nationalökonomische, statistische, hygienische, volkserzieherische Gesichtspunkte, in seinen handelspolitischen Maßnahmen und Landesmeliorationen, in seinem fortschrittlichen Strafrecht, das der Folter enge Grenzen setzte, in der zunehmenden Verschriftlichung der Verwaltung und des

---

168 Voigt 1871. On the transformation of this legend; see Thomsen 2005, 57–61, 154–56.
169 The Italian policy of these medieval emperors was the subject of one of the most famous debates in nineteenth century German historiography, the so-called Sybel-Ficker controversy, in which Nationalist historians (who favoured national unification under Prussian leadership to the exclusion of Austria) such as Heinrich von Sybel (1817–1895) accused past emperors including Frederick II of failing in their national duty to lay the foundations of a nation-state north of the Alps, while the German-Austrian historian Julius von Ficker (1826–1902) defended the policies of the Medieval Emperors. See the collection of texts edited in Schneider 1941; additionally Brechenmacher 2003.
170 On the following, see with further examples and references Thomsen 2005, 93–210.
171 Burckhardt [1860], 2. The German original is slightly different however, describing Frederick as the first modern man to sit on a throne *(der erste moderne Mensch auf dem Throne)*, Burckhardt 1996 [1860], 3.
172 Gregorovius 1978 [1871], 408. For 'enlightened absolutism' see Hampe 1899, 15; Hampe 1909, 225. For 'enlightened despotism' see Winckelmann 1863, 379.

Gerichtsverfahrens – in all diesem kühlen Rationalismus mutet er uns doch wenig mittelalterlich an und weist weit in das siebzehnte Jahrhundert hinein.[173]

[And it was not a whimsical tyranny, but an enlightened absolutism that took reason alone as its yardstick. In its all-encompassing care, its freedom from dogmatism and mysticism, its influence through national economic, statistical, hygienic, and educational points of view, his commercial policies and land improvements, his progressive criminal law that limited the use of torture, increasing the use of writing in the administration and court proceedings – in all this cool rationalism, he seems to us to be not so medieval after all and points towards the seventeenth century.]

It should now be clear that the concept of enlightened absolutism (or despotism) developed an associative dimension that could encompass rulers from different epochs and link them in a series. These rulers were said not only to have shared similar political principles and philosophical ideas about how to govern a state, but also to have had certain personal traits in common. As seen in the first chapter of this work, there was no evolutionary historical scheme behind the various series of great historical men that were established in the nineteenth and early twentieth centuries, and this is also true of the lists of 'enlightened rulers' to which Hammurapi was now added. The portrayal of the Old Babylonian king as a forerunner of the two Fredericks did not imply that he was more 'primitive' than his medieval respectively early modern successors: all appeared equally enlightened within their historical contexts. The inclusion of Hammurapi in these series of admired rulers, of course, said less about kingship in ancient Babylonia than it did about concepts of the ideal monarchy and the ideal ruler in modern Germany. The political dimension of the debate about Hammurapi's role in his 'enlightened' state can thus only be understood by contextualising it within political ideas regarding good and just kings in modern societies in general and the constitutional position of monarchs in late nineteenth century German states in particular. As we shall see, this was indeed one of the most sensitive and controversial issues of the new German empire at the time of the discovery of the Code of Hammurapi.

2.2 The Monarch

In terms of political history, the nineteenth century saw the rise of 'monarchical constitutionalism'.[174] Before the French Revolution, the monarchs of Europe ruled

---

173 Hampe 1909, 225.
174 On the concept of monarchical constitutionalism see Kirsch 1999; additionally Kraus 2004.

as 'sovereigns' by the grace of God; that is, without formal rules (such as constitutions) to limit their power. In theory, their rule was absolute, though in practice their actual power had always been limited by informal rules and social power relations, as critics of the concept of absolutism have rightly pointed out. The first written constitutions were adopted in the United States (1787), Poland (1791) and France (1791); the first of these led to the establishment of a modern republic, the following two to constitutional monarchies (though that of France lasted only until execution of Louis XVI and the adoption of a republican constitution in 1793). After the French Revolution and the wars that followed, the idea that a nation should possess a constitution spread throughout Europe, initially as a result of the Napoleonic conquests. The first constitutional monarchy in Germany was established in 1807 in the Napoleonic satellite state of Westphalia.[175] Independent constitutions followed in the southern and south-western German states after the Congress of Vienna.[176] The two largest German states however, Prussia and Austria, were without constitutions until the revolution of 1848, and thus formally remained absolutist regimes.

The constitutions of the early nineteenth century typically rejected the concept of popular sovereignty that had been embraced during the age of revolution. However, a straightforward return to pre-revolutionary absolutism, with a sovereign at the top embodying the 'divine right' of kings, was no longer feasible either. The *Charte constitutionnelle* of 1814, the constitution of the relatively short-lived French Bourbon monarchy, presented an elegant solution to this dilemma. This constitution was based neither on the idea of popular sovereignty nor on the concept of a contract between the monarch and his subjects. Instead, it was enacted by the king, who in taking this step voluntarily limited his own power – at least in theory, as the social balance of power no longer permitted him to rule as his absolutist predecessors had. Even the preamble of this constitution clearly indicates that it is based on a compromise to which the king was compelled; after pointing out that in France "all power resides in the person of the King," it continues by saying that the "exercise of this power must be adapted to the various needs of the times," and that the King will fulfil the wishes of his people for a constitution.[177] Thus, the theoretical distinction between the possession of power and

---

[175] On Napoleonic influence upon German constitutionalism, see Huber 1957, 88–90; Grimm 2015, 55–58.

[176] On these early German constitutions, see Huber 1957, 314–87; Grimm 2015, 71–76; Frotscher and Pieroth 2022, 117–48.

[177] See https://www.verfassungen.eu/f/fverf14-i.htm, accessed 10 February 2025.

its exercise, a model that can be traced back to the French jurist and political philosopher Jean Bodin (1530–1596), was crucial to the whole construction.[178]

The *Charte constitutionnelle* strongly influenced European constitutionalism in the first half of the nineteenth century and served as a model for the constitutions adopted in the southern German states of Bavaria, Baden, and Württemberg.[179] Its basic idea, the fiction of the King as the sole sovereign who restrains himself by enacting a constitution of his own free will, became known in Germany as the 'monarchical principle' *(monarchisches Prinzip)*. It was first articulated in the Bavarian Constitution of 1818, whose preamble states that Bavaria is a "sovereign monarchical state in accordance with the provisions of the present constitutional charter." As decreed by King Maximilian I: "The King is the head of the state, unites in himself all rights of state authority, and exercises them under the conditions laid down by him in the present constitutional charter."[180] Although most nineteenth-century European constitutions differed little from the German ones in this respect, scholars such as the reactionary political philosopher Friedrich Julius Stahl (1801–1861) presented the monarchical principle as a distinctly German contribution to political theory, positively contrasting it with the parliamentary principle already established in Britain:

> Die Nation in ihrer parlamentarischen Vertretung regiert sich selbst, und der König steht nur darüber, indem er dieser Regierung (formell) die Sanktion erteilt [...]. Dies ist es, was wir das parlamentarische Prinzip nennen. [...] Im Unterschiede dazu werden wir daher das monarchische Prinzip darin finden müssen, daß die fürstliche Gewalt dem Rechte nach undurchdrungen über der Volksvertretung stehe, und daß der Fürst tatsächlich den Schwerpunkt der Verfassung, die positiv gestaltende Macht im Staate, der Führer der Entwicklung bleibe. Hierin zeigt sich, daß das monarchische Princip etwas Anderes und zwar ein Mehrers ist als die Souveränität des Königs.[181]
>
> [The nation, in its parliamentary representation, governs itself, and the king stands above it only by (formally) sanctioning this government [...]. This is what we call the parliamentary principle. [...] By contrast, we must therefore find the monarchical principle in the fact that

---

178 On Bodin's theory of the state, see among others Denzer 1973.
179 See Kirsch 1999, 299–373; additionally Frotscher and Pieroth 2022, 44–46.
180 See Verfassungsurkunde für das Königreich Bayern (26 May 1818), https://www.jura.uni-wuerzburg.de/lehrstuehle/muenkler/verfassungsdokumente-von-der-magna-carta-bis-ins-20-jahrhundert/verfassung-des-koenigreichs-bayern-26-mai-1818, accessed 10 February 2025. On the monarchical principle, see Heun 2001; additionally Böckenförde 2024a [1967], 277–91; Grimm 2015, 113–16; Thiele 2021, 187–98.
181 Stahl 1845, 10–12. On Stahl as political and legal theorist, see Kersten 2010. Even liberal scholars such as Otto Hintze underlined the advantages of the German monarchical principle. See Hintze 1970 [1911]. In contrast to his stance, monarchical constitutionalism was actually a common European idea, as evidenced by Kirsch 1999.

the princely power stands, in law, impenetrable above the people's representation, and that the prince remains the centre of gravity of the constitution, the positively creative power in the state, the leader of development. This shows that the monarchical principle is something other and, indeed, something more than the sovereignty of the king.]

According to nationalist historians such as Treitschke, there was a traditional German "monarchical attitude," which was strengthened by the "enlightened despotism" of Frederick II: "[T]hat is why the German people [...] remained the most loyal to monarchs among the great cultural nations."[182] Following these ideas, the monarchical constitutions of the nineteenth century contained central royal prerogatives, including control of the military and decisions regarding foreign policy, as well as the right to declare war, or a state of emergency. Such constitutions did not provide for a separation of powers but instead granted the monarch significant legislative and executive authority. Laws required both the monarch's assent and parliamentary approval. Most importantly, the government was accountable solely to the monarch, not to parliament; it was the monarch who appointed the head of the government and had the power to dismiss him at any time. Despite such prerogatives, these new constitutions did represent the limitation of royal power. Moreover, the king's 'gift of his own free will' was a one-off act: once granted, a constitution could not simply be revoked.[183]

The most important monarchical constitution in the German Confederation (*Deutscher Bund*), the association of sovereign states that existed between 1815 and 1866, was the Prussian one imposed in 1850 by Frederick William IV (1795–1861) after the failed revolution of 1848. In contrast to the revolutionary *Paulskirchenverfassung* (Frankfurt Constitution), which was intended for a new national state, and the *Charte Waldeck*, a draft for a liberal Prussian constitution, the imposed one of 1850 explicitly rejected the concept of popular sovereignty in favour of the monarchical principle.[184] Against the background of Prussia's complex position as the most powerful state by far in the German Reich, which had been established in 1871, the Prussian constitution influenced the German political system until its abolition in 1918.[185] Monarchical prerogatives, such as the government's dependence (in the person of the Chancellor) on the monarch, were also central to the constitution the German Reich. However, the monarchical

---

[182] Treitschke 1879, 99.
[183] This led to a famous constitutional conflict in the state of Hanover in 1837, after King Ernst August I (1771–1851) announced that he did not feel bound by the 1833 constitution. See Ipsen 2017.
[184] See Huber 1961, 304–24.
[185] On the Prussian constitution, see Huber 1970, 54–128; additionally Siemann 1990, 78–83; Grimm 2015, 214–17; Frotscher and Pieroth 2022, 185–93.

principle was compromised there to the extent that the monarch did not act (as in Prussia) as the sole representative of state authority. The Reich was a federal state composed of sovereign federal states. State sovereignty was therefore formally vested in the *Bundesrat* (federal chamber), over which the Kaiser presided as King of Prussia. The position of the Kaiser was clearly defined in the Constitution of the Reich Article 11: "The Presidency of the Confederation belongs to the King of Prussia, who bears the name of German Emperor."[186] Nevertheless, the constitution of the German Reich established a strong executive position for the monarch: he was not subject to democratic parliamentary control and he appointed the government (i.e., the Chancellor of the Reich). In practice however, the dualism of monarch and chancellor required cooperation and informal arrangements. This worked reasonably well under the first German emperor, Wilhelm I, as he left most of the business of government to his chancellor, Otto von Bismarck (1815–1898). In the era of his grandson Wilhelm II however, the disadvantages of this informal arrangement became apparent, as the young Kaiser was by no means willing to leave day-to-day politics to others and confine himself to his constitutional role as 'president' of the federal chamber. Rather, he wanted to be 'his own chancellor' and sought to reduce the chancellors he appointed to mere executors of his political ideas.[187]

The political ambitions of the young Kaiser were far from uncontroversial, leading to heated discussions about the monarch's 'personal rule' *(persönliches Regiment)* throughout his entire reign. This term had been introduced by Wilhelm II himself in the early 1890s to signify the style of politics he wished to pursue. The Kaiser was clearly influenced by certain ideas I have discussed above, such as the role of great men in history, with whom the emperor identified. The phrase 'personal rule' was soon adopted by the circle of advisers and friends surrounding the Kaiser, who increasingly gained informal political influence, bypassing a constitution that did not provide for a royal court.[188] Historians agree that Wilhelm II did not truly determine German politics but rather intervened in them, often with negative results. However, it has long been debated whether the term 'personal rule' meaningfully describes his political role or whether it should be seen as the neo-absolutist fantasy of a megalomaniacal monarch and

---

[186] See https://en.wikisource.org/wiki/Constitution_of_the_German_Empire, accessed 20 February 2025; for the German original version, see https://de.wikisource.org/wiki/Verfassung_des_Deutschen_Reichs_(1871), accessed 20 February 2025.
[187] The phrase that Wilhelm II wanted to be his own chancellor was already widespread at the time. See Fehrenbach 1969, 90–92.
[188] On the establishment of Wilhelm's 'personal monarchy', see the seminal second volume of the biography by John Röhl 2004; on Wilhelm's court society see Röhl 1995.

his entourage.[189] The contemporary debate regarding this issue reached its climax during the chancellorship of Bernhard von Bülow (1900–1909), coinciding with the Babel-Bible controversy and the discovery of Hammurapi's stele.[190] It was during this period that the term 'personal rule' entered the political vocabulary and became a widely used slogan. Unsurprisingly, the expression also featured prominently in contemporary representations of the Kaiser himself, including cartoons, as demonstrated by an example from the social democratic magazine *Der wahre Jacob* and published in 1910 (fig. 3).[191] For the liberal and democratic opponents of

Figure 3: The cartoon was published in 1910 by the left-wing magazine *Der wahre Jacob*. The text (in Berlin dialect) reads as follows: "Look, that's the first guard regiment" - "And who is riding ahead?" - "This is the personal regiment".

the emperor, the phrase 'personal rule' was used polemically or as a warning against leaving the fate of the Reich to the whims of a ruler perceived as unpredictable.

A famous example is the historian Ludwig Quidde's (1858–1941) biographical sketch of the Roman Emperor Caligula (12–41 AD) published in 1894, which became the most popular anti-monarchical pamphlet to appear in the Reich.[192] It is also a powerful reminder of the importance of historical references and the assertion of direct parallels between figures from very different eras in the political discourse at the turn of the twentieth century. The identification of political leaders with Caligula, the epitome of a mad and megalomanic despot since antiquity,

---

189 On this debate, see Hull 1991; additionally Nipperdey 2013 [1992], 475–85.
190 See Lerman 1982, 1990.
191 On this magazine, see Ege 1990; for cartoons featuring Wilhelm II see Rebentisch 2000.
192 Quidde 1894. For the scandal it provoked see Holl, Kloft and Fesser 2001; Kohlrausch 2005, 118–54; Kloft 2020 [2000]. The pamphlet went through 34 editions with a total print run of over 200,000 copies. It was also published as an article in several liberal and social democratic journals. Attempts by the authorities to ban or confiscate the text were not very successful and probably contributed to its popularity. See Kohlrausch 2005, 124.

remains a popular trope today, as evidenced by recent articles and cartoons about US President Donald Trump.[193] That Quidde's *Studie über Cäsarenwahn* ("Study on the Madness of Emperors") was less about the ancient Roman emperor than about the current German one became clear to his contemporaries from the very first pages of the text: The description of how the ruler set up "his own regiment" after his "leading statesman" had "fallen out of favour" contained a clear allusion to the dismissal of Bismarck and the beginning of Wilhelm's assumed personal rule.[194] As Quidde later admitted, his clear aim with this work was "to warn the German people of the dangers inherent in the emperor's unpredictable personality."[195] The term *Cäsarenwahnsinn*, a political buzzword that had become popular via a novel by the nationalist writer Gustav Freytag (1816–1895) a few years before, did not refer to an individual mental disease of the ruler, but to a specific political situation that Quidde considered typical of monarchies: "*Cäsarenwahnsinn* is the product of conditions that can only flourish in the moral degeneration of monarchist-minded peoples."[196]

Harsh criticism of Wilhelm's personal rule was not confined to the political left. A few years later, the *völkisch* and antisemitic writer and politician Graf Ernst Reventlow (1869–1943) penned a fierce critique of Wilhelm's personal rule that was, in many ways, similar to Quidde's. Significantly, however, he chose a different historical parallel, complaining of the monarchy's "Byzantinism", which he defined as a "pathological relationship between a ruler and his people" that only produces servility and encourages flatterers.[197] However, both examples demonstrate that terms such as 'Byzantinism' and 'Caesarism' played a central role in the German debate, serving as expressions of the dangers and perils of the monarchical system (though they were rarely accompanied by calls for a republican state).[198] By evoking the turmoil of Caligula's reign and assassination, as well as the long decline of the Byzantine Empire, these comparisons – far from being meaningless decoration – clearly shaped the political perception

---

193 Among others Bryant 2024. These parallels were already popular during his first term. See "Donald Trump has 'fascinating parallels' with Caligula," The Guardian, 1 June 2016. Whether these comparisons are accurate is, of course, beyond the scope of this study. However, as historians have recently argued, Caligula's supposed madness may have been a posthumous creation of his opponents in antiquity. See Winterling 2011.
194 Quidde 1894, 4.
195 Quidde 1926, 54.
196 Quidde 1894, 7.
197 Reventlow 1906, 3. Although Reventlow was an important political figure he remains underresearched. See Kimmel 2009 for basic information.
198 Until the late twentieth century, both terms were used uncritically in German historiography. See for instance Pezold 1971.

of Wilhelm's reign. It is instructive to note the historical epochs that were *not* invoked in this context: apparently, neither the ancient Near East nor the Islamic Middle East seemed suitable for illustrating monarchy in a state otherwise characterised as despotic. I am also not aware of any instance in which Wilhelm's identification with Hammurapi's Babylonia was used to emphasise the dangers of autocracy or tyranny.

However, the relationship between political discourse on the monarchy and contemporary representations of Hammurapi became more apparent in other fields. One important point of reference for such analogies was the correspondence between individual citizens, provincial administrators, and the Babylonian king, which provides fascinating insights into the legal practices of the Old Babylonian period.[199] As mentioned above, many of these ancient letters were known prior to the discovery of Hammurapi's Law Code, and the first significant publication of their contents (by Leonard King) had appeared in 1898. A German translation of the letters, edited by Arthur Ungnad, followed in 1914.[200] Ungnad had already completed a popular selection of Hammurapi's correspondence and intended to publish it the same year, but the First World War broke out and delayed its appearance. This volume was finally published in 1919 with a very insightful introduction in which he identified strong affinities between ancient Babylonia and modern Germany.[201] According to Ungnad, his letters demonstrate not only Hammurapi's "high sense of justice and impartiality"[202] but also his personal involvement and intervention in individual legal cases on behalf of the poor and weak:

> Wenn jedoch jemand glaubte, sein Recht bei den Richtern seiner Stadt nicht gefunden zu haben, so war es ihm gestattet, an einen höheren Gerichtshof zu appellieren, an die Richter des Königs zu Babylon. Ja, der König selbst griff als oberster Richter häufig in Rechtsfragen ein. Das lehren nicht nur gelegentlich Bemerkungen in Rechtsurkunden, sondern die Briefe Hammurapis selbst. [...] Immer wieder bestätigt sich auch in diesen Briefen der unwandelbare Gerechtigkeitssinn des Herrschers und seine unablässige Sorge um das Wohl seiner Untertanen.[203]

> [However, if someone believed that he had not found justice with the judges of his city, he was allowed to appeal to a higher court, to the judges of the king of Babylon. Indeed, the king himself frequently intervened as supreme judge in legal matters. This is taught not only by occasional remarks in legal documents, but also by Hammurapi's letters themselves. [...]

---

199 See with further references Charpin 2021, 146–49.
200 King 1898; King 1900a; King 1900b; Ungnad 1914.
201 Ungnad 1919, 3–4.
202 Ungnad 1919, 49.
203 Ungnad 1919, 62–63.

> Again and again, these letters confirm the ruler's unchanging sense of justice and his unceasing concern for the welfare of his subjects.]

It was this image of Hammurapi as a king who tirelessly worked for the good of his state and subjects, distinguished by his expertise and in-depth knowledge, that most captivated contemporary scholars. Josef Kohler, Ungnad's co-editor of the Code of Hammurapi, could hardly contain his enthusiasm in this regard and portrayed the king as a fervent worker embodying a modern bourgeois ethos:

> Seine Thätigkeit ist eine geradezu fieberhafte; was er befiehlt, soll sofort sein. [...] Alles dieses bietet uns die Charakteristik eines ausserordentlich umsichtigen, Tag und Nacht thätigen, temperamentvollen Herrschers, der in alles und jedes eingreift und offensichtlich die ganze Staatsverwaltung Babylons auf eine bisher nicht erreichte Höhe gebracht hat.[204]
>
> [His activity is almost feverish; whatever he orders must be immediate. [...] All this gives us the characterisation of an extraordinarily prudent, day and night active, spirited ruler, who intervenes in everything and anything and has obviously brought the entire state administration of Babylon to a hitherto unattained height.]

Against the backdrop of an idealized image of enlightened rulers it is not surprising that the legal historian drew a direct parallel between Hammurapi and the Prussian kings of the eighteenth century: "In these letters we sometimes have the impression that we have before us the records of Frederick II or Frederick William I."[205] In fact, the concept of the humble and fervently dedicated monarch is a fundamental aspect of the myth of enlightened absolutism. In particular, Frederick II of Prussia deliberately cultivated such an image of himself, and this image was uncritically adopted by later historians, who saw him as the ideal type of enlightened ruler.[206] Most influential in this respect was Frederick's *Politisches Testament* ("Political Testament") of 1752, in which he famously claimed that "the ruler is the first servant of the state. [...] He must listen to all complaints, and he must quickly right the wrongs of those threatened with violence."[207] This demand included direct intervention in individual cases, even against his own administration:

> Man darf mit den Pflichtvergessenen kein Erbarmen haben: die Stimme der Witwen und Waisen fordert Vergeltung, und Sache des Fürsten ist es, die Beamten zu ihrer Pflicht

---

204 Kohler and Peiser 1904, 2–3.
205 Kohler and Peiser 1904, 2. For a similar parallelisation, see Wilhelm II 1938, 27.
206 Some historians were still arguing this way in the 1980s, see Birtsch 1987. For a critique of the focus on Frederick II, see Aretin 1988.
207 Friedrich der Große 1912, 155.

anzuhalten und streng gegen die vorzugehen, die seine Autorität mißbrauchen und das öffentliche Vertrauen unter dem Vorwand von Recht und Gerechtigkeit täuschen. Gerade gegen solche Art von Pflichtvergessenheit muß ich die äußerste Strenge anraten; denn der Herrscher macht sich gewissermaßen zum Mitschuldigen an den Verbrechen, die er unbestraft läßt.[208]

[No mercy must be shown to the negligent: the voice of the widows and orphans demands retribution, and it is the prince's duty to urge the officials on to do their duty and to take strict action against those who abuse his authority and deceive the public trust under the pretext of law and justice. I must advise the utmost severity against such negligence, for the ruler makes himself complicit in the crimes he allows to go unpunished.]

The myth surrounding Frederick II, which had originated during his lifetime, was largely based on stories, some real, some legendary, that depicted him as a selfless caregiver, genuinely concerned for the welfare of each of his subjects.[209] The most famous example in this respect was the so-called Müller-Arnold case. Christian Arnold operated a water-powered grain mill in Brandenburg and sought justice for an alleged upstream diversion of water from his mill by a nobleman, which rendered his mill inoperable. Although the miller and his wife lost all court cases related to the matter in the 1770s, their fortunes changed when they appealed to Frederick II. The king not only overturned the decisions of the Prussian courts but also imprisoned some of the judges and key figures in the administration of justice, ultimately restoring the mill and its water supply to the Arnolds.[210]

In the same way, the Code of Hammurapi seemed to bear witness to a similar enlightened spirit that was both practical and devoted to the specific concerns of royal subjects, as Winckler pointed out: "The formulation of the individual paragraphs [of the Law Code] is transparent, the provisions are clear and avoid sophistry; they have arisen from practice and are intended to serve practice directly."[211] Kohler went even further, seeing in the "paternal despotism" of Hammurapi certain "social blessings" that made ancient Babylonia appear as a precursor of the Prussian-German welfare state established by Bismarck's social legislation in the 1870s.[212] Wilhelm II adopted this view in his later book on Mesopotamian kingship. According to him, "social welfare" was a defining feature of the Old Babylonian state and he particularly praised Hammurapi's role as a

---

[208] Friedrich der Große 1912, 119.
[209] See, for instance, Frank 1926.
[210] On this famous case and its historical context see Dießelhorst 1984; additionally Luebke 1999; Prümm 2012; Wienfort 2012.
[211] Winckler 1913, 39.
[212] Kohler 1914, 57. On the foundation of the German welfare laws, see among others Stolleis 2014, 29–82.

"warm-hearted father to his people."[213] Perhaps this reveals more about Wilhelm's own chosen self-image as a socially minded and just Emperor, which he strove to achieve particularly during the early years of his reign, though usually without any concrete political results. One of the earliest examples was his political intervention in a miners' strike in the Ruhr in May 1889. While Bismarck was adamantly against state intervention, Wilhelm verbally sided with the workers, portraying himself as a patriarchal arbiter. This dispute contributed to Bismarck's dismissal a few months later but did nothing to prevent the workers' bitter defeat.[214] However, it is important to remember that the German social reforms were introduced 'from above', not least in order to undermine the rising Social Democrats. Wilhelm II's state was an authoritarian welfare state that aimed to decouple welfare from democracy and political liberalism.[215] Following that model, social justice could only be assured by a strong state led by a strong king who cares for all his subjects as would a good father.

This patriarchal idea of welfare is, of course, much older than the German Reich or 'enlightened absolutism'. Michel Foucault famously coined the term 'pastoral power' to refer to this particular conception of the relationship between God and man, or between a ruler and his subjects, rightly pointing to the ancient Near Eastern roots of a concept that later found its way into Western political theory.[216] The idea of "pastoral power" in his sense is "defined by its beneficence", with the "salvation of the flock," or the sovereign's subjects, as its ultimate goal.[217] However, the French philosopher did not refer to the Code of Hammurapi in this respect, which in fact could have strongly underscored his arguments, as 'pastoral power' can be identified as its driving principle. In the prologue to his law Code, the Babylonian king identifies himself as the "shepherd of the people," a traditional royal title that had been used by Mesopotamian kings before him.[218] The positive image of the king as a good shepherd or herdsman likely originated in the ancient Near East and spread to the Mediterranean, where it found its way into Greek poetry

---

213 Wilhelm II 1938, 27.
214 See Mommsen 2002, 35–38.
215 This should be emphasised in contrast to recent interpretations that have unilaterally focused on the modern, democratic, and reformist aspects of the German Reich. See especially Richter 2021, 62–72; critique of this approach by Conze 2020, 103–34.
216 Foucault 2009, 115–34. See also Bröckling 2017.
217 Foucault 2009, 126.
218 On the concept of the shepherd-king, see with further references Murray 1990; Naiden 2013, 88–95; in general also Patterson 1988.

and philosophy.[219] However, the most important source for disseminating the pastoral ideal into European literature on kingship was undoubtedly the Bible, perhaps best exemplified by Psalm 23: "The Lord is my Shepherd, I shall not want."

Fundamental to the pastoral ideal of kingship in the ancient Near East was the concept of social justice, which the king was expected to uphold, or, if disrupted, to restore.[220] Accordingly, Mesopotamian kings positioned themselves as protectors of the weak against the strong, often in the prologues and epilogues of law collections, as Hammurapi did: "In order that the mighty not wrong the weak, to provide just ways for the waif and the widow, I have inscribed my precious pronouncements upon my stela." (LH, epilogue).[221] Thus, the proverbial reference to widows and orphans as particularly worthy of protection in European writings on kingship, such as Frederick II's Political Testament, is rooted in traditions that are much older than the Bible, which of course, became the main source of this expression for later reception.[222] However, ancient Near Eastern conceptions of social justice should not be confused with the modern ideal of social equality. According to Jan Assmann, the principle underlying ancient Egyptian and Mesopotamian notions of justice is "vertical solidarity", which presupposes a hierarchical social order that it aims to preserve and defend by mitigating excesses. (In contrast, modern "horizontal solidarity" aims to abolish social hierarchies). The idea of social progress or improvement did not exist; instead, appeals to 'justice' sought to restore the 'original' social order. What the weak expected from the king in ancient Near Eastern society was protection against exploitation by the strong, while the king expected obedience and loyalty from the weak.[223] It then becomes clear that Hammurapi's self-presentation on the stele as 'King of Justice' was not least part of a highly successful royal propaganda strategy.[224] The extraor-

---

[219] See with further references Haubold 2000, 17–20. Against this backdrop, Foucault's stark contrast between Near Eastern and biblical pastoralism on the one hand, and Greek political thinking on the other, seems exaggerated. See Foucault 2009, 115–34.
[220] The central Akkadian terms in this respect were *kittum* (truth) and *mīsharum* (equity). On these terms and on Babylonian ideas of (social) justice in general, see among others Foster 1995; Cancik-Kirschbaum 1999; Neumann 2008; Westbrook 2009c [1995]; with a focus on the Code of Hammurapi Barmash 2020, 49–86; Charpin 2021, 150–52. The Mesopotamian conceptions seem to be similar to the ancient Egyptian concept of *Ma'at*, as Assmann 2001 [1990] argues.
[221] Quoted from the translation by Roth 1995b, 80, 133.
[222] See Fensham 1962.
[223] Assmann 2001 [1990], 245–52. This aspect is also strongly emphasised by Westbrook 2009c [1995].
[224] This was the central argument of American Assyriologist Jacob J. Finkelstein against the legislative character of the Code of Hammurapi. See Finkelstein 1961. For more on this thesis, see (among others) Barmash 2020, 6–8.

dinary status the Code achieved in later periods supported Hammurapi's rise to become, in the words of Marc Van de Mieroop "the paradigm of a just king," – a status he held in antiquity, long before his modern rediscovery.[225]

Against this backdrop, the enthusiasm of German scholars, particularly that of the Kaiser himself, for 'pastoral' conceptions of monarchy and their historical roots becomes understandable. The ideology of pastoralism appeared to offer a way of tackling social injustices and exploitation while simultaneously affirming the existing political and social order. Given the desperate living conditions of large sections of the population during the age of industrialisation, there was therefore more at play than a traditional concept of governance. The fierce class struggles of the mid-to-late nineteenth century, along with the looming shadow of social revolution, had given rise to a new notion of 'social monarchy,' often legitimised by historical and sometimes racial speculation. In this vein, the legal scholar Lorenz von Stein (1815–1890), regarded as the founder of the concept of a socialist German kingdom, advocated a return to an allegedly ancient Germanic kingship which "by its very nature […] does not allow the absolute rule of one class over another, but stands above both."[226] Von Stein argued that only this idea could reignite the popularity of the institution of monarchy "The true, powerful, lasting and most beloved kingdom is the kingdom of social reform."[227] Similar arguments were later used by the theologian and liberal politician Friedrich Naumann (1860–1919) to argue that the German Reich should be a social monarchy *(soziales Kaisertum)*.[228] Wilhelm II was far from the first monarch to draw on the ideas that were circulating. The French emperor Napoleon III was, before his seizure of power, himself the author of social-reformist pamphlets, and had already attempted to establish a 'democratic' monarchy, based on plebiscite support for his policies and heavily reliant on the support of the lower classes.[229]

These ideas – or ideologies – of 'social' and 'democratic' monarchs should be considered in the context of how the monarchy reinvented itself during the long nineteenth century.[230] Such reinventions became necessary due to the severe crisis of legitimacy that the institution of monarchy had faced since the French Revolution. The appeal to divine favour became increasingly unconvincing, although it

---

225 Van de Mieroop 2005, 111.
226 Stein 1850, 21.
227 Stein 1850, 48. On the idea of a 'socialist monarchy' in the nineteenth century, see Sellin 2011, 241–61.
228 Naumann 1900, 216–25. On Naumann's conception of a 'national socialism,' see among others Fehlberg 2012, 317–426.
229 See, for example Napoleon III 1854. For more on this topic see Sellin 2011, 242–49.
230 Osterhammel 2014, 579–93.

was used by most European monarchs until the First World War, and with particular emphasis by Wilhelm II, it had in fact been reduced to a mere formula of monarchical constitutionalism, lacking any practical significance.[231] Even as a 'traditional type' of legitimacy in the Weberian sense, divine favour could by no means compete with the revolutionary idea of popular sovereignty. Against this background, the concept of the monarchy as the only institution above class antagonisms and able to unite a nation emerged as an attractive new source of legitimacy. This transformation had already been observed by Max Weber, whose concept of 'plebiscitary rule' was modelled after the rule of Napoleon III.[232] In the early twentieth century, these ideas increasingly merged with the aforementioned notions of charismatic leadership, particularly on the political right.[233] Especially after Germany's defeat in the First World War, these concepts also became applied to the 'great rulers' of history, who thus became politically charged figures. A notable example of this is the new cult surrounding Frederick II of Sicily during the Weimar Republic.[234] Admired as an enlightened ruler in the nineteenth century, he was now chosen by right-wing inellectuals as a symbol of salvation, as demonstrated by the biography written by the famous medievalist Ernst Kantorowicz (1895–1963), who was then a fervent nationalist and opponent of democracy and liberalism.[235]

Unlike Frederick II of Sicily (and his supposed Prussian counterpart in the eighteenth century), Hammurapi of Babylon did not achieve national saviour status for obvious reasons: his prominence was too recent and his appropriation for nationalist purposes was too challenging given his Semitic origin. It should be clear however, that modern discourse regarding the Old Babylonian king and debates surrounding the conception of monarchy were converging in an era when the latter had become severely challenged. Contemporary scholars did not simply impose modern conceptions of monarchy on ancient Babylonian material, neither did the ancient materials directly influence modern politics. Through translations and interpretations, the ancient material did, however, affect contemporary discourse and was used to legitimise certain ideas of governance and monarchical traditions, by demonstrating their supposed roots in ancient Babylonia. In this re-

---

[231] On this development see the sketch by Brunner 1968.
[232] Weber 2019, 406.
[233] On these ideas see Breuer 2001, 105–46; with a focus on the Weimar period Schreiner 1998.
[234] See Thomsen 2005, 211–86.
[235] Kantorowicz 1927. There has been long-running and controversial debate regarding Kantorowicz's early and later works and the relationship between them. See with further references Greiert 2017.

spect, the discovery of the Code of Hammurapi seemed to be good news for the German monarch and his supporters.

Apart from the concepts of enlightened kingship, social monarchy and the authoritarian welfare state, law itself, along with its assumed position within state and society, provided another basis for drawing parallels between the political systems of Old Babylonia and modern Germany. The key concept in this respect was the *Rechtsstaat*.

2.3 The *Rechtsstaat*

The term *Rechtsstaat* occurs quite often in German descriptions of Hammurapi's Babylonia from the beginning of the twentieth century. As early as his first lecture on *Babel und Bibel* ("Babel and the Bible") – delivered almost precisely at the time of the excavation of the Law Code, which was therefore still unknown to him – Delitzsch referred to the "highly developed *Rechtsstaat*" of the Babylonians and argued that this indicated they possessed a "culture comparable to ours".[236] Subsequently, the Assyriologist viewed the discovery of the stele as confirmation of this thesis and again wrote enthusiastically about an "exemplary *Rechtsstaat*" under Hammurapi.[237] However, referring to ancient Babylonia as a *Rechtsstaat* was not only anachronistic in terms of legal history (a fact of which scholars were well aware), but the application of a modern term to an ancient Near Eastern context served to further link Hammurapi's Babylonia to modern Prussia and Germany, thereby influencing contemporary discourse on the rule of law, its theoretical foundation, and its historical roots.

The concept of *Rechtsstaat* is central to German political and legal discourse and has certain national peculiarities.[238] For this reason, the term has no equivalent in other languages; neither 'rule of law' nor 'constitutional law,' the two most commonly proposed translations, adequately convey the meaning and implications of the German concept, as they are based on different premises of legal the-

---

236 Delitzsch 1902, 25.
237 Delitzsch 1905, 19; see also Delitzsch 1903, 21–25.
238 On the *Rechtsstaat* as a uniquely German idea, see Ullerich 2011, 44; Mecke 2013, 36; additionally Grote 1999. For the history of the *Rechtsstaat* concept, see Stolleis 1990; Böckenförde 1992, 2024a [1967]; Hofmann 1995; with a different perspective Maus 1978; additionally Pieroth 2011; and most recently Pichl 2024, 21–64. For the classical objections to general claims of a German *Sonderweg*, see Blackbourn and Eley 1984.

ory, though these differences need not be overemphasised.[239] Legal philosophy today closely associates the *Rechtsstaat* concept with the principles of liberal (parliamentary) democracy and fundamental human rights, rendering it inseparable from a specific political order and a universal set of values. This idea is most prominently represented by Jürgen Habermas, who argues for the "intrinsic connection between *Rechtsstaat* and democracy."[240] In German legal theory, two spheres are distinguished: on the one hand the 'formal' *Rechtsstaat* encompasses institutional rules, legal certainty, and administrative legality; on the other hand the 'material' *Rechtsstaat* binds the state to certain fundamental principles or values, particularly the fundamental rights outlined in the first 19 articles of the German constitution, the "Basic Law" *(Grundgesetz)* which defines the Federal Republic of Germany as a democratic and social *Rechtsstaat* (Article 28).[241]

However, Habermas' thesis of the 'synchronicity' *(Gleichursprünglichkeit)* of the rule of law and democracy cannot be interpreted historically, as they have different origins and backgrounds.[242] Unlike today, the term *Rechtsstaat* was not originally associated with any particular form of government or universal values during the nineteenth and early twentieth centuries.[243] As the legal scholar and constitutional judge Ernst-Wolfgang Böckenförde has shown in an influential article, *Rechtsstaat* is one of those basic or "gateway" concepts in legal theory that defy clear definition and are interpreted and adapted differently across various political and historical contexts.[244] While the term was coined in the early nineteenth century, its essential idea can be traced back to Kant. In his 1797 *Metaphysik der Sitten* ("Metaphysics of Morals"), the philosopher linked the concepts of state and law almost intrinsically, defining the state as the "union of a multitude of human beings under laws of right"[245] Liberal legal theorists of the early nine-

---

[239] On the national and conceptional differences, see Kriele 1995, 328–30; Grote 1999; Denninger 2002; Kirste 2013; Mecke 2013. For a perspective on the similarities and common ground, see MacCormick 1984.
[240] Habermas 1999. See in general among others Becker, Lauth and Pickel 2001.
[241] Note that the term *Rechtsstaat* does not appear until Article 28 of the German Constitution. On the constitutional *Rechtsstaatsprinzip*, see (among others) Heintschel von Heinegg 1996; Huber 2019; Holterhus 2022; (briefly) Koetter 2013.
[242] Habermas 1999, 299.
[243] Habermas therefore distinguished three steps in the development of this concept in his *Theory of Communicative Action:* the bourgeois *Rechtsstaat*, the democratic *Rechtsstaat*, and the democratic and social *Rechtsstaat*. See Habermas 1995 [1981], 527–47 (in the English edition, the term *Rechtsstaat* is translated as 'constitutional state,' see Habermas 1987, 359–73).
[244] Böckenförde 2024b [1969], 143.
[245] Kant 2917 [1797], 99. German original: "Ein Staat (Civitas) ist die Vereinigung einer Menge von Menschen unter Rechtsgesetzen [...]."(Kant 1907 [1997], 313 (§45).

teenth century, such as Carl Welcker (1790–1869) and Robert von Mohl (1799–1875), followed the Königsberg philosopher and introduced the term *Rechtsstaat* as a fundamental principle or spirit of the state, rooted in the concepts of reason and rationality: "Reason is now the supreme law, and the law commands only what reason commands."[246] Liberal legal theory holds that a state of non-rational law, or even lawlessness, can occur not only in a monarchy but also in a democracy. According to this view, the antitheses of the *Rechtsstaat* were despotism and theocracy; two forms of government founded not on the principles of rational law but on the arbitrary passions of an uncontrolled ruler or on blind faith devoid of reason. For the liberal theorists of the nineteenth century, however, the actual antonym of the legal state was the police state *(Polizey-Staat)*, as established by the absolutist rulers of the eighteenth century and defined as a state with unrestricted executive power and a police force that interferes in the private and economic sphere of the people.[247] What these positions reflected was the juridification of the social and political that had been taking place since the late eighteenth century. The aim of the liberal jurists of the early nineteenth century was thus to institutionalise the achievements of this process in a formal *Verrechtsstaatlichung*, a term coined by Habermas in this context.[248]

The liberal concept of the *Rechtsstaat* has always included the recognition and respect of rational law by the state itself, especially by the executive branch of the state. Legal certainty *(Rechtssicherheit)* inherently requires the state to be bound and constrained by law. Indeed, restricting state arbitrariness was the central aim of liberal scholars of the nineteenth century, even if democratic participation or the implementation of the welfare state were not yet integral aspects of their political program.[249] The demand for *Rechtssicherheit* becomes understandable considering the policy of restoration during the *Vormärz* period between the Napoleonic Wars and the revolution of 1848, which was characterised by the persecution of political opponents, especially liberals and democrats. Closely connected with legal certainty was the idea of judicial independence and the corresponding demand to limit (and ultimately to prohibit) the monarch's intervention in

---

246 Welcker 1813, 25. See also Mohl 1829, 8–9.
247 See Mohl 1844. In the eighteenth and early nineteenth centuries, the responsibilities of the police *(Polizey)* extended beyond security and order to encompass areas that would later form part of the welfare state. See among others Stolleis 1996. Against this backdrop, the bourgeois nature of liberal legal theorists became evident as they rejected any form of state intervention, including the concept of the modern welfare state. See on this aspect Maus 1978, 18–29.
248 Habermas 1995, 528 (in the Englisch edition with the German original: Habermas 1987, 359).
249 The concept of the social *Rechtsstaat* was only developed during the Weimar Republic by the social democratic legal scholar Hermann Heller (1891–1933). See Heller 1930.

court proceedings in the form of so-called *Machtsprüche* (power decrees). Against this background, the limits of the concept of enlightened absolutism as applied to the Prussian state of the eighteenth century, at least as far as they encompassed the central principles of the rule of law, become clear. On the one hand, the admired ruler Frederick II was famous for his measures that established an independent and incorruptible judiciary, such as the training of judges and the creation of a professional justice administration. On the other hand, Frederick II was also famous for interfering in legal proceedings in ways that were clearly incompatible with the rule of law.[250] The most notable example of this was his overturning of the verdict in the Müller-Arnold case, as described above. For legal scholars – and not only those with liberal views – this was not seen as proof of the king's commitment to the poor and weak, but rather as a cautionary tale that emphasised the need to avoid monarchical intervention as much as possible.[251] In practice, such cases were rare after 1800, but it was not until the Prussian Constitution of 1850 that the principle of judicial independence was enshrined.[252]

The insistence of liberal scholars on the incorruptibility and independence of the judiciary as an integral part of the concept of *Rechtsstaat* was clearly a critical reaction to the political and legal situation during the *Vormärz*. However, following Böckenförde, most modern legal historians critically describe how in the second half of the nineteenth century the concept of the *Rechtsstaat* increasingly lost both its normative function (as a goal to be achieved) and its critical function, which led, in part, to legal positivism becoming the dominant school of thought regarding law at the turn of the twentieth century. Indeed, from the mid-nineteenth century onwards, legal scholars began to restrict the meaning of the term *Rechtstaat* to certain formal aspects, such as transparent judicial procedure, explicitly excluding notions of 'natural' or 'rational' law.[253] The main proponent of this shift was the aforementioned conservative political and legal scholar Friedrich Julius Stahl, who provided the most renowned definition of the *Rechtsstaat* in German legal studies:

> Der Staat soll Rechtsstaat seyn, das ist die Losung und ist auch in Wahrheit der Entwicklungstrieb der neueren Zeit. Er soll die Bahnen und Gränzen seiner Wirksamkeit wie die freie Sphäre seiner Bürger in der Weise des Rechts genau bestimmen und unverbrüchlich sichern und soll die sittlichen Ideen von Staatswegen, also direkt, nicht weiter verwirklichen

---

250 See, with further references, Prümm 2012; Wienfort 2012.
251 See Kotulla 2007.
252 See Kotulla 1992.
253 See Böckenförde 2024b [1969], 150–58.

(erzwingen), als es der Rechtssphäre angehört, d.i. nur bis zur nothwendigen Umzäumung. Dieß ist der Begriff des Rechtsstaats, nicht etwa, daß der Staat bloß die Rechtsordnung handhabe ohne administrative Zwecke, oder vollends bloß die Rechte der Einzelnen schütze, er bedeutet überhaupt nicht Ziel und Inhalt des Staates, sondern nur Art und Charakter, dieselben zu verwirklichen.[254]

[The state should be a *Rechtsstaat*; that is the slogan and, in truth, the driving force behind modern development. It should precisely define and inviolably secure the boundaries of its power and the free sphere of its citizens in accordance with the law, and it should not realise (enforce) moral ideas through state action; i.e., directly, beyond what belongs to the sphere of law; i.e., only to the extent necessary for necessary regulation. This is the concept of the *Rechtsstaat*, not that the state merely administers the legal system without administrative purposes, or merely protects the rights of individuals; it does not mean the goal and content of the state, but only the manner and character of realising them.]

Its focus on legal procedures connects the concept of *Rechtsstaat* with that of the *Verwaltungsstaat* (administrative state), as the implementation of and compliance with formal legal procedures depend on a functioning administration. Leading scholars of administrative law in the Wilhelmine era, such as Otto Mayer (1846–1924), thus equated the two concepts, so that a smooth and well-organised administration soon became the central feature of the concept of a *Rechtsstaat*.[255] However, against the claim that the political and normative idea of the *Rechtsstaat* had degenerated into formalism and legal positivism, it should be noted that legal certainty and formal elements were essential to its conception and that criticism of these ideas has always been highly ambivalent. It is perhaps worth pointing to the current global crisis regarding the rule of law here, due to the rise of authoritarian rule and the attack on the rule of law by right-wing political parties, even in long standing liberal democracies.[256] More problematic than the formalist conception of the *Rechtsstaat* was the fact that the whole idea became an integral part of German nationalism during the early twentieth century; German scholars were certain that their country was the most advanced *Rechtsstaat* and most

---

254 Stahl 1846, 106.
255 See Mayer 1895, 53–63.
256 For this reason, see the different perspective of Maus 1978. She rightly emphasised that a critique of formalism and legal positivism was essential to the nationalist and antisemitic scholars of the early twentieth century, most notably Carl Schmitt (1888–1985), who viewed pure legalism as inherently Jewish. After 1945, mostly conservative legal scholars attempted to blame legal positivism, whose most prominent representative in the German-speaking world was Austrian-Jewish Heinz Kelsen (1881–1973) a jurist and the main enemy of Carl Schmitt during the 1920s and 1930s, for the defenselessness of the *Rechtsstaat* against demolition by the Nazis. However, recent scholarship has exposed this as one of the founding myths of the German judicial system in the postwar years. See among others Dreier 2011.

agreed that this was due to the policies of the Prussian kings in the eighteenth and early nineteenth centuries. According to the historian Otto Hintze, Frederick II laid the foundations of the modern German constitutional and administrative state by ordering a new legal code in which "the spirit of enlightened despotism [...] found classic expression in its benevolent, humane tendencies and conservative social policies."[257]

Scholars at the turn of the twentieth century were well aware that the establishment of the modern Prussian *Rechtsstaat* had been a long and arduous journey and one that had included several key steps, such as the creation of a functional and efficient legal administration, the prohibition of monarchical interference, and the development of an independent and incorruptible judiciary. Therefore, it must have seemed all the more astonishing that many of the same things had already been achieved in ancient Babylonia. While Delitzsch did not elaborate on his claim regarding Babylonia as an "exemplary *Rechtsstaat*," others sought to justify the anachronistic use of this term by referring to certain legal practices and rules under Hammurapi. The multi-volume collection of Babylonian laws edited by Kohler, Peiser and Ungnad was aimed in this direction.[258] Ungnad, for example, emphasised the supposed impartiality of the Babylonian judges and enthusiastically praised Hammurapi for enforcing the "incorruptibility of the judiciary" (although not its independence from himself).[259] However, against the background of the development and transformation of the concept in the later nineteenth century, the claim that Old Babylonia was a *Rechtsstaat* in the modern sense primarily indicated that Hammurapi had established a modern *Verwaltungstaat*. The emphasis on trade and commerce in his code seemed to support this claim, as a thriving economy, such as was assumed to have existed in ancient Babylonia, depends on a high level of legal certainty. Consequently, German scholars praised the organised, efficient and excellent administration in Babylonia, which they thought had cleary reached an unprecedented level. Through the lens of contemporary legal positivism, they all assumed that the provisions in the Code of Hammurapi constituted normative legislation that was more or less applied by Babylonian judges in a manner similar to how modern judges apply contemporary law.[260]

---

[257] Hintze 1915, 397, 400. The code was adopted by his successor Frederick William II in 1792 as the *Preußisches Allgemeines Landrecht*.
[258] See Kohler and Peiser 1904; Kohler and Ungnad 1909b; Kohler and Ungnad 1909a; Kohler and Ungnad 1910, 1911.
[259] Ungnad 1919, 64.
[260] See especially Kohler and Peiser 1904, 3; Winckler 1913, 14; Meissner 1926, 57.

Just as the authoritarian and patriarchal conceptions of monarchy that circulated during the Wilhelmine period were solidified by their supposed Babylonian roots, the imposition of the modern concept of the *Rechtsstaat* onto the Code of Hammurapi contributed to the historical legitimisation of the founding principles of the German state. Furthermore, it reinforced the notion of an elective affinity between ancient Babylonia and modern Germany.

3 Religion and Ethics

From today's perspective, it is not always easy to understand why the discovery of objects from the ancient Near East had such a profound impact on late nineteenth and early twentieth century religious discourse. In a general sense, it should be noted that Christianity remained a central force in that period, shaping European cultures, societies and politics to a much greater extent than it does today. Then, the discovery of a past not mentioned in the Bible and difficult to reconcile with its narratives appeared much more problematic. However, important transformations and trends, often described as secularisation or de-Christianisation, were already active at the time, alongside the emergence of new religious practices and movements. These developments provoked endless debates regarding the significance of religion in general – for society, culture, law, politics, science, etc., and of Christianity in particular.[261]

Moreover, there were additional reasons for the specific importance of religion in the field of Ancient Near Eastern Studies.[262] One of these was the personal and disciplinary background of many scholars, a high proportion of whom were trained theologians or were employed by theological institutions. But more important was the subject itself: as Christianity had its origins in the ancient Near East, the study of religion and religious practices in the context of the biblical world proved delicate. Due to the overlap with central narratives of the Hebrew Bible, German Jewish scholars were actively involved in these debates. They often found themselves caught between the conflicting positions of the Christian apologists and the secularists and were required to defend themselves against these stances as well as the anti-Jewish tropes and narratives prevalent on both sides.[263] This became evident when the discovery of the Code of Hammurapi immediately raised the question of its relationship to biblical law. There were two issues at stake: Firstly, the historical relationship between Hammurapi and Moses needed to be defined; behind this problem stood the question of to what extent Babylonian law was a source for biblical law. The second issue hinged on whether biblical law was ethically superior to other legal traditions. This latter

---

[261] For an overview with a focus on the German context (among many others), see Nipperdey 2013 [1990], 428–530; Graf 2004, 133–78.
[262] On the importance of religion in the field of German oriental studies, see in general Marchand 2009. With a focus on Britain, see Holloway 2001; Malley 2012.
[263] On German-Jewish scholars in the fields of Ancient Near Eastern Studies, see Renger 2001. The topic of German-Jewish Orientalism has been well researched over the last two decades. See among others Efron 2004; Peleg 2005; Aschheim 2010; Heschel 2018; Wittler 2019.

issue was closely related to the broader question of the relationship between positive law and morality; a topic that continues to be extensively debated in legal theory and the philosophy of law to this day. The entire issue resurfaced in the philosophical debate between Kant's concept of morality and Hegel's concept of *Sittlichkeit*. Notably, both sides of the debate – those seeking to establish a completely secular form of law and morality, and those insisting on the religious foundation of both – were interested in ancient Babylonian law and its connection to the Bible.

3.1 Hammurapi and Moses

Before the discovery of ancient Mesopotamian legal sources, biblical law was thought to be the oldest written law in human history. For this reason alone, the Code of Hammurapi provoked comparisons with biblical law, believed by the faithful to have been handed directly to Moses from God.[264] The question of the relationship between Hammurapi and Moses becomes even more inescapable when considering the significant parallels between the two sources.[265] The most notable example is the law of retaliation, also known as the *lex talionis*, which is encapsulated in the biblical phrase "an eye for an eye and a tooth for a tooth" (Ex 21:23–27). This idea of reciprocal justice is also the fundamental principle of the penal regulations in the Code of Hammurapi (see LH §§1–5), but, as we know from earlier legal codes such as the Code of Ur-Nammu (LU §1), it has much older origins.[266]

Upon its discovery, there was no doubt that the Code of Hammurapi was much older than the Mosaic Law; even the most orthodox theologians did not question this fact. The commonly accepted chronology (no longer considered accurate today) placed the era of Hammurapi in the early third millennium BC. In contrast, the Exodus, the mass migration led by Moses, was usually dated to the reign of the Egyptian pharaoh Ramses II in the thirteenth century BC. For this reason, the similarities between the two law collections were potentially grist for the mills of certain fervent Orientalists who tried to decentralise Christianity (and Judaism) in history in favour of the pre-biblical ancient Near East.[267] In this respect, there was certainly a triumphant edge to the subtitling of Winckler's edition of the Code

---

[264] This chapter is based on an article that has already been published. See Wiedemann 2024a.
[265] For an overview of the parallels, see the tables by Wright 2009, 7–11.
[266] On the *lex talionis* in Babylonian law, see (among others) Harke 2007; on the *lex talionis* in the Bible, see Jacobs 2014, 68–189; additionally Otto 1996; Westbrook 2009b [1986].
[267] See in general Marchand 2009, 212–51.

of Hammurapi as "the world's oldest statute book," as before 1902, this epithet had been reserved for Mosaic law. Delitzsch's rhetorical question as to whether the "Israelite laws" had been influenced by, or even copied from, the much older Babylonian laws was heading in the same direction.[268] With regard to both scholars, it is reasonable to suspect that their scorn was motivated by antisemitism and anti-clericalism, sentiments which often went hand in hand during the Wilhelmine era. However, the frontlines of this debate were more complex and did not follow specific ideological and political lines of thinking.

One might expect those Christian and Jewish scholars who insisted on the uniqueness and authenticity of the Hebrew Bible and the historical truth of its narratives to have taken a hostile view of assertions concerning parallels between Babylonian law and biblical law, given the potential of such claims to detract from the glory of the latter. Quite the opposite was true, however. At least initially, conservative theologians were among those who particularly welcomed the discovery of the Code of Hammurapi. To understand this positive reaction, it is important to take into account the relationship that existed between Assyriology and the Bible *before* the eruption of the Babel-Bible controversy. Until the late nineteenth century theologians usually welcomed the sensational discovery of ancient Near Eastern monuments and texts because they saw these as corroborating the authenticity and historical truth of the biblical narratives. The search for external proofs of the Bible had a long history and went hand in hand with the rise of modern Biblical Studies in the middle of the eighteenth century. The most famous example of such proof-seeking is the Danish expedition to Arabia between 1761 and 1767, of which the German mathematician and cartographer Carsten Niebuhr (1733–1815) was the only survivor. The project was initiated and planned by the Göttingen biblical scholar Johann David Michaelis (1717–1891) who wanted to use empirical knowledge of the languages, geography, and ethnography of the (modern) Middle East to illuminate the biblical past.[269] The further exploration of the Middle East over the course of the nineteenth century went hand in hand with its imperial penetration by European powers and led to an explosion of knowledge regarding the ancient Near East.

For Biblical Studies, sources dating from the mid-second to the mid-first millennium BC were of special interest, because this was the period illuminated by the so-called historical books of the Bible. It was during this time that the stories of the biblical Patriarchs, the Exodus of the Israelites from Egypt, the so-called

---

[268] Delitzsch 1903, 25.
[269] On Niebuhr and his expedition, see Rasmussen 1986; Wiesehöfer and Conermann 2002. On Michaelis and the formation of modern German Biblical Studies, see Rauchstein 2017; for more general perspectives see Sheehan 2005, 182–217; Carhart 2007, 27–68; Legaspi 2010, 79–155.

Landnahme (the conquest and settlement in Canaan), the Kingdom of David and Salomon, the division of the United Monarchy into Israel and Judah, attacks by the Assyrians and Babylonians, and the Babylonian Exile occurred. In the early twentieth century, scholars were particularly fascinated by the geographical and political position of ancient Israel and Judah, as they lay between the major powers of the ancient Near East: Egypt, Assyria, Babylonia, and Persia. They sought to analyse this constellation using geopolitical concepts and the narratives established by contemporary imperialist geographers and historians. The geohistorical narratives they developed in turn significantly reshaped imperial perceptions of the Middle East. One notable example is the concept of the 'Fertile Crescent,' a term originally coined by the American Egyptologist James Henry Breasted (1865–1935).[270]

As the archaeological exploration of Egypt preceded that of other Middle Eastern countries, the hopes of biblical scholars had initially rested on excavations centring on the Nile. With the story of Joseph and his brothers, as well as that of the Exodus, Egypt seemed to have been the historical setting of some of the most important biblical narratives. Even in the seventeenth and eighteenth centuries, European scholars speculated on the connection of Joseph and Moses to the history of Egypt and looked for external evidence of events like the Exodus. Biblical Egypt remained a central topic of scholarship in the nineteenth century.[271] However, neither the modern excavations there nor ancient Egyptian texts seemed to testify to the veracity of the biblical narratives.[272] Disappointed by Egypt, European scholars hoped that Mesopotamian remains would prove to be more useful for Biblical Studies. Especially the later parts of the Old Testament, the prophets and writings, include a lot of concrete and detailed references to Assyrian, Babylonian and Persian places, names, and historical events dating to the middle of the first millennium BC, when the kingdoms of Israel and Judah were influenced, or outright controlled, by Eastern Empires. In 722 BC, Israel became part of the Assyrian Empire and ceased to exist as a political entity; Judah suffered the same fate in 587 BC when it was conquered by the Neo-Babylonian empire.

---

[270] Breasted 1916, 100–101. On the background of this metaphor, see Scheffler 2003; on the influence of geopolitics to Ancient Near Eastern Studies, see with further references Wiedemann 2020, 256–84.

[271] See among others Assmann 1998.

[272] The most important object in this respect was the Merneptah Stele, also known as the Israel Stele, excavated in 1896 by the British archaeologist Wlllliam Matthew Flinders Petrie (1853–1942) in Thebes. The text on the stele – an account of the victories of pharaoh Merneptah (ca. 1213–1203 BC) over his enemies – represents the oldest mention of Israel as a collective entity but remained the only textual reference from ancient Egypt at all. See among others Hasel 2008; Nestor 2015.

With the following Babylonian Exile the entire setting of the biblical narrative shifted from Palestine to Babylonia. For this reason, the spectacular excavations led by Paul-Émile Botta and Austin Henry Layard that took place at various Assyrian sites in the 1840s were closely followed by biblical scholars, who generally became convinced that these confirmed the biblical narratives. What is more, discoveries such as the famous Lachish reliefs from the South-West Palace of Sennacherib at Nineveh, which depicts the Assyrian siege of the Judean city in 701 BC, seemed to shed light on incidents that the Bible only briefly mentioned (2 Kings 18:13–15).[273] As a result, these discoveries have been viewed as extra-biblical sources for interpreting the text.[274] In a certain sense, though, ancient Near Eastern archaeology practiced during the nineteenth and early twentieth centuries was in fact always 'biblical archaeology,' although most of the scholars involved did not pursue any direct apologetic goals.[275]

For conservative Christians of the late nineteenth century however, uncovering material evidence to corroborate the biblical text became particularly urgent, as it could be used as a weapon against their major adversary in the field of Biblical Studies: philological or 'higher' criticism.[276] As has rightly been emphasised, biblical criticism is one of the modern sciences that undermined modern Europeans' sense of certainty, thus contributing heavily to the crisis of historicism in the field of theology at the turn of the twentieth century.[277] The application of the same methodological tools to the Bible as to any other textual source appeared to be an inevitable path to its disenchantment. Thus, when Nietzsche argued in his polemic against historicism, that Christianity, "under the influence of historical treatment" became "denaturalised" and resolved into "pure knowledge about Christianity," something he believed would ultimately lead to its destruction (a process he welcomed), he was undoubtedly primarily referring to biblical criticism.[278] Already in the eighteenth century, scholars had begun to distinguish the Old Testament into different textual layers and to develop a chronological schema that differs from the traditional order of the books. In

---

[273] The reliefs were discovered by Layard during his excavations between 1845–1847. He ordered them to be completely removed, after which they were transported to England, where they remain on display in the British Museum.
[274] See Ussishkin 1980.
[275] See Zink MacHaffie 1981. On the history of biblical archaeology, see (among others) Thompson 1999; Davis 2004; Cline 2009.
[276] On the history of biblical criticism in the nineteenth century, see (among others) Thompson 1970; Frei 1974; Kraus 1982; Rogerson 1984; Reventlow 2001; Sæbø 2013.
[277] Otto 2010, 1. On the reactions to historicism in contemporary German theology, see (among others) Nowak 1987; Graf 1997.
[278] Nietzsche 1991, 96 (original German Nietzsche 1988, 297).

the late nineteenth century, philological criticism was most prominently associated with Julius Wellhausen (1844–1918) whose textual criticism of the Old Testament became the starting point of a new narrative that revolutionised the historiography of ancient Israel. Following this, central biblical events like the Exodus or the conquest of Canaan, were called into question and began to appear more mythical than historical.²⁷⁹ However, it was the traditional view of biblical law that was most challenged by Wellhausen's new arrangement of the text. Instead of being revealed to Moses on Mount Sinai, biblical law now appeared to be a late product of textual composition, written during the Babylonian exile or even later.²⁸⁰

The rejection of Wellhausen and his supposed attack on the foundation of Christian faith was particularly strong among conservative Protestants in Great Britain. Significantly, his most prominent scholarly opponent was an Anglican cleric who was at the same time one of the founding fathers of British Assyriology. Archibald Henry Sayce (1845–1933) wrote several monographs (some of them translated into German) on the contemporary discoveries in the Middle East that were aimed at refuting biblical criticism in general. According to Sayce, the "verdict of monuments" came down entirely on the side of the biblical narratives.²⁸¹ The most influential German scholar with a similar agenda was Fritz Hommel. Due to his Pan-Babylonian theory, Hommel's exegesis of the Old Testament was considerably less literal than that of other conservative scholars; nevertheless, like Sayce, he completely rejected decontextualised philological criticism.²⁸²

Against this backdrop, the initially positive reactions of conservative Christians to the discovery of the Code of Hammurapi are not surprising. For instance, Eduard König (1846–1936), an Old Testament scholar and a fierce opponent of Wellhausen and Delitzsch, argued that the Hammurapi stele demonstrated not only that complex legal systems existed in the early periods of Near Eastern his-

---

279 Wellhausen 1878, 1894. There is a huge body of literature on Wellhausen and his school. Most recently with further references Kurtz 2018, 19–166; on his biography Smend 1989, 99–113; Bauer 2005.
280 Wellhausen 1885. In many respects, Wellhausen built on the work of Wilhelm Martin Leberecht de Wette (1780–1849) who had already shown that the Book of Deuteronomy could only have been written much later than other biblical books. For short information, see (among others) Smend 1989, 38–52; Huwyler 2013. For more on the highly negative impact this new perspective had on the Protestant view of Jews and Judaism, see Pasto 2003.
281 See Sayce 1884a; Sayce 1884b; Sayce 1894. See on these writings Zink MacHaffie 1981. On Sayce and his intellectual context, see Belton 2007.
282 His attack was published in German and English at the same time. See Hommel 1897a; Hommel 1897b.

tory but also that the ancient Hebrews were not primitive nomads before settling in Canaan. Instead, he believed that they had long before attained a high level of cultural achievement.[283] In this respect, there was no difference between König's views and those of Jewish Orthodox scholars like Seligmann Meyer (1853–1925), another active participant in the Babel-Bible-controversy, who expressed the hope that the Babylonian code would contribute to a better understanding of what he termed "Jewish antiquity" and confirm the historical truth of the Hebrew Bible.[284] Hommel went even further: whereas Wellhausen and the liberal biblical scholars placed 'the Law after the Prophets' Hommel used the Hammurapi Code as evidence for a longstanding tradition of written law in the ancient Near East.[285] Early on in his polemical attack on Wellhausen, he adopted the identification of Hammurapi as the biblical King Amraphel, a theory initiated by French scholars that was pivotal in establishing the strong connection Hommel drew between Babylonia and the Bible.[286] Once the Code was found, Hommel became convinced that Abraham was responsible for bringing elements of Babylonian law to the Holy Land – an argument which fit in with his Pan-Babylonian convictions very well as adherents of this school of thought contended that all cultural achievements stemmed from ancient Mesopotamia.

The strategy of conservative scholars to use objects and texts from the ancient Near East as a weapon against the supposed dangers of liberal biblical criticism was subject to pitfalls, however. It could only work if these objects were accepted as sufficient evidence for the historicity of biblical narratives, and certain of the new finds were proving ambivalent in this respect. Prior to the excavation of the Hammurapi stele, the most significant case was the discovery of clay tablets containing fragments of the Epic of Gilgamesh by the British Assyriologist George Smith (1840–1876) in 1872. The eleventh tablet contains a story about a big flood that is very similar to the account of the Flood in the Book of Genesis (Gen 6–9). The unmistakable parallels between these two accounts allowed for the possibility of regarding the Bible as merely reproducing an older Mesopotamian myth.[287] While conservative Christians and advocates of biblical archaeology saw the biblical version of the Flood story as being verified by an external source, Delitzsch, in his lectures on Babel and the Bible, supported the primacy of the Mesopotamian narrative. For most scholars the parallels he drew upon were any-

---

283 König 1903.
284 Meyer 1903, 8.
285 Hommel 1904, 238.
286 See the references to "KHammurapi" in the index of Hommel 1897b. On this identification see above.
287 See Smith 1876. On the contemporary debate, see Cregan-Reid 2006; McGeough 2015, 392–406.

thing but new, but the sharpness of his questions and his polemical tone was unknown before. "Is it any wonder," Delitzsch asked with reference to the parallels between the Mesopotamian and biblical Flood accounts, "that a whole series of biblical stories now suddenly emerge from the night of the Babylonian treasure hills in a *purer* and *more original* form?"[288] By insinuating that parts of the Old Testament were based on older Mesopotamian sources he undermined the Bible's theological and philological value. Neither a divine revelation nor a primary source, the Bible was now a mere copy of something 'purer' and 'more original'.

For conservative Christians and Jews however, placing the Bible within the context of the ancient Near East, as Delitzsch did, appeared to confirm Nietzsche's prediction that a consistent "historical treatment" of religion would ultimately lead to its destruction.[289] The antiquity of the Code of Hammurapi thus posed a similar problem in this respect, as it could be perceived as questioning the originality of biblical law. As the theologian Eduard König stated, the origin and authenticity of the laws outlined in the Pentateuch were at stake.[290] Thwarting the argument that Moses, was a mere copyist, adorned with laurels that rightly belonged to Babylonia, was of great importance to the Christian and Jewish defenders of the Bible, who needed to demonstrate that biblical law did not depend on Babylonian law. If the parallels could not be ignored, they needed to be explained by other means than via direct borrowing. One such possibility was to deny the existence of historical connections between the two codes and to explain any similarities as being due to ideas universal to the history of law. In this vein, the German-Jewish legal historian Georg Cohn (1845–1918), president of the University of Zürich, referred to the theory of general "elementary ideas" (*Elementargedanken*), developed by the German ethnologist Adolf Bastian (1826–1905).[291] However, there were few other scholars who followed this line of argument, as reference to universals did not seem to convincingly explain certain of the detailed similarities recognised between Babylonian and biblical law. Furthermore, even among German anthropologists and ethnologists, Bastian's ideas became increasingly unpopular after the turn of the century and were ultimately replaced by the paradigm of cultural diffusion, which sought to explain cultural similarities through direct borrowing.[292] The version of diffusionism prevalent in Ancient Near Eastern Studies had its own name, the aforementioned 'Pan-Babylonism'.

---

288 Delitzsch 1902, 29 (emphasises mine).
289 Nietzsche 1991, 96–97.
290 König 1903, 172.
291 Cohn 1903, 39. On the concept of *Elementargedanken*, see Bastian 2007 [1895].
292 On the rise of cultural diffusionism, see (among others) Smith 1991; Müller 1993.

A much more convincing means of explaining the parallels between the Code of Hammurapi and biblical law was an elegant solution put forward by the Austrian-Jewish Orientalist David Heinrich Müller (1846–1912). In his 1904 investigation *Die Gesetze Hammurabis und ihr Verhältnis zur mosaischen Gesetzgebung* ("The Laws of Hammurapi and their Relation to Mosaic Law"), via analogy with the methods of comparative linguistics, Müller developed a new approach for the systematic comparison of different law codes:

> Wie in der vergleichenden Sprachforschung der grammatische Bau hauptsächlich für die Verwandtschaft zweier Sprachen entscheidend ist, so müssen bei der vergleichenden Rechtsforschung nicht Einzelbestimmungen, sondern ganze Komplexe von Gesetzen in Betracht gezogen werden.[293]
>
> [As in comparative linguistics, grammatical structure is the main factor in determining the relationship between two languages, therefore in comparative legal research it is not individual provisions that need to be considered, but entire complexes of laws.]

During his studies, Müller had become more and more convinced that the Laws of the Twelve Tables, the legislation that was the foundation of Roman law, was also heavily influenced by the "old-Semitic" tradition of written law.[294] This argument was presumably a general revaluation of the ancient Near East, but of course did little to clarify the question of the relationship between the two Near Eastern codes involved in the debate. To facilitate systematic comparisons, Müller created tables juxtaposing the provisions contained in the laws of Hammurapi, in Mosaic law and in the Twelve Tables. At first glance, his findings were contradictory: he emphasised the close connection and the strong parallels between law collections while at the same time arguing that the Code of Hammurapi could not have been the source of Mosaic law because the formulation and arrangement of the biblical laws seemed more "original".[295] For these reasons, Müller concluded that there were no direct historical links between the two codes, but that both stemmed from a common source – an "original law" *(Urgesetz)* laid down at an earlier time.[296] Some years later, this idea was taken up by the Austrian legal historian Paul Koschaker, although he did not assume the existence of a single original law but considered it more likely that the Code of Hammurapi was a compilation of many different ancient sources.[297] Moreover, unlike Müller, Koschaker went to

---

293 Müller 1903, 6.
294 Müller 1903, 7.
295 Müller 1903, 241.
296 Müller 1903, 7.
297 See Koschaker 1917, 3–5.

great lengths to avoid discussing the relationship between biblical and Babylonian law. In fact, the crux of Müller's argument was his claim that the rules of the *Urgesetz* were better preserved in the Bible than in the Babylonian tradition: "The legislation of Moses took the whole system of the *Urgesetz* and faithfully preserved the wording, arrangement and order where it had no reason to make changes."[298] Within this framework, it became possible to concede that the Code of Hammurapi was indeed the oldest written text ever found and at the same view Mosaic law as more original and more authentic. What now appears to have been an awkward compromise became widely accepted by Christian and Jewish scholars of the time.

The debate regarding the historical relationship and possible dependency of biblical law on Babylonian sources was only one aspect of the discourse surrounding Hammurapi and Moses. Even more important was the question of the meaning and relative positions of the two codes in the wider history of human civilisation. Therefore, the relationship between law and ethics, especially the question of whether both developed separately or not, quickly became focus of the discussion.

3.2 Law, Morality and *Sittlichkeit*

A concession that biblical law was, to a certain degree, influenced by Babylonian law, did, of course, not necessarily imply a cultural and religious devaluation of biblical law. Such a conclusion was drawn only by certain fervent Orientalists, anticlericalists, and antisemites who certainly did not represent the majority of the German academic world during the Wilhelmine era. Thus, the preference of scholars like Winckler, Kohler, and Delitzsch for Hammurapi at the expense of Moses was far from uncontested. Theologians and biblical scholars were by no means alone in their attempts to uphold the unique importance of the biblical lawgiver. What they desired was a definite assessment of the cultural and ethical implications of Babylonian law versus biblical law. More broadly, this problem concerned the general relationship between law, ethics and religion, as discussed not only in theology but also within studies of legal philosophy and theory.

The main line of argument in this respect was developed again by Müller in his seminal work on the relationship between biblical law and the Code of Hammurapi. As mentioned above, Müller conceded that Moses had taken over the "entire systematic" of the original Semitic tradition.[299] What mattered to the Austrian

---

298 Müller 1903, 242.
299 Müller 1903, 242.

Orientalist however, were what he saw as the "substantive amendments" Moses had made in certain areas. Noting that the treatment of slaves under biblical law was far more lenient than that advised by the Code of Hammurapi, he argued that Moses was responsible for introducing certain key elements that had not existed in law before him, namely "wisdom, mercy, and ethical greatness."[300] At this point in time, it becomes clear that the early twentieth century Hammurapi vs. Moses debate encompassed broader questions about the normative and religious foundations of modern law. In a long review of Müller's book published in the *Monatsschrift für Geschichte und Wissenschaft des Judentums*, Rabbi David Feuchtwang (1864–1936) of Vienna expanded on this point, highlighting a moral gulf between the codes of Hammurapi and Moses and strongly denying any ethical continuity between them:

> Unendlich gross ist die Ähnlichkeit und Übereinstimmung in beiden Gesetzen; unendlich tief ihr Gegensatz; viele Fäden spinnen formell hinüber und herüber, kein Steg führt aber über die sittliche Kluft, die Moses von Hammurapi trennt [...] Von hier aus hätte kein direkter Weg zur Blüte aller Gesetzgebungen, zum weltbezwingenden Dekalog geführt.[301]
>
> [Infinitely great is the similarity and agreement in both laws; infinitely profound their contrast; many threads formally spin back and forth, but no bridge spans the moral chasm that separates Moses from Hammurapi [...] No direct path would have led from him to the flowering of all laws, to the world-transcending Ten Commandments.]

It is worth noting that there was no division between Christian and Jewish religious scholars regarding the *cultural* achievements of the Babylonians: neither group had any difficulty accepting the priority of the Babylonians over the ancient Israelites in the fields of science, technology, economy, and politics, as this view aligned well with the biblical narrative. However, while 'modernist' scholars such as Kohler, Winckler, Delitzsch, and Lehmann-Haupt interpreted this as indicating a general Babylonian superiority over the Hebrews, Jewish and Christian scholars distinguished between cultural achievements and ethical and religious ones. They asserted an ethical and moral exceptionalism of the Israelites, which ultimately led to a similar notion of supremacism. The superiority of biblical law was especially emphasised by Samuel Oettli (1846–1911), a protestant professor of Old Testament studies at the University of Greifswald:

> Ohne Frage spiegelt sich im C[odex]H[ammurapi] ein viel entwickelteres staatliches Leben, als im Bundesbuch; aber ebenso unzweifelhaft ringt sich in diesem und in den späteren Gesetzessammlungen der Thora ein anderer, ein wahrhaft humaner Geist empor, der seinen

---

300 Müller 1903, 242.
301 Feuchtwang 1904, 393–94.

Quellort in dem unvergleichlich reineren und sittlich fruchtbareren religiösen Glauben Israels hatte. [...] In allen diesen Beziehungen und zumal in der durchaus religiösen Fundierung der Einzelforderungen hat eben in der Thora Israels der Geist gewaltet der freilich nicht auf den Bau eines festgefügten, Völker bezwingenden Weltreichs, aber auf die Gründung einer Gottesherrschaft des Friedens und der Gerechtigkeit unter den Menschen hin arbeitet.[302]

[There is no question that the civil life reflected in the Codex of Hammurapi is far more developed than that reflected in the Covenant Code; but it is equally beyond doubt that a different, a truly humane spirit struggles forth in this [latter] and in the later law collections of the Thora, one whose source lies in the religious faith of Israel, which is incomparably purer and more fruitful ethically. [...] In all these relationships, and especially in the thoroughly religious foundation of the individual demands, it is precisely in the Torah of Israel that the spirit has prevailed, which, of course, does not work towards the construction of a firmly established empire that conquers nations, but towards the founding of a divine rule of peace and justice among people.]

In fact, the main intention of many of the Christian scholars engaging in these debates was not to defend the ancient Israelites (let alone the modern Jews). Their apologia was rooted in a Christian-centred narrative in which the alleged ethical exceptionalism of the Israelites was seen as their central contribution to human history, as it ultimately led to the Christian mission of the world.

At the core of this debate were fundamental questions regarding the religious foundations of both ancient and modern law. The relationship between the Old Babylonian king and the gods became central in this respect. Various deities are mentioned on Hammurapi's stele, but the sun god Shamash stands out as the most significant, being named eight times in the prologue and epilogue to the laws. In the ancient Mesopotamian pantheon, Shamash was responsible for justice and was revered as the divine judge and protector of the law.[303] It is likely that Hammurapi's stele had been erected at the main temple of Shamash in the southern Babylonian city of Sippar and stood there for five hundred years before it was stolen by the Elamites. The scene depicted on the stela is highly illustrative of an Old Babylonian king's role as law-giver (fig. 4). Hammurapi stands before Shamash, who sits on a throne, and receives the god's insignia of justice, the rod and ring.[304] At first glance, this scene appears to be similar to the common

---

302 Oettli 1903, 88.
303 For short information with further references, see Krebernik 2006–2008; Krebernik 2009–2011.
304 On the iconography of this relief, see with further references Elsen-Novak and Novak 2006; on Mesopotamian representations of Shamash, see Kurmangaliev 2009–2011; on the meaning of the rod and ring, see Wiggermann 2006–2008.

Figure 4: The relief of the stele of Hammurapi shows the Babylonian king standing in front of the sun god Samas.

conception of the divine revelation of Mosaic Law to Moses on Mount Sinai (Ex 19–20); a fact emphasised by Delitzsch.[305] However, the striking difference between the two stories is that Moses receives the written law itself directly from God, and delivers these to the Israelites, whereas Hammurapi only receives insignia that authorises him to administer justice himself. Unlike the Bible, the Ham-

---

305 Delitzsch 1903, 23–24.

murapi stela makes no claim that its laws were of divine authorship; in ancient Mesopotamia, it was the kings who set down the law, not the gods.[306] Theologians noticed this distinction early on and used it as a basis for asserting fundamental theological and ethical differences. The Leipzig pastor Johannes Jeremias (1865–1942), for example, drew a sharp distinction between the Babylonian and Biblical revelation narratives, arguing that the relief on the Hammurapi stele demonstrated the pagan character of Babylonian law by illustrating a despotic relationship between God and man: "This pagan revelation lacks the spiritually and morally free acceptance of faith; it does not rise above the forms of ancient Oriental despotism."[307] Following Jeremias, Babylonian law remained despotic, while only Moses, and ultimately, of course, Jesus, were considered to have reveal a truly ethical law that superseded despotism.

Like Jeremias, the overwhelming majority of Christian scholars who engaged in discussions of Hammurapi vs. Moses had Protestant backgrounds. Catholic scholars were much less involved in these debates. Hubert Grimme, then professor of Semitic studies at the University of Fribourg in Switzerland, was an exception in this respect, though his arguments do not seem to reflect any distinctly Catholic theological positions. As a specialist in Islamic history and a renowned biographer of Muhammad, he adopted a broader perspective on 'Oriental law,' which allowed him to develop a new argument for the alleged moral superiority of the Israelites.[308] In his 1903 book *Das Gesetz Chammurapis und Moses* ("The Law of Hammurapi and Moses"), he adopted Müller's theory that Babylonian and biblical law had a common ancestor and identified this supposed shared source with the customary law practiced by the ancient Semitic tribes of the desert.[309] In keeping with the European variant of the myth of the noble Bedouin and widespread narratives of cultural pessimism in fin-de-siècle Europe, Grimme contrasted the supposedly pure and noble customs of desert nomads with those of the decadent Babylonian civilisation.[310] Grimme then argued that Mosaic law was closer to this original Semitic law, which in his view ruled out any direct connec-

---

306 On this important difference, see with further references Naiden 2013.
307 Jeremias 1903, 56–57. This is one of the rare instances in which Hammurapi is associated with (oriental) despotism. It should be noted however, that it was not the Babylonian king but the sun god Shamash who Jeremias considered to be the despot.
308 See Grimme 1892; Grimme 1895; Grimme 1904.
309 Grimme 1903, 25.
310 See Grimme 1903, 27. On the romanticisation of the Bedouin in European writings, see Tidrick 1981. As Isabel Toral-Niehoff has shown, the myth of the 'noble Bedouin' emerged from a mixture of European and Middle Eastern imagination, and clearly drew on Arabic sources. See Toral-Niehoff 2002; on its relevance for Ancient Near Eastern Studies of the time, see Wiedemann 2012.

tion between Moses and Hammurapi. Furthermore, he considered the Code of Hammurapi, with its detailed rules for trade and commerce, as only suitable for a feudal society based on a slave-holding economy. In contrast, he believed that Mosaic law reflected an egalitarian society of free nomads.[311]

The association of Moses with nomadic life was anything but new in Biblical Studies, and can be traced back to Michaelis' works in the late eighteenth century.[312] This theme continued to play a central role in German Biblical Studies throughout the latter part of the twentieth century. For instance, the Old Testament scholar Albrecht Alt (1883–1956) aimed to differentiate the 'casuistic' elements of biblical law, which he believed were adopted from surrounding civilisations, from the 'apodictic' sections that he traced back to the supposedly original laws of Semitic nomads.[313] The notion of a stark contrast between city dwellers and nomads was almost always morally charged in philosophical and theological writings. For Grimme, the nomadic background of the Israelites became the central criterion for his claim that Moses was ethically superior to Hammurapi; which he said ultimately "paved the way for the Christian law of morality."[314] Thus, Grimme attributed Moses' superiority not in terms of the divine revelation granted him, as other scholars did, but to a purer way of life, undistorted by civilisation – in contrast to the hyper-civilised and decadent Babylonians:

> Babels Gesetz hat niemals die bis an die Babels Tore streifenden Beduinen bezwungen: trennte doch beide eine Welt von Anschauungen und Lebensbedingungen. Ähnlich muß man sich das Verhältnis zwischen Babel und Altisrael denken. [...] Betrachtet man daher endlich den Geist, welchen die israelitische und babylonische Gesetzgebung atmet, so erscheint selbst das hüben und drüben äußerlich Verwandte durch eine tiefe Kluft getrennt.[315]
>
> [Babel's law never prevailed over the Bedouins, who grazed their flocks as far as the gates of Babel: the two were worlds apart in terms of outlook and living conditions. We must think of a similar relationship between Babel and ancient Israel [...]. If we consider the spirit that breathes through Israelite and Babylonian legislation, even what appears to be superficially related, was in fact separated by a deep chasm.]

---

311 Grimme 1903, 29.
312 Michaelis' work on Mosaic Law appeared in six volumes and went through several editions. See for the first edition Michaelis 1770–1775. There is a huge body of literature on Michaelis and his studies of the Mosaic law. See among others Hess 2000; Neis 2003, 507–49; Carhart 2007, 27–68; Sheehan 2005, 182–217; Legaspi 2010, 79–155; Rauchstein 2017.
313 Alt 1934. For a critique of this thesis, see (among others) Crüsemann 2005, 18–20.
314 Grimme 1903, 45.
315 Grimme 1903, 27.

By pitting the civilised against the non-civilised, Grimme employed a classic strategy that historian Rainer Kipper aptly termed the "reassessment of primitiveness in morality" *(Umwertung von Primitivität in Moralität).*[316] Its similarity to German national myths of the nineteenth and early twentieth centuries were all too evident, as the Bedouins (standing in for the Israelites) were cast in the same role as the ancient Teutons in relation to the 'civilised' Romans.

The anchoring of Mosaic law in Bedouin customs and a supposedly ethically purer nomadic way of life led to the emergence of another problem for German philosophical discourse related to ethics and religion: the distinction between *Moralität* (morality or ethics) on one hand and *Sittlichkeit* on the other. At the turn of the twentieth century, when German scholars were writing about morality or ethics, they often used the word *Sittlichkeit*, a term which is quite difficult to translate into other languages. Derived from the German word *Sitte* (meaning a custom or tradition), *Sittlichkeit* combines the ideas of morality and custom and could thus be used to refer, as Hegel did, to customary morality as opposed to reflective morality.[317] Today, even native speakers of German would find it difficult to understand the meaning this term once conveyed, because it has nearly vanished from modern German-language discourse regarding culture, history, or politics.[318] The complexity of *Sittlichkeit* in the late nineteenth and early twentieth centuries becomes evident when one looks at the Hammurapi vs. Moses debate. *Sittlichkeit* was employed as a term both by those who argued for the moral or ethical superiority of Mosaic law and the Israelites as well as by the modernists who insisted on the cultural (technological, economic, secular etc.) superiority of Hammurapi and the Babylonians. The Moses vs. Hammurapi debate thus reflects various, and even contradictory, understandings of *Sittlichkeit* within German discourse of the time. While most seemed to believe that the meaning of the term was obvious, its usage was often contradictory and sometimes contested, making it resistant to simple definitions. Similar to the concept of the *Rechtsstaat* analysed above, *Sittlichkeit* was omnipresent in contemporary discourse but rarely explained.

For several reasons, *Sittlichkeit* was particularly important to discourse regarding history, religion, and (ancient) law.[319] Roughly understood as a form of morality shaped by custom, the concept of *Sittlichkeit* was always surrounded

---

[316] Kipper 2002, 272–74.
[317] For more on the history of the concepts of customary vs. reflective morality, see Ilting 1983, 238–84; Ilting 1984.
[318] The term is still present in juridical language. The best known examples are *Sittlichkeitsvergehen* (acts of indecency) or *Sittlichkeitverbrechen* (sex crimes).
[319] See for instance Gierke 1916/17.

by questions of its historical genesis, its variations across different eras and cultures, its connection to religion and religious practices, and its relationship to written law. The forms these questions took were certainly shaped by the highly influential philosophical distinction between *Moralität* and *Sittlichkeit* Hegel made in his critique of Kant's moral philosophy.[320] Kant had used the two terms more or less synonymously to characterise actions that are motivated solely by duty *(Pflicht)* to the moral law; thereby contrasting duty with mere conformity with law.[321] But the most important aspect was that Kant's principles of morality were universal, unconditional, and formal, based on the idea of rational agents who autonomously impose moral law upon themselves. This Hegel criticised as being too abstract and only formal, calling it "an empty principle of moral subjectivity," and thereafter introducing a sharp distinction between *Moralität* and *Sittlichkeit* in his own work.[322] He reserved the term *Sittlichkeit* for a more objective form of ethics, referring to those moral obligations that people have to the communities of which they are a part, something he then contrasts with abstract and subjective morality. Thus, Hegel took social entities like the family, civil society, and the state as expressions of this highest form of moral life: "The ethical is a subjective disposition, but of that right which has being in itself."[323] There were two aspects of Hegel's concept of *Sittlichkeit* that were of particular relevance to German discourse regarding history, law and religion in the nineteenth century; firstly, an insistence on concrete social and historical contexts, and secondly, the historisation of moral beliefs and values that results from this dependence. Hegelian *Sittlichkeit* differs not only from one society to the next but also from one era to another. Moreover, as Hegel's followers were convinced, it evolved over the course of history.

---

320 Most famously expressed in his "Philosophy of Right;" see Hegel 1991 [1820], 133–275 (German original: Hegel 1986 [1820], 203–91). There is a huge body of literature on Hegel's distinction. See (among others) Ritter 1977 [1966]; Amengual 2001; see also the articles in Kuhlmann 1986. This differentiation is still at work in more recent social and moral philosophical debates. See (among others) Habermas 2021; Honneth 2021.
321 Kant 1907a [1797], 219. Consequently, in the English of edition of *Metaphysik der Sitten*, the terms *Moralität* and *Sittlichkeit* are both translated as morality. See Kant 2017 [1797], 23.
322 Hegel 1991 [1820], 191 (§ 148, see also §135). In English editions the term *Sittlichkeit* is usually translated as "ethics" or "ethical life." See the remarks of the translator (pp. 403–404); also Charles Taylor 1975, 376–78; others prefer to use the German term as a loanword. See, for example, Kain 2018, 83–137. On Hegel's critique of Kant's concept of morality, see with further references Wood 2017.
323 Hegel 1991 [1820], 186 (§ 141). German original: "Das Sittliche ist subjektive Gesinnung, aber des an sich seienden Rechts." (Hegel 1986 [1820], 287).

As a result, in later nineteenth century writings, differences in the way the term *Sittlichkeit* was used across various topics, such as culture, statecraft, law, religion, etc. became increasingly vast, leading to the term ultimately losing its connection with ethics. This can be demonstrated by examining how *Sittlichkeit* was used in historiographical works. The most influential contribution in this respect came from the historian and neo-Hegelian Johann Gustav Droysen (1808– 1884) who, alongside Ranke, is considered one of the founding fathers of German historicism. Compared to other historians of the nineteenth century, the level of theoretical reflection in Droysen's still-relevant *Historik* is certainly extraordinary. Although his epistemology primarily followed that of Kant, some of his key concepts were clearly borrowed from Hegel. Most important in this respect was the idea of *sittliche Mächte* (which roughly translates to "ethical powers"), a term Droysen coined to refer to the historical 'powers' that shape individuals into social units, including family, nation (*Volk*), religion, and the state. Highly sceptical of notions such as progress or development, which since the Enlightenment have conventionally served as foundations for the concept of continuity and the belief in a unified history, Droysen maintained that the *sittliche Mächte* were the only fundamental and universal categories that allowed historians to write coherent history.[324] Unlike Droysen however, most historians of the time used the term *Sittlichkeit* without further clarification. For them, the concept's appeal lay in the possibility of identifying different stages or levels in various societies and epochs, thereby elevating *Sittlichkeit* as an indicator of cultural progress. Against this backdrop, scholars who insisted on the modernity and superiority of Babylonian law often found evidence of a high level of *Sittlichkeit* within it, viewing Babylon as the cradle of civilisation and the most advanced society of the ancient Near East.[325]

Sittlichkeit remained a contested concept in scholarly writings, however. Furthermore, with the rise of philosophical neo-Kantianism in the late nineteenth century, the use of the term as a synonym for morality (in the sense of universal ethic) gained new currency. For some scholars, Kant's internal moral law of reason appeared to be an enlightened and modern variant of the idea of divine law revealed to Moses. For this reason, neo-Kantianism proved particularly attractive to Jewish scholars, especially those who were highly assimilated into German bourgeois culture (as a consequence, this school of thought was increasingly identified by its antisemitic opponents as a Jewish school of philosophy).[326] The most

---

324 Droysen 1977, 290–362. On Droysen's theory of history, see (among others) Rüsen 1993, 226–75.
325 See, specifically, Lehmann-Haupt 1905, 6.
326 On the Jewish contribution to Neo-Kantianism, see with further references Daub 2016.

important neo-Kantian thinker at the turn of the twentieth century was the German-Jewish philosopher Hermann Cohen (1842–1919). When, in his remarkable article *Religion und Sittlichkeit* (1907), he identified the "nature of God" with the "nature of human *Sittlichkeit*" and calls God himself an "archetype and model" *(Urbild und Vorbild)* of human *Sittlichkeit*, it is clear that Cohen is using the term to denote a universal concept of morality in the Kantian sense of the word.[327] Although Christian theologians like Hommel, Jeremias, or Oettli would certainly not have concurred with Cohen's insistence on the originally Jewish character of ethical monotheism, from which Christianity deviated in some respects, they shared his understanding of *Sittlichkeit* as a synonym for universal ethics.[328]

Remarkably, all German scholars, whether religious or non-religious, progressives or conservatives, agreed that the cultural superiority of the Babylonians was not accompanied by superior morality (in the sense of a humane and universal ethic). This can be best demonstrated through the writings of Josef Kohler, who is not only regarded as one of the forerunners of the so-called neo-Hegelian school of law but who also paved the way for comparative studies on the ethnology of law.[329] Though very interested in the customs and rules of so-called primitive or natural peoples, Kohler was convinced that progress was present in the history of law (the final stage of which was modern Western law), progress that corresponded to general social and economic development. To Kohler, it was beyond doubt that Babylonian law was more highly developed than that of the Bible, not least because of Babylonia's perceived modernity in other respects. Thus, in a highly critical review of Oettli's book on Hammurapi and Moses, Kohler explicitly linked economic progress with the rise of private property and self-interest. He further asserted that it would be unhistorical to consider the more altruistic and humane (in terms of modern morality) provisions of biblical law to be indications of its 'higher' character:

> Mit diesem Kommunismus sind natürlich eine Menge altruistischer Wendungen verbunden, die man als humane Züge hervorzuheben pflegt, und auf die auch der Verfasser [Oettli] aufmerksam macht. Allein unrichtig ist, wenn man behauptet, dass derartige menschenfre-

---

327 Cohen 1924.
328 See for instance Jeremias 1903, 25; Oettli 1903, 88; for Jewish scholars, see Feuchtwang 1904, 393. On the debates among Jewish scholars regarding the biblical foundations of ethics see Krone 2012, 327–74.
329 See for instance Kohler 1885; Kohler 1904a [1899]. On Kohler as a forerunner of the neo-Hegelian school of law, see Spendel 1983, 5. On the neo-Hegelian school of law in general, the main proponents of which became strong supporters of the Nazis, see (among others) Hurstel 1996; Mährlein 2000; Großmann 2010.

undliche Einrichtungen eine gesteigerte höhere Kultur bezeugten, sondern im Gegenteil: die Kultursteigerung drängt zunächst zu einer scharfen Ausgestaltung des Privatvermögens und, damit verbunden, zum Egoismus des Vermögens- und Geschäftsverkehrs. Dieser scharfe Vermögensegoismus ist das charakteristische Zeichen einer bestimmten hervorragenden Kulturstufe. [...] Es ist daher ungeschichtlich, wenn man von dem entwickelten babylonischen Rechte die sog. Menschenfreundlichkeit, d. h. die kommunistischen Züge erwartet, die sich in der Thora finden.[330]

[Of course, this communism [of the Mosaic law] is associated with a lot of altruistic phrases, which one tends to regard as more humane, and which the author [Oettli] also draws attention to. But it is not correct to say that such philanthropic institutions would evidence a more advanced culture, on the contrary: the progress of culture initially pushes towards a well-defined form of private property, and, as a result, towards the egoism of property and commercial transactions. This decisive egoism in the use of property is characteristic of a more advanced stage of civilisation. [...] It is therefore unhistorical to expect the so-called philanthropism (i. e. the communist features), of the Thora within highly developed Babylonian law.]

The modernist Kohler's exclusion of ethics from the concept of historical progress led him to a conclusion similar to that of religious scholars: though Babylonian law was less egalitarian and less just than biblical law, it represented a higher level of civilisation. Where these two groups differed was in their historical judgements; religious scholars were repulsed by Babylonian civilisation while Kohler and others were attracted to it. A central aspect of their fascination was that Babylonia appeared to them to be an almost secular society, characterised by an almost secular form of monarchical rule.

3.3 Babylonian Secularism

The relationship between the Old Babylonian ruler and the gods, along with his religious function in society, were central aspects of the debate over Hammurapi in the early twentieth century. In some respects, such questions also reflected political issues that were highly controversial in contemporary Germany, as the religious function of the German Kaiser and his constitutional position within the structure of the Protestant Church were complex problems, which, fuelled by his own religious pronouncements, remained the subjects of constant political debate.[331] At the national level, the Emperor had no religious or ecclesiastical functions; however, the German Emperor was also King of Prussia, where the situation

---

330 Kohler 1903, 1547.
331 See in general the articles in Samerski 2001.

was different. As previously mentioned, the religious legitimacy of the ruler – his divine right – was explicitly stated in the preamble of the Prussian constitution of 1849/1850. Furthermore, the Prussian king (and thus the German Kaiser) served as the supreme bishop *(summus episcopus)* of the "Evangelical State Church of Prussia's Older Provinces" and in this role exercised what was known as ecclesiastical government *(Kirchenregiment)*.[332] Thus, in Prussia (as in other Protestant German states), state and church, throne and altar, were not separate but closely interwoven, and the Prussian kings were determined to maintain their monarchical prerogatives and sovereign control over the Church.[333] Wilhelm II however, adopted a stance that went beyond traditional claims to the divine right of kingship and ecclesiastical government, and it was in this context that Hammurapi became relevant to him. As discussed above, the monarch conceived of the Babylonian king as at the beginning of a series of extraordinary historical figures through whom God had revealed himself.[334] It is clear that he saw in this heroic lineage not only his revered grandfather, but also himself. This perspective, clearly influenced by Chamberlain, was far less traditional and therefore a subject of public dispute.[335]

Among those who saw these matters differently from the German emperor were undoubtedly most of the scholars. They were not interested in a genealogy of divine rulers stretching from the present back to the Old Babylonian kings. Instead, scholars such as Winckler, Kohler and Lehmann-Haupt were fascinated by the supposedly non-religious or even secular aspects of Hammurapi's kingship. It was again the concept of enlightened absolutism that served as the narrative framework for his view. The historian Roscher had previously emphasised that the subjugation of the church to the reason of the state was one of the central aims of enlightened rulers.[336] Frederick II of Prussia and Joseph II of Austria had both pursued purely pragmatic policies of religious tolerance that should not be confused with the actual acceptance of those who were religiously differ-

---

332 The *Evangelische Kirche der altpreußischen Union* was an important Protestant ecclesiastical body, created in 1817 via a series of decrees by Frederick William III (1770–1840) of Prussia which united both Lutheran and Reformed denominations. Although not the first of its kind, the Prussian Union was the first to be established in a major German state. It grew to become the largest independent religious body in the German Empire and later within Weimar Germany, with some 18 million parishioners. The term 'Old Prussia' thus refers to the territory of Prussia before 1866, as neither the churches of Hesse-Kassel, Nassau and Frankfurt, nor the Lutheran churches of Schleswig-Holstein and Hanover, were incorporated into the Prussian state church after the annexations of 1866.
333 See the short description in Nipperdey 2013 [1990], 480–86.
334 Wilhelm II 1903, 495. See also above chapter 1.
335 See Markschies 2021.
336 Roscher 1874, 381.

ent. These policies were based solely on state interests. Frederick, who was widely regarded by his contemporaries as an atheist, intervened in church politics on several occasions.[337] Such actions were much easier in Protestant Prussia than in Catholic Austria, where Joseph II nevertheless took decisive action against the influence of the Catholic church and pursued a determined policy of secularising church property.[338] Similar deeds were performed by other historical rulers to whom the extended version of enlightened absolutism was applied. In particular, Frederick II of Sicily was known for his constant battles with the Church and the Pope, while his policies towards his Muslim subjects (and Islam in general) earned him a reputation as a tolerant ruler. Popular accounts, clearly infused with nationalism and anti-clericalism, even praised his "hatred of the omnipotent priesthood," something which had aligned him with the German national will (despite the fact that Frederick's struggles with the Pope were centred on his Sicilian state).[339]

In this way, Hammurapi's appeal in the early twentieth century for modernists was largely attributed to his supposedly anti-religious policies and his portrayal as a thoroughly political realist *(Realpolitiker)*, a perspective noted appreciatively by Wilhelm II.[340] Scholars such as Winckler and Kohler went even further, characterising Hammurapi's rule as being just as non- or even anti-religious as that of Frederick of Sicily and other so-called enlightened rulers. The famous Law Code Stele itself seemed to bear witness to this. The relief depicting Hammurapi receiving the insignia of justice from Shamash was commonly interpreted as showing the Babylonian king as the god's "equal," which was then contrasted with the supposed subservience of Moses, as the biblical God passed the tablets down to him.[341] According to Winckler, Hammurapi's reference to numerous gods in his Code was merely traditional, as the king was clearly the one who promulgated the law and introduced new principles to legitimise his rule:

> Trotz aller Betonung seiner Berufung durch die Götter und seiner Ergebenheit, zeigt sich Hammurapi damit doch als ein König, der seine Macht auf andere Dinge stützt als die Anerkennung durch die Priesterschaft allein. Er läßt den weltlichen Teil seiner Aufgabe stark hervortreten und ordnet die weltlichen Angelegenheiten in seinem eigenen Namen, im Namen der königlichen Gewalt, nicht in dem der Gottheit. Seine Gesetze sind daher ein Ergebnis praktischer Bedürfnisse, ein Erzeugnis der Entwicklung der Dinge, nicht ein solch-

---

337 See with further references Kerautret 2012.
338 See with further references Pranzl 2008.
339 Schirrmacher 1865, 340–42. On this author, see Thomsen 2005, 138, 164–65.
340 Wilhelm II 1938, 28.
341 See Lehmann-Haupt 1905, 46.

es der geistigen und geistlichen Spekulation mit Idealforderungen, wie sie Teile der biblischen Gesetzgebung darstellen.[342]

[Despite all the emphasis on his divine appointment and his devotion to the gods, Hammurapi shows himself to be a king who bases his power on other things than the recognition of the priesthood alone. He emphasises the secular nature of his duties, ordering secular affairs in his own name and in the name of royal power rather than in the name of a deity. His laws are therefore a result of practical needs, a product of the development of things, not of spiritual and intellectual speculation with ideal demands, as is the case with some parts of biblical legislation.]

Hammurapi was believed to have maintained a strong opposition between the ruler and the "old religion" of his country, particularly that upheld by the priests of the temple of Marduk, the chief Babylonian god. For Winckler, Hammurapi's laws stood in sharp contrast to the irrational and highly complex rules that he believed were typical of oriental religions and oriental thought: "His legislation is purely practical and mundane; it avoids all ideals and theories and is secular in nature."[343] In his view, it was Hammurapi's secularism that ultimately distanced him from the ancient Near East and aligned him with the enlightened rulers of European modernity. However, Winckler's portrayal may also be seen as a de-orientalisation of the exceptional Babylonian king; one that does not contradict stereotypical views of oriental history but ultimately confirms them.

The legal historian Kohler made a similar argument to that of Winckler, but went even further by elevating the supposed contrast between Hammurapi and his oriental context to the level of moral and legal philosophy. Adopting key assumptions from the German historical school of jurisprudence *(Historische Rechtsschule)* established by Carl von Savigny (1779–1861) in the early nineteenth century, Kohler argued against deriving law from nature or reason.[344] As a legal historian and legal ethnologist, he focused on the diverse historical origins of positive law and its varied manifestations across different societies and found that in its empirical form, law proved to be something constantly changing, depending on the historical and cultural context. This result appeared to challenge the normative concept of law, thus raising the issue of relativism; also a topic of concern in other areas of historicism. Consequently, the historical approach provoked much debate in legal studies and led to an anti-historicist revolt in the 1920s,

---

[342] Winckler 1904, XXXI.
[343] Winckler 1904, XXXII.
[344] On the German historical school, which experienced a kind of revival in the 1870s and 1880s, see (among others) Haferkamp 2018.

akin to that which occurred in the discipline of theology.³⁴⁵ What mattered most for Kohler's analysis of ancient Babylonian law however, was his strict distinction between law and morality, which, along with his rejection of natural law, somewhat resembles conceptions of legal positivism developed later in the twentieth century by scholars such as Hans Kelsen (1881–1973) and Herbert L. A. Hart (1907–1992).³⁴⁶ The crucial point was that Kohler viewed any fusion of law and morality – or law and religion – as the indicator of either a pre-modern legal system or an oriental one, characterising oriental systems as those containing both theocratic and despotic elements. For him, it was the separation of law and morality, which he believed the Code of Hammurapi had achieved, that emancipated ancient Babylonian law from its oriental context and rendered it superior to it. The following section deserves attention:

> Bei einem orientalischen Gesetze kommt vor allem die Frage in Betracht, ob das Gesetz ein reines Rechtsgesetz ist oder ob es einen theokratisch-religiösen, das ganze Leben des Menschen erfassenden Charakter in sich trägt. [...] Völlig theokratischer Art und Recht und Sittlichkeit miteinander verbindend sind die indischen Gesetzbücher, theokratisch sind aber insbesondere auch die gesetzlichen Bestimmungen des israelitischen Rechts, namentlich des sogen. Bundesbuches, des Deuteronomiums und des priesterlichen Gesetzes. Hier wechseln Rechts- und Sittlichkeitsvorschriften mit einander [...]. Diese theokratische Art findet sich noch viel später im Koran. Ganz im Gegensatz dazu steht das Gesetz Hammurapis. In geradezu moderner Weise ist das Juristische aus dem Gesamtlebensvorschriften herausgenommen, und alles, was die Moralllehre angeht, insbesondere die Erörterungen über den sittlichen und unsittlichen Gebrauch des Rechts sind vollkommen bei Seite gelassen, denn dies sollte der religiös sittlichen Betrachtungsweise anheim gestellt bleiben.³⁴⁷

> [With an Oriental law, the primary question to be considered is whether the law is a purely legal act or whether it is of a theocratic-religious character, addressing the whole life of human beings. [...] The Indian law books are of an entirely theocratic type and link morality and law together; but the legal provisions of Israelite law, specifically those of the so-called Covenant Code, the Book of Deuteronomy and the priestly law, are also theocratic. Legal provisions alternate with ethical prescriptions therein [...]. This theocratic type [of law] appears again, much later, in the Koran. The law of Hammurapi is quite the opposite of this. In an almost modern way, the juridical has been extracted from the prescriptions governing other aspects of life and anything to do with moral doctrine is left out entirely, particularly the debates on the moral and immoral use of law, because these should be left to the purview of religious morality.]

---

345 On the debate of the problem of historicism and relativism in legal studies at the turn of the twentieth century, see with further references Wittkau 1992, 80–95.
346 See Hart 1958; Hart 1961, 181–207; Kelsen 1967 [1960].
347 Kohler and Peiser 1904, 137–38.

Therefore, Kohler's association of theocracy with the Orient should not be reduced to a mere strategy of othering. The mixture of law and ethics he rejected was not limited to Oriental societies but encompassed significant portions of European legal history as well. However, it is significant that, with regard to the biblical confluence of ethics and law, his views did not differ greatly from those of religious scholars who asserted the moral superiority of the Bible. While Kohler saw the lack of distinction between law and morality in Mosaic law as a sign of its backwardness and Oriental inferiority, many religious scholars argued that the same lack of distinction demonstrated its progressiveness and superiority. The issue here was the theologisation and ethicisation of law, which indeed is a central feature of biblical law and is alien to older conceptions of law in the ancient Near East wherein the law was given by the king, not the gods.[348] Nevertheless, the claim that Babylonian law was secular in contrast to biblical law, a contrast that has been put forward until recently, remains highly problematic.[349] Such a claim presupposes the modern distinction between the religious and the secular, an idea that was entirely foreign to the ancient Near Eastern world.

In a more general sense, the scorn directed against biblical law by Kohler and Winckler clearly reflects a tradition of European antinomism; a school of thought that rejects laws, morality and social norms in the name of complete freedom.[350] Within this perspective, the law is seen as an imposition that undermines individual autonomy. Writings involving antinomism often also involve antisemitism, as the revelation of Mosaic law to the people of Israel as narrated in the Bible seems to symbolise an original subjugation of humanity to external principles imposed by God. A negative portrayal of Jewish legalism, in contrast to a supposedly Christian freedom from the law, is therefore deeply rooted in Christianity and has been emphasised particularly strongly in German Protestantism. Even philosophers such as Kant denounced Judaism as "the epitome of mere static laws."[351] Kohler's assessment of the Talmud, published in a short article in 1907, followed the same line of thinking and was largely negative. Although he managed to distance himself from antisemitism, Kohler's description of the Talmud nevertheless contains numerous anti-Jewish tropes. It reinforced the stereotype of 'dry Jewish legalism'

---

[348] On this difference, see (among others) Albertz 2003; Schmid 2021; Brague 2007.
[349] As a more recent example see Paul 1970, 6–8.
[350] See in general Palmer 1999; most recently Zwiep 2024.
[351] Kant 1907b [1793/94], 125. Antinomism, although recognized by many scholars as a central motif of European antisemitism, remains under-researched as a phenomenon. See the numerous references to this trope in Nirenberg 2013.

and portrayed the Talmud as exhibiting the flaws of oriental law while negatively contrasting it with the Western tradition, as first demonstrated by Roman law.[352]

The overall negative view of oriental theocracy (from which Hammurapi's Babylonia was said to be so different) had also long been shaped by anti-clerical and anti-Catholic ideologies which portrayed the (Catholic) Church as a purely theocratic, and, in this respect, truly oriental institution. Contemporaries certainly recognised the anti-clerical insinuations in the negative descriptions of priesthood and theocracy by scholars such as Kohler and Winckler, who themselves had been influenced by the era of anti-Catholic *Kulturkampf* the German state had engaged in during the 1870s and 1880s.[353] While Winckler repeatedly made anti-clerical statements, but otherwise does not appear to have engaged in religious debate, Kohler was an outspoken representative of the 'free religion' movement *(freireligiöse Bewegung)* and advocated for the establishment of purely secular rituals and cultic practices.[354] In particular, he campaigned for the right to cremate the dead, which was not legalised until the late nineteenth century.[355] A growing rejection of theocratic rule, with its supposed conflation of morality and law, mirrored the position of these two scholars in the debates regarding the status of (Christian) religion in contemporary German society and underpinned the ideological formation of German secularism.

---

352 Kohler 1907, 163–64.
353 See (among many others) M. Gross 2005; Borutta 2010; Dittrich 2014.
354 On the formation of German secularism, see (among others) Weir 2014; Weir 2015; Habermas 2019.
355 See Spendel 1983, 45.

Summary and Outlook

Although excavated by French archaeologists, the discovery of the stele bearing the Code of Hammurapi was a much bigger media event in Wilhelmine Germany than it was across the Rhine. In Germany, the find was widely discussed and attracted considerable scholarly and public attention, well beyond the small circle of specialists in the niche discipline of Assyriology. Hammurapi could not have chosen a better time and place to be resurrected from oblivion, as Romantic Orientalism was deeply rooted in German literature and scholarship and the Reich was ruled by a monarch with a particular interest in the history and politics of the Middle East. In addition, the prolific German excavations at the ancient site of Babylon had begun only a few years before Hammurapi's stele came to light, and had themselves sparked a Babylomania that was further intensified by media events such as the Babel-Bible-controversy.

In this context, Hammurapi and his law collection became significant reference points for discussions on a wide range of topics, some of which, at first glance, seem to have little to do with the history of the ancient Near East. Modern scholars began to identify striking similarities between the Babylonian king of the eighteenth century BC, the Prussian kings of the eighteenth century AD, and their own monarch; depicting all of these characters according to the model of enlightened absolutism. This historical entanglement of very different rulers and societies was not the result of a lack of historical reflection; of course, everyone recognised the considerable differences between the societies of the ancient Near East and modern Europe. Rather, what made these temporal entanglements attractive were specific issues and problems, particularly in the areas of politics, law, and religion, which contemporary German scholars believed both ancient Babylonia and their own society had in common. The notions of historical continuity, progress, and development that are usually associated with specific modern understandings of time and history were already being challenged by the turn of the twentieth century (in fact, these notions have always been less dominant than our postmodern perspective on the 'classical' modern period assumes). The discovery of a historical era that appeared almost modern – or rather, as an ancient version of modernity – contributed to a crisis in the traditional conception of history. Alternative ways of representing history and relating different eras to one another, such as the concept of key-epochs, brought to life by a few (male) heroic individuals, seemed to offer new solutions. One of the conceptual frameworks used to link together certain 'bright' epochs stemming from various historical contexts was enlightened absolutism. Differences in the social, technological, and economic status of the historical contexts to which the concept was applied (i.e., Old

Babylonia, medieval Sicily, eighteenth-century Prussia, modern Germany) mattered far less than the alleged common spirit of these ages, or *Zeitgeist*, characterised by rational administration, strong economies, and social welfare. The most important element of the concept of enlightened absolutism, however, was a rulers' personal will to mould their realm according to their wishes. This last point, which appeared to be substantiated by Hammurapi's interventions and decisions in individual law cases (as evidenced by his letters), attracted significant public attention during the first decade of the twentieth century due to its political ramifications. After all, the German Kaiser and his supporters had sought to establish an autocratic and anti-democratic form of government in modern Germany, which they described as *persönliches Regiment* and attempted to legitimise this principle by linking it to ancient Babylonia. In his ultimately unsuccessful attempt to modify the political system of the German Reich to his advantage, the Kaiser exploited the ambiguity in the German constitution regarding the definition of the monarch's position. Though scholars of the time did not compare the Code of Hammurapi with modern constitutions (as the CH does not address the position of the monarch in the Babylonian political system) they did compare its spirit to that of certain modern law codes and constitutions. This included making analogies between the Babylonian and German rule of law, or *Rechtsstaatlichkeit*, usually by focusing on formal aspects such as legal certainty and judicial independence.

In terms of the broader history of law however, the main question raised by the discovery of the Laws of Hammurapi concerned their relationship to biblical law. This aspect gained a highly political dimension due to the concurrent Babel-Bible controversy, in which the Code of Hammurapi became a central reference point for both sides of the debate. For those taking the view of Delitzsch, the Code of Hammurapi seemed to testify to the Bible's dependence on Babylonia and thus to contribute to its general disenchantment. In contrast, Delitzsch's opponents sought to identify differences between the two law traditions that would ultimately prove the superiority of biblical law. These opposing viewpoints reflected longstanding debates in German legal theory and philosophy regarding the relationship between law, morality (*Sittlichkeit*), and religion. Again, the Code of Hammurapi served as a reference point for various positions. For proponents of the German historical school and pioneers of legal positivism, the apparent absence of moral rules and any normative framework in Babylonian law, along with its generally 'secular' character, seemed to demonstrate its modernity, whereas proponents of natural and rational law theory considered these features to be a major weakness of Babylonian law as compared to biblical law.

If the Code of Hammurapi had been discovered only twenty years later, these discussions may have been entirely different. While the larger debate did not end with the outbreak of the First World War, one can nevertheless observe a clear discursive break between the Wilhemine period and the new Weimar era. One reason for this was a generational change; many of the thinkers who dominated the German debate involving the Hammurapi Stele in the first decade following its discovery died before, during or shortly after the First World War: The theologian Samuel Oettli in 1911, the Orientalist David Heinrich Müller in 1912, the Assyriologist Hugo Winckler in 1913, the legal historian Josef Kohler in 1919, and the Assyriologists Friedrich Delitzsch and Felix Peiser in 1921. Others, such as the Assyriologist Fritz Hommel retired and ceased to publish. The great editions of Babylonian law, initiated by Kohler and Peiser, were continued by Koschaker and Ungnad, while younger scholars such as Benno Landsberger (1890–1968) further contributed to the study of the Code of Hammurapi.[356] The ongoing political situation in Germany deeply affected the fields of Ancient Near Eastern Studies, Biblical Studies and Legal History, to name those most relevant to this monograph. German Middle Eastern Studies, which had been expanding rapidly in the Wilhemine era and were both admired and envied by international colleagues, suddenly lost their leading position due to a lack of financial support and new difficulties in gaining access to scholarly materials. The loss of Germany's colonial and imperial infrastructure was particularly hard on these disciplines, as Middle Eastern sites were no longer part of an allied country such as the Ottoman Empire. Instead, previous study areas now belonged either to the newly formed Turkish nation state or were under the control of Western colonial empires, as was the case for archaeological sites in Syria and Mesopotamia. Furthermore, the First World War resulted in a breakdown in international scholarly cooperation, thereby, complicating the study of objects in British, French, and American museums and university collections by German scholars.[357]

Most importantly however, was the changed political, cultural, and intellectual landscape after 1918, which resulted in a different public reception and level of attention paid to such issues, as compared to before the war. Although nearly all of the general ideas that shaped German Orientalism in the 1920s were present before the First World War, the discursive constellations shifted during the Weimar Republic. It was primarily political radicalisation that reshuffled the cards in the great game of ideas and ideologies. For example, whereas legal positivism had previously been found among both conservative and liberal scholars, by the 1920s it was restricted to democratic defenders of the democratic status quo, with the Austrian-Jewish jurist and political philosopher Kelsen as its most promi-

---

356 Koschaker and Ungnad 1923; Landsberger 1939.
357 See Marchand 2009, 476–87.

nent representative.³⁵⁸ Conversely, legal scholars still sympathetic to the old monarchy questioned the legitimacy of the new republican order, referring to supposedly higher principles of law than the written Weimar constitution. As a result, legal positivism became the central bogeyman for nationalist and antisemitic scholars, who denounced it as 'Jewish' legalism, its most prominent detractor being the future Nazi jurist Carl Schmitt, who drew heavily on the tradition of Christian antinomism.³⁵⁹ Therefore, Weimar anti-positivism did not lead to the return of the normative into law; rather, it paved the way for the "normativity of the ideological" under the Nazis, to borrow a phrase from the legal scholar Bernd Rüthers.³⁶⁰

The 'great men' paradigm, which had significantly influenced the discourse on Hammurapi during the Wilhelmine period, also underwent an important transformation after the First World War. As noted above, in the nineteenth and early twentieth centuries, this concept was closely linked to similar ideas about so-called geniuses, particularly in the fields of art and science. During the Weimar years however, the study of great men was increasingly refined into an authoritarian notion of political leadership, characterised by a strong (male) leader presiding over masses who blindly followed his will. The ideology and cult of political leadership became core elements of right-wing and fascist movements across Europe during the 1920s. Consequently, the older concept of enlightened monarchs favouring pastoral and patriarchal styles of authoritarianism while promoting the rule of law (though they themselves were of course above the law), did not align with this new framework. For this reason, neither the two Fredericks nor Hammurapi were suitable for fascist appropriation. Lastly, new tides of antisemitism became a major factor in the increasing radicalisation of politics. Even during the Babel-Bible controversy, siding with Babel against the Bible had often (but not always) coincided with antisemitic prejudices. By the 1920s, this polarisation had intensified, as the radical rejection of the Old Testament emerged as an important signifier of political antisemitism. This sentiment frequently appeared intertwined with notions of a *völkisch* religion, either Christian or neopagan, that was purged of all 'Jewish' elements.³⁶¹

Since 1902, Mesopotamian law collections older than the Code of Hammurapi have come to light, with the oldest known being the Laws of Ur-Namma, written c.

---

358 See (among others) Dreier 2019.
359 See with further references R. Gross 2005; Maus 2011 [1995].
360 Rüthers 1988, 65.
361 On *völkisch* conceptions of religion, see (among others) Schnurbein and Ulbricht 2001; Cancik and Puschner 2004; Puschner and Vollnhals 2012.

2100 BC.³⁶² This means that the laws of Hammurapi have lost their status as the oldest of human history; furthermore, given the long tradition of Mesopotamian law, the erection of the stele can no longer be considered the heroic act of one individual, as early twentieth-century scholars held. However, several other issues raised by the Code of Hammurapi continue to be subjects of ongoing debate in the fields of Ancient Near Eastern Studies, Biblical Studies, and Legal History, partly due to their general nature. Questions such as whether law, ethics, and religion developed separately, and at what date they became intertwined, are perhaps not ultimately answerable and so are revisited by every new generation of scholars. The general positions of the 'Hammurapi vs. Moses' debate from the early twentieth century are still identifiable in some scholarly writings of today. There are modern scholars who claim that biblical law strongly depends on the Laws of Hammurapi and portraying the Israelites as mere imitators.³⁶³ Conversely, a German Old Testament scholar recently made a sharp distinction between an "ethos of ruling and serving," as represented by Hammurapi and the Babylonians, and an "ethos of freedom and equality," as represented by Moses and the Bible. These perspectives clearly echo the polemics of early twentieth century Christian and Jewish defenders of Moses against Delitzsch and his followers.³⁶⁴ To take another problem, the historical relationship between customary or common law and positive or written law and how each developed remains a subject of debate. This debate includes the related questions of which aspects of Babylonian and biblical law can be attributed to which traditions, and whether a common source for both of these ancient Near Eastern law codes should be assumed.³⁶⁵

However, the context in which these questions are being discussed at the beginning of the twenty-first century is very different from that of Wilhelmine Germany, which gives this scholarly discourse a different significance. To begin with the most obvious point, although the concept of secularism (understood as a teleological category intrinsically linked to modernity), has been rightly criticised, there is no doubt that the importance of religion to almost all European societies dramatically decreased over the course of the twentieth and twenty-first centuries (this does, however, not apply to other regions of the world in a similar way).³⁶⁶ In Germany, persons who do not belong to one of the Christian churches now make up the majority of the population; in Berlin, almost 70% of residents are con-

---

362 See (among others) Roth 1995b; for the Laws of Ur-Namma Roth 1995a, 13–22.
363 See especially Wright 2009, but also the critique by Otto 2010.
364 Lux 2003, 112–13.
365 See the overview of current scholarship by Otto 2006, 2010; Schmid 2021.
366 For criticism of the concept of secularism, see Asad 2003.

sidered non-denominational.³⁶⁷ As knowledge of the Bible comes to be increasingly rare, it is difficult to envision major public debates like those of the Babel-Bible controversy occurring today. Moreover, any current discussion of the relationship between Babylonian and biblical law or the figures of Hammurapi and Moses are only followed by a small segment of society.³⁶⁸ Even radical criticism of the Bible and the outright rejection of biblical religion do not provoke society anymore. But it is not only Moses who has faded from public discourse, Hammurapi has almost completely lost his relevance as well, largely due to a lack of knowledge about the ancient Near East, which is no longer included in the school curriculum. Therefore, while biblical and ancient Near Eastern scholars continue to debate some of the questions raised following the discovery of Hammurapi's stela, their discussions rarely attract attention beyond academia.

Though the religious issues related to the Code of Hammurapi have lost their political and cultural relevance, it is more challenging to address the political and constitutional issues that characterised German debates involving the Code of Hammurapi at the beginning of the twentieth century. The problems surrounding the monarchy and its historical legitimacy have become irrelevant since the Kaiser abdicated in 1918, though a small minority on the far right (the so-called *Reichsbürger*) may still dream of a new German monarchy.³⁶⁹ The 'monarchical principle' is now a matter for historians rather than constitutional lawyers, and journalists no longer need to speculate about benefits or disadvantages of the 'personal rule' of a monarch who claims divine right. The decline of monarchism does not mean, however, that the appeal of autocratic and authoritarian rule has disappeared. Calls for strong leaders (still usually conceived of as men) and authoritarian conceptions of the welfare state are gaining new currency. These tenden-

---

367 See Forschungsgruppe Weltanschauungen in Deutschland, Kirchenmitglieder und Konfessionsfreie in Berlin, 2019, https://fowid.de/meldung/kirchenmitglieder-und-konfessionsfreie-berlin-1867-2017, accessed 15 May 2025.
368 However, it seems that there are national and cultural differences and this observation should not be generalised. Though both articles are of a similar length, the English Wikipedia article on Hammurapi includes a paragraph discussing the relationship between the Code of Hammurapi and biblical law which is absent from the German version. This difference may reflect the different levels of importance placed on religious issues in German and American contexts.
369 See, for instance the extremist group *Königreich Deutschland* (Kingdom of Germany), https://koenigreichdeutschland.org/de, accessed 01 April 2025. The website is no longer accessible as the group was banned in May 2025 by the German Minister of the Interior. See https://www.bmi.bund.de/SharedDocs/pressemitteilungen/DE/2025/05/verbot-koenigreich-deutschland.html, accessed 30 May 2025. On the organisation and ideology of the *Reichsbürger*-movement, see the brief summary in Bundesministerium des Innern und für Heimat 2023, 30–34.

cies have been accompanied by a steady decline in the rule of law worldwide over the past decade, including in liberal democracies.[370] Without repealing liberal constitutions as neo-absolutist monarchs did in the nineteenth century, current authoritarian movements have found ways to disrupt constitutional structures and institutions and have been quite successful in certain countries, such as Hungary. Rather than relying on democratic and constitutional procedures, the current "authoritarian constitutionalism", as defined by legal scholar Günter Frankenberg, depends on special mandates and decrees, as well as the disempowerment of the judiciary and an abolition of the separation of powers.[371]

It is true that the ongoing debates regarding threats to democracy are now conducted without reference to ancient Near Eastern or biblical history, as these references are no longer considered relevant. Given the current situation however, an acknowledgement of the long history and evolution of law has acquired new political urgency. While there may be no need to declare the Code of Hammurapi the historical origin of our modern *Rechtsstaat*, as German scholars did at the beginning of the twentieth century, it is important that the rule of law not be taken for granted. It is rather a historical achievement worth defending. For this reason, reflections on the long history of law, sometimes going back to the era of Hammurapi, remain relevant in the 21st century.

---

[370] See the latest (2024) "Global rule law report" by the World Justice Project (WJP): https://worldjusticeproject.org/rule-of-law-index, accessed 30 March 2025. There is a huge body of literature on this topic, see (among others) Huber 2019; Schmidt and Zabel 2021; Pichl 2024.
[371] Frankenberg 2020, 134–69.

References

Albertz, Rainer. 2003 [1997]. Die Theologisierung des Rechts im Alten Israel. In Rainer Albertz. *Geschichte und Theologie. Studien zur Exegese des Alten Testaments und zur Religionsgeschichte Israels*, edited by Ingo Kottsieper, and Jakob Wöhrle, 187–208. Berlin: De Gruyter.
Alt, Albrecht. 1934. *Die Ursprünge des israelitischen Rechts*. Leipzig: Hirzel.
Amengual, Gabriel. 2001. Der Begriff der Sittlichkeit. Überlegungen zu seiner differenzierten Bedeutung. *Hegel-Jahrbuch* 2001:197–203.
Aretin, Karl O. F. von. 1988. Aufgeklärter Herrscher oder aufgeklärter Absolutismus? Eine notwendige Begriffsklärung. In *Gesellschaftsgeschichte. Festschrift für Karl Bosl zum 80. Geburtstag*. Vol. 1, edited by Ferdinand Seibt, 78–87. Munich: Oldenbourg.
Aretin, Karl O. F. von, ed. 1974. *Der aufgeklärte Absolutismus*. Cologne: Kiepenheuer & Witsch.
Arnold, Bill T. 2021. A Centennial Review of "Die Große Täuschung". Friedrich Delitzsch's Final Reflections on the Babel-Bibel-Controversy. In *Der Babel-Bibel-Streit und die Wissenschaft des Judentums*, edited by Eva Cancik-Kirschbaum, and Thomas L. Gertzen, 45–62. Münster: Zaphon.
Arnold, Bill T., and David B. Weisberg. 2002. A Centennial Review of Friedrich Delitzsch's "Babel und Bibel" Lectures. *Journal of Biblical Literature* 121:441–57.
Asad, Talal. 2003. *Formations of the Secular. Christianity, Islam, Modernity*. Stanford: Stanford University Press.
Aschheim, Steven E. 2010. *The Modern Jewish Experience and the Entangled Web of Orientalism*. Amsterdam: Menasseh ben Israel Instituut.
Assmann, Jan. 1998. *Moses the Egyptian. The Memory of Egypt in Western Monotheism*. Cambridge [MA]: Harvard University Press.
Assmann, Jan. 2001 [1990]. *Ma'at. Gerechtigkeit und Unsterblichkeit im Alten Ägypten*. Munich: Beck.
Barmash, Pamela. 2020. *The Laws of Hammurabi. At the Confluence of Royal and Scribal Traditions*. Oxford: Oxford University Press.
Bastian, Adolf. 2007 [1895]. *Ethnische Elementargedanken in der Lehre vom Menschen. Ausgewählte Werke*. Vol. 7, edited by Peter Bolz, and Manuela Fischer. Hildesheim: Olms-Weidmann.
Bauer, Michael. 2005. Julius Wellhausen. In *Klassiker der Theologie*. Vol. 2, edited by Friedrich W. Graf, 123–40. Munich: Beck.
Baumgart, Peter. 2000. Absolutismus ein Mythos? Aufgeklärter Absolutismus ein Widerspruch? Reflexionen zu einem kontroversen Thema gegenwärtiger Frühneuzeitforschung. *Zeitschrift für historische Forschung* 27:573–89.
Bauriedl, Sybille. 2007. "Der Orient" als Raumkonstruktion in der Geographie. In *Orient- und IslamBilder. Interdisziplinäre Beiträge zu Orientalismus und antimuslimischem Rassismus*, edited by Iman Attia, 137–54. Münster: Unrast.
Becker, Michael, Hans-Joachim Lauth, and Gert Pickel, eds. 2001. *Rechtsstaat und Demokratie. Theoretische und empirische Studien zum Recht in der Demokratie*. Wiesbaden: Westdeutscher Verlag.
Beckmann, Klaus. 2002. *Die fremde Wurzel. Altes Testament und Judentum in der evangelischen Theologie des 19. Jahrhunderts*. Göttingen: Vandenhoeck & Ruprecht.
Belton, Roshunda L. 2007. *A Non-Traditional Traditionalist: Rev. A. H. Sayce and His Intellectual Approach to Biblical Authenticity and Biblical History in Late-Victorian Britain*. Doctoral Dissertation. Baton Rouge. Available from https://repository.lsu.edu/gradschool_dissertations/1655, accessed 15 March 2025.

Berg, Nicolas, ed. 2023. *Der Berliner Antisemitismusstreit. Eine Textsammlung von Walter Boehlich.* Berlin: Jüdischer Verlag.
Bernasconi, Robert. 2000. With What Must the Philosophy of World History Begin? On the Racial Basis of Hegel's Eurocentrism. *Nineteenth-Century Contexts* 22:171–201.
Bezold, Carl. 1903. *Ninive und Babylon.* Bielefeld: Velhagen & Klasing.
Birtsch, Günter. 1987. Der Idealtyp des aufgeklärten Herrschers. Friedrich der Große, Karl Friedrich von Banden und Joseph II. im Vergleich. In *Der Idealtyp des aufgeklärten Herrschers*, edited by Günter Birtsch, 9–47. Stuttgart: Meiner.
Birtsch, Günter. 1996. Aufgeklärter Absolutismus oder Reformabsolutismus? *Aufklärung* 9:101–9.
Blackbourn, David, and Geoff Eley. 1984. *The Peculiarities of German History. Bourgeois Society and Politics in Nineteenth-Century Germany.* Oxford: Oxford University Press.
Blänkler, Reinhard. 2011. *"Absolutismus". Eine begriffsgeschichtliche Studie zur politischen Theorie und zur Geschichtswissenschaft in Deutschland (1830–1870).* Frankfurt a. M.: Peter Lang.
Böckenförde, Ernst-Wolfgang. 1992. Rechtsstaat. In *Historisches Wörterbuch der Philosophie.* Vol. 8, edited by Joachim Ritter, and Karlfried Gründer, 332–42. Darmstadt: Wissenschaftliche Buchgesellschaft.
Böckenförde, Ernst-Wolfgang. 2024a [1967]. Der deutsche Typ der konstitutionellen Monarchie im 19. Jahrhundert. In Ernst Wolfgang Böckenförde. *Recht, Staat, Freiheit. Studien zur Rechtsphilosophie, Staatstheorie und Verfassungsgeschichte.* Erweiterte Ausgabe, 273–305. Frankfurt a. M.: Suhrkamp.
Böckenförde, Ernst-Wolfgang. 2024b [1969]. Entstehung und Wandel des Rechtsstaatsbegriffs. In Ernst Wolfgang Böckenförde. *Recht, Staat, Freiheit. Studien zur Rechtsphilosophie, Staatstheorie und Verfassungsgeschichte.* Erweiterte Ausgabe, 143–69. Frankfurt a. M.: Suhrkamp.
Bohrer, Frederick N. 2003. *Orientalism and Visual Culture. Imagining Mesopotamia in Nineteenth-Century Europe.* Cambridge: Cambridge University Press.
Borutta, Manuel. 2010. *Antikatholizismus. Deutschland und Italien im Zeitalter der europäischen Kulturkämpfe.* Göttingen: Vandenhoeck & Ruprecht.
Brague, Rémi. 2007. *The Law of God. The Philosophical History of an Idea.* Chicago: University of Chicago Press.
Breasted, James H. 1916. *Ancient Times. A History of the Early World. An Introduction to the Study of Ancient History and the Career of Early Man.* Boston: Ginn.
Brechenmacher, Thomas. 2003. Wieviel Gegenwart verträgt historisches Urteilen? Die Kontroverse zwischen Heinrich von Sybel und Julius Ficker über die Bewertung der Kaiserpolitik des Mittelalters (1859–1862). In *Historisierung und gesellschaftlicher Wandel in Deutschland im 19. Jahrhundert*, edited by Ulrich Muhlack, and Christian Mehr, 87–112. Berlin: Akademie Verlag.
Breuer, Stefan. 2001. *Ordnungen der Ungleichheit. Die deutsche Rechte im Widerstreit ihrer Ideen 1871–1945.* Darmstadt: Wissenschaftliche Buchgesellschaft.
Bröckling, Ulrich. 2017. Von Hirten, Herden und dem Gott Pan. Figurationen pastoraler Macht. In Ulrich Bröckling. *Gute Hirten führen sanft. Über Menschenregierungskünste*, 15–44. Berlin: Suhrkamp.
Brunner, Otto. 1968. Vom Gottesgnadentum zum monarchischen Prinzip. In Otto Brunner. *Neue Wege der Verfassungs- und* Sozialgeschichte, 160–86. Göttingen: Vandenhoeck & Ruprecht.
Bryant, Nick. 2024. Trump Is America's Caligula. His Mission Is to Destroy What Made America Great. *The Sydney Morning Herald*, 2 December 2024. Available from https://www.smh.com.au/

world/north-america/trump-is-america-s-caligula-his-mission-is-to-destroy-what-made-america-great-20241202-p5kv0h.html, accessed 15 March 2025.
Bundesministerium des Inneren und für Heimat. 2023. Brief Summary: 2023 Report on the Protection of the Constitution. Facts and Trends. Available from https://www.verfassungsschutz.de/EN/home/home_node.html, accessed 15 March 2025.
Burckhardt, Jacob. N. d. [1860]. *The Civilization of the Renaissance in Italy*, translated by S. G. C. Middlemore. Vienna: Phaidon; Oxford: Oxford University Press.
Burckhardt, Jacob. N. d. 1943 [1905]. *Force and Freedom. Reflections on History*, edited by James H. Nichols. New York: Pantheon.
Burckhardt, Jacob. N. d. 1978 [1905]. *Weltgeschichtliche Betrachtungen*, edited by Rudolf Marx. Stuttgart: Kröner.
Burckhardt, Jacob. N. d. 1996 [1860]. *Die Kultur der Renaissance in Italien*. Essen: Phaidon.
Butler, Eliza M. 1935. *The Tyranny of Greece over Germany. A Study of the Influence Exercised by Greek Art and Poetry over the Great German Writers of the Eighteenth, Nineteenth and Twentieth Centuries*. Cambridge: Cambridge University Press.
Cancik, Hubert, and Uwe Puschner, eds. 2004. *Antisemitismus, Paganismus, Völkische Religion*. Berlin: De Gruyter.
Cancik-Kirschbaum, Eva. 1999. "König der Gerechtigkeit". Ein altorientalisches Paradigma zu Recht und Herrschaft. In *Torah – Nomos – Ius. Abendländischer Antinomismus und der Traum vom herrschaftsfreien Raum*, edited by Gesine Palmer, 52–68. Berlin: Vorwerk.
Cancik-Kirschbaum, Eva. 2007. "Menschen ohne König ...": Zur Wahrnehmung des Königtums in sumerischen und akkadischen Texten. In *Das geistige Erfassen der Welt im Alten Orient. Sprache, Religion, Kultur und Gesellschaft*, edited by Claus Wilcke, 167–90. Wiesbaden: Harrassowitz.
Cancik-Kirschbaum, Eva. 2008. Mittelalter – Alter Orient. Eine Perspektive Friedrich Heers. In *Die geistige Welt des Friedrich Heer*, edited by Richard Faber, and Sigurd P. Scheichl, 87–106. Vienna: Böhlau.
Cancik-Kirschbaum, Eva, and Thomas L. Gertzen, eds. 2021. *Der Babel-Bibel-Streit und die Wissenschaft des Judentums*. Münster: Zaphon.
Carhart, Michael C. 2007. *The Science of Culture in Enlightenment Germany*. Cambridge [MA]: Harvard University Press.
Carlyle, Thomas. 1897 [1841]. *The Works of Thomas Carlyle in Thirty Volumes. Vol. 5: On Heroes, Hero-Worship and the Heroic in History*, edited by Henry D. Traill, and Thomas Carlyle. Cambridge: Cambridge University Press.
Chamberlain, Houston S. 1928. *Briefe 1882–1924 und Briefwechsel mit Kaiser Wilhelm II*. Vol. 2. Munich: Bruckmann.
Charpin, Dominique. 2010. *Writing, Law, and Kingship in Old Babylonian Mesopotamia*. Chicago: University of Chicago Press.
Charpin, Dominique. 2020. L'élection du P. Scheil au Collège de France en 1905. In *From Mari to Jerusalem and Back. Assyriological and Biblical Studies in Honor of Jack Murad Sasson*, edited by Annalisa Azzoni, Alexandra Kleinerman, Douglas A. Knight, and David I. Owen, 26–68. University Park [PA]: Eisenbrauns.
Charpin, Dominique. 2021. *Hammurabi of Babylon*. London: Bloomsbury Academic.
Charpin, Dominique. 2023. Hammu-rabi, ein babylonischer Herrscher, der in seinem gesamten Reich Gerechtigkeit spricht. *Zeitschrift für Altorientalische und Biblische Rechtsgeschichte* 29:1–18.

Cline, Eric H. 2009. *Biblical Archaeology. A Very Short Introduction.* Oxford: Oxford University Press.
Cohen, Hermann. 1924 [1907]. Religion und Sittlichkeit. Eine Betrachtung zur Grundlegung der Religionsphilosophie. In Hermann Cohen. *Jüdische Schriften. Dritter Band: Zur jüdischen Religionsphilosophie und ihrer Geschichte*, edited by the Akademie für die Wissenschaft des Judentums, 96–168. Berlin: Schwetschke & Sohn.
Cohn, Georg. 1903. *Die Gesetze Hammurabis.* Zürich: Orell Füssli.
Conze, Eckart. 2020. *Schatten des Kaiserreichs. Die Reichsgründung 1871 und ihr schwieriges Erbe.* Munich: Deutscher Taschenbuchverlag.
Cook, Stanley A. 1903. *The Laws of Moses and the Code of Hammurabi.* London: Adam & Charles Black.
Cooper, Jerold S. 1993. Sumerian and Aryan. Racial Theory, Academic Politics and Parisian Assyriology. *Revue d'Histoire de Religiones* 210:169–205.
Cregan-Reid, Vybarr. 2006. Discovering Gilgamesh. George Smith and the Victorian Horizon of History. In *The Victorians and the Ancient World. Archaeology and Classicism in Nineteenth-Century Culture*, edited by Richard Pearson, 109–23. Cambridge: Cambridge Scholars Press.
Crüsemann, Frank. 2005. *Die Tora. Theologie und Sozialgeschichte des alttestamentlichen Gesetzes.* Gütersloh: Gütersloher Verlagshaus.
Crüsemann, Nicola. 2001. *Vom Zweistromland zum Kupfergraben. Vorgeschichte und Entstehungsjahre (1899–1918) der Vorderasiatischen Abteilung der Berliner Museen vor fach- und kulturpolitischen Hintergründen.* Berlin: Mann.
Danguy, Laurence. 2009. *L'ange de la jeunesse. La revue " Jugend " et le Jugendstil à Munich.* Paris: Éditions de la Maison des sciences de l'homme.
Daniels, Peter T. 1995. The Decipherment of Ancient Near Eastern Scripts. In *Civilizations of the Ancient Near East. Vol. 1*, edited by Jack M. Sasson, 81–94. New York: Scribner.
Daub, Adiran. 2016. Neukantianismus. *Enzyklopädie jüdischer Geschichte und Kultur.* Available from https://doi.org/10.1163/2468-2845_ejgk_COM_0581, accessed 15 April 2025.
Davies, William W. 1905. *The Codes of Hammurabi and Moses.* Cincinnati: Jennings & Graham.
Davis, Thomas W. 2004. *Shifting Sands. The Rise and Fall of Biblical Archaeology.* Oxford: Oxford University Press.
Décultot, Élisabeth, and Daniel Fulda, eds. 2016. *Sattelzeit. Historiographiegeschichtliche Revisionen.* Berlin: De Gruyter.
Delgado, Mariano, Klaus Koch, and Edgar Marsch, eds. 2003. *Europa, Tausendjähriges Reich und Neue Welt. Zwei Jahrtausende Geschichte und Utopie in der Rezeption des Danielbuches.* Stuttgart: Kohlhammer.
Delitzsch, Friedrich. 1902. *Babel und Bibel. Ein Vortrag.* Leipzig: Hinrichs.
Delitzsch, Friedrich. 1903. *Zweiter Vortrag über Babel und Bibel.* Stuttgart: Deutsche Verlagsanstalt.
Delitzsch, Friedrich. 1904. *Babel und Bibel. Ein Rückblick und Ausblick.* Stuttgart: Deutsche Verlagsanstalt.
Delitzsch, Friedrich. 1905. *Babel und Bibel. Dritter (Schluss-)Vortrag.* Leipzig: Hinrichs.
Delitzsch, Friedrich. 1920. *Die große Täuschung. Kritische Betrachtungen zu den alttestamentlichen Berichten über Israels Eindringen in Kanaan, die Gottesoffenbarung am Sinai und die Wirksamkeit der Propheten.* Stuttgart: Deutsche Verlagsanstalt.
Delitzsch, Friedrich, and Friedrich Mürdter. 1891. *Geschichte Babyloniens und Assyriens. Zweite Auflage des gleichnamigen Werkes von F. Mürdter revidiert und größtenteils neubearbeitet von Friedrich Delitzsch.* Stuttgart: Verlag der Vereinsbuchhandlung.

Demel, Walter. 2010. *Vom aufgeklärten Reformstaat zum bürokratischen Staatsabsolutismus*. Munich: Oldenbourg.
Demel, Walter. 2015. Enlightened Absolutism. *Encyclopaedia of Early Modern History Online*. Available from https://doi.org/10.1163/2352-0272_emho_COM_026289, accessed 31 January 2025.
Demel, Walter. 2019. Reformabsolutismus. *Encyclopaedia of Early Modern History Online*. Available from https://doi.org/10.1163/2352-0248_edn_COM_334922, accessed 31 January 2025.
Denninger, Erhard. 2002. "Rechtsstaat" oder "Rule of Law" – was ist das heute? In *Festschrift für Klaus Lüderssen zum 70. Geburtstag am 2. Mai 2002*, edited by Cornelius Prittwitz, 41–54. Baden-Baden: Nomos.
Denzer, Horst. 1973. Bodins Staatsformenlehre. In *Jean Bodin*, edited by Horst Denzer, 233–44. Munich: Beck.
Dießelhorst, Malte. 1984. *Die Prozesse des Müllers Arnold und das Eingreifen Friedrichs des Großen*. Göttingen: Schwartz.
Dittrich, Lisa. 2014. *Antiklerikalismus in Europa. Öffentlichkeit und Säkularisierung in Frankreich, Spanien und Deutschland (1848–1914)*. Göttingen: Vandenhoeck & Ruprecht.
Doblhofer, Ernst. 2008. *Die Entzifferung alter Schriften und Sprachen*. Stuttgart: Reclam.
Dörner, Friedrich K., and Eleonore Dörner. 1989. *Von Pergamon zum Nemrud Daǧ. Die archäologischen Entdeckungen Carl Humanns*. Mainz: Zabern.
Dreier, Horst. 2011. Zerrbild Rechtspositivismus. Kritische Bemerkungen zu zwei verbreiteten Legenden. In *Vom praktischen Wert der Methode. Festschrift Heinz Mayer zum 65. Geburtstag*, edited by Clemens Jabloner, Gabriele Kucsko-Stadlmayer, Gerhard Muzak, and Ludwig Adamovich, 61–91. Vienna: Manz.
Dreier, Horst. 2019. *Kelsen im Kontext. Beiträge zum Werk Hans Kelsens und geistesverwandter Autoren*, edited by Matthias Jestaedt, and Stanley L. Paulson. Tübingen: Mohr Siebeck.
Droysen, Johann G. 1977. *Historik Band 1: Rekonstruktion der ersten vollständigen Fassung der Vorlesungen (1857). Grundriß der Historik in der ersten handschriftlichen (1857/1858) und der letzten gedruckten Fassung (1882)*, edited by Peter Leyh. Stuttgart: Frommann.
Duncan, George S. 1904. The Code of Moses and the Code of Hammurabi. *The Biblical World* 23:188–93.
Efron, John M. 2004. From Mitteleuropa to the Middle East. Orientalism through a Jewish Lens. *The Jewish Quarterly Review. New Series* 94:490–520.
Ege, Konrad. 1990. *Karikatur und Bildsatire im Deutschen Reich. Der Wahre Jacob. Hamburg 1879/80, Stuttgart 1884–1914: Mediengeschichte, Mitarbeiter, Chefredakteure, Grafik*. Münster: Literatur Verlag.
Elsen-Novak, Gabriele, and Mirko Novak. 2006. Der "König der Gerechtigkeit". Zur Ikonologie und Teleologie des "Codex Hammurapi". *Baghdader Mitteilungen* 37:131–55.
Emerson, Ralph W. 1850. *Representative Men. Seven Lectures*. Boston: Phillips, Sampson & Company.
Engels, Eve-Marie, ed. 2009. *Charles Darwin und seine Wirkung*. Frankfurt a. M.: Suhrkamp.
Escher, Anton. 2011. Die geographische Gestaltung des Begriffs "Orient" im 20. Jahrhundert. In *Orient – Orientalistik – Orientalismus. Geschichte und Aktualität einer Debatte*, edited by Burkhard Schnepel, Gunnar Brands, and Hanne Schönig, 132–52. Bielefeld: transcript.
Eschweiler, Peter. 2022. *Hegels Ägypten. Die Sphinx und der Geist in der Geschichte*. Paderborn: Fink.
Fehlberg, Frank. 2012. *Protestantismus und Nationaler Sozialismus. Liberale Theologie und politisches Denken um Friedrich Naumann*. Bonn: Dietz.
Fehrenbach, Elisabeth. 1969. *Wandlungen des Deutschen Kaisergedankens 1871–1918*. Berlin: De Gruyter.

Fensham, Charles F. 1962. Widow, Orphan, and the Poor in Ancient Near Eastern Legal and Wisdom Literature. *Journal of Near Eastern Studies* 21:129–39.
Feuchtwang, David. 1904. Moses und Hammurabi. *Monatsschrift für Geschichte und Wissenschaft des Judentums* 48:385–99.
Figueira, Dorothy M. 1995. Oriental Despotism and Despotic Orientalisms. *Bucknell Review* 38:182–99.
Finkelstein, Jacob J. 1961. Ammiṣaduqa's Edict and the Babylonian "Law Codes". *Journal of Cuneiform Studies* 15:91–104.
Fischer, Rudolf. 1985. *Babylon*. Stuttgart: Thienemann.
Forst, Rainer, and Klaus Günther, eds. 2021. *Normative Ordnungen*. Berlin: Suhrkamp.
Foster, Benjamin. 1995. Social Reform in Ancient Mesopotamia. In *Social Justice in the Ancient World*, edited by K. D. Irani, and Morris Silver, 165–78. Westport: Greenwood.
Foucault, Michel. 2009. *Security, Territory, Population. Lectures at the Collège de France, 1977–1978*, edited by Michel Senellart. New York: Picador.
Frahm, Eckart. 2007. Images of Assyria in Nineteenth- and Twentieth-Century Western Scholarship. In *Ohrientalism, Assyriology and the Bible*, edited by Steven W. Holloway, 74–94. Sheffield: Phoenix Press.
Frank, Bruno. 1926. *Friedrich der Große als Mensch im Spiegel seiner Briefe, seiner Schriften, zeitgenössischer Berichte und Anekdoten*. Berlin: Deutsche Buch-Gemeinschaft.
Frankenberg, Günther. 2020. *Autoritarismus. Verfassungstheoretische Perspektiven*. Berlin: Suhrkamp.
Frei, Hans W. 1974. *The Eclipse of Biblical Narrative. A Study in Eighteenth and Nineteenth Century Hermeneutics*. New Haven: Yale University Press.
Friedrich der Große. 1912. Das politische Testament von 1752. In *Die Werke Friedrichs des Großen in deutscher Übersetzung. Siebenter Band: Antimachiavell und Testamente*, edited by Gustav B. Volz, 118–99. Berlin: Reimer.
Frotscher, Werner, and Bodo Pieroth. 2022. *Verfassungsgeschichte. Von der nordamerikanischen Revolution bis zur Wiedervereinigung Deutschlands*. Munich: Beck.
Fügert, Anja, and Helen Gries, eds. 2020. *Glazed Brick Decoration in the Ancient Near East*. Oxford: Archaeopress.
Galton, Francis. 1875. *Hereditary Genius. An Inquiry into Its Laws and Consequences*. New York: Appleton and Company.
Gerdmar, Anders. 2009. *Roots of Theological Anti-Semitism. German Biblical Interpretation and the Jews, from Herder and Semler to Kittel and Bultmann*. Leiden: Brill.
Gierke, Otto v. 1916/17. Recht und Sittlichkeit. *Logos. Internationale Zeitschrift für Philosophie der Kultur* 6:211–64.
Goez, Werner. 1958. *Translatio Imperii. Ein Beitrag zur Geschichte des Geschichtsdenkens und der politischen Theorien in Mittelalter und in der frühen Neuzeit*. Tübingen: Mohr Siebeck.
Gossman, Lionel. 2000. *Basel in the Age of Burckhardt. A Study in Unseasonable Ideas*. Chicago: University of Chicago Press.
Graber, Rolf. 2006. Aufgeklärter Absolutismus. Historiographiegeschichtliche Aspekte und forschungspolitische Konsequenzen eines umstrittenen Epochenbegriffs. In *Aufklärung – Vormärz – Revolution*, edited by Helmut Reinalter, 15–25. Frankfurt a. M.: Peter Lang.
Graf, Friedrich W. 1997. Geschichte durch Übergeschichte überwinden. Antihistoristisches Geschichtsdenken in der protestantischen Theologie der 1920er Jahre. In *Geschichtsdiskurs. Band 4: Krisenbewusstsein, Katastrophenerfahrungen und Innovationen 1880–1945*, edited by Wolfgang Küttler, Jörn Rüsen, and Ernst Schulin, 217–44. Frankfurt a. M.: Fischer.

Graf, Friedrich W. 2004. *Die Wiederkehr der Götter. Religion in der modernen Kultur.* Munich: Beck.
Gregorovius, Ferdinand. 1978 [1871]. *Geschichte der Stadt Rom im Mittelalter vom V. bis zum XVI. Jahrhundert. Band II: Siebentes bis zwölftes Buch*, edited by Waldemar Kampf. Munich: Beck.
Greiert, Andreas. 2017. Innovation und Ressentiment. Ernst Kantorowicz im historiographischen Diskurs der Weimarer Republik. *Historische Zeitschrift* 305:393–419.
Grimm, Dieter. 2015. *Deutsche Verfassungsgeschichte 1776–1866.* Frankfurt a. M.: Suhrkamp.
Grimme, Hubert. 1892. *Mohammed. Erster Teil: Das Leben nach den Quellen.* Münster: Aschendorffsche Buchhandlung.
Grimme, Hubert. 1895. *Mohammed. Zweiter Teil: Einleitung in den Koran. System der koranischen Theologie.* Münster: Aschendorffsche Buchhandlung.
Grimme, Hubert. 1903. *Das Gesetz Chammurabis und Moses. Eine Skizze.* Cologne: Bachem.
Grimme, Hubert. 1904. *Mohammed.* Munich: Kirchheimsche Verlagsbuchhandlung.
Gross, Michael B. 2005. *The War Against Catholicism. Liberalism and the Anti-Catholic Imagination in Nineteenth-Century Germany.* Ann Arbor: University of Michigan Press.
Gross, Raphael. 2005. *Carl Schmitt und die Juden. Eine deutsche Rechtslehre.* Frankfurt a. M.: Suhrkamp.
Großmann, Andreas. 2010. Recht verkehrt. Hegels Rechtsphilosophie im Neuhegelianismus. In *Recht ohne Gerechtigkeit? Hegel und die Grundlagen des Rechtsstaates*, edited by Mirko Wischke, and Andrzej Przyłębski, 191–208. Würzburg: Königshausen & Neumann.
Grote, Rainer. 1999. Rule of Law, Rechtsstaat and "Etat de droit". In *Constitutionalism, Universalism and Democracy. A Comparative Analysis*, edited by Christian Starck, 269–306. Baden-Baden: Nomos.
Grotsch, Klaus. 1984. Naturvölker/Kulturvölker. In *Historisches Wörterbuch der Philosophie.* Vol. 6, edited by Joachim Ritter, and Karlfried Gründer, 635–41. Basel: Schwabe.
Habermas, Jürgen. 1987. *The Theory of Communicative Action. Vol. 2: Lifeworld and System. A Critique of Functionalist Reason.* Cambridge: Polity.
Habermas, Jürgen. 1995 [1981]. *Theorie des kommunikativen Handelns. Band 2: Zur Kritik der funktionalistischen Vernunft.* Frankfurt a. M.: Suhrkamp.
Habermas, Jürgen. 1999. Über den internen Zusammenhang von Rechtsstaat und Demokratie. In Jürgen Habermas, *Die Einbeziehung des Anderen. Studien zur politischen Theorie*, 293–305. Frankfurt a. M.: Suhrkamp.
Habermas, Jürgen. 2021. Noch einmal: Zum Verhältnis von Moralität und Sittlichkeit. In *Normative Ordnungen*, edited by Rainer Forst, and Klaus Günther, 25–41. Berlin: Suhrkamp.
Habermas, Rebekka. 2019. Secularism in the Long Nineteenth Century between the Global and the Local. In *Negotiating the Secular and the Religious in the German Empire. Transnational Approaches*, edited by Rebekka Habermas, 115–43. New York: Berghahn.
Haferkamp, Hans-Peter. 2018. *Die Historische Rechtsschule.* Frankfurt a. M.: Klostermann.
Hagner, Michael. 2004. *Geniale Hirne. Zur Geschichte der Elitenforschung.* Göttingen: Wallstein.
Hampe, Karl. 1899. Kaiser Friedrich II. *Historische Zeitschrift* 83:1–42.
Hampe, Karl. 1909. *Deutsche Kaisergeschichte in der Zeit der Salier und Staufer.* Leipzig: Quelle & Meyer.
Harbsmeier, Michael. 2002. Orientreisen im 18. Jahrhundert. In *Carsten Niebuhr (1733–1815) und seine Zeit*, edited by Josef Wiesehöfer, and Stephan Conermann, 63–84. Stuttgart: Steiner.
Harke, Jan D. 2007. *Das Sanktionssystem des Codex Hammurapi.* Würzburg: Ergon.
Harper, Robert F. 1904. *The Code of Hammurabi, King of Babylon about 2250 B.C. Autographed Text, Transliteration, Translation, Glossary, Index of Subjects, Lists of Proper Names, Signs, Numerals,*

Corrections, and Erasures with Map Frontispiece and Photograph of Text. Chicago: University of Chicago Press.

Hart, Herbert L. A. 1958. Positivism and the Separation of Law and Morals. *Harvard Law Review* 71:593–629.

Hart, Herbert L. A. 1961. *The Concept of Law*. Oxford: Clarendon Press.

Hartog, François. 2015. *Regimes of Historicity. Presentism and Experiences of Time*. New York: Columbia University Press.

Hartung, Fritz. 1955. Der aufgeklärte Absolutismus. *Historische Zeitschrift* 180:15–42.

Hasel, Michael G. 2008. Merenptah's Reference to Israel. Critical Issues for the Origin of Israel. In *Critical Issues in Early Israelite History*, edited by Richard S. Hess, Gerald A. Klingbeil, and Paul J. Ray Jr., 47–60. University Park [PA]: Penn State University Press.

Haubold, Johannes. 2000. *Homer's People. Epic Poetry and Social Formation*. Cambridge: Cambridge University Press.

Hegel, Georg W. F. 1914. *Lectures on the Philosophy of History*, translated and edited by John Sibree. London: Bell and Sons.

Hegel, Georg W. F. 1970. *Vorlesungen über die Philosophie der Geschichte*. G. W. F. Hegel. Werke 12, edited by Eva Moldenhauer, and Karl Markus Michel, Frankfurt a. M.: Suhrkamp.

Hegel, Georg W. F. 1975. *Lectures on the Philosophy of World History. Introduction: Reason in History*, translated by Hugh Barr Nisbet and edited by Johannes Hoffmeister. Cambridge: Cambridge University Press.

Hegel, Georg W. F. 1986 [1820]. *Grundlinien der Philosophie des Rechts*. G. W. F. Hegel. Werke 7, edited by Eva Moldenhauer, and Karl Markus Michel. Frankfurt a. M.: Suhrkamp.

Hegel, Georg W. F. 1991 [1820]. *Elements of the Philosophy of Right*, translated by Hugh Barr Nisbet and edited by Allen W. Wood. Cambridge: Cambridge University Press.

Hegel, Georg W. F. 2018. *Vorlesungen über die Ästhetik II*. G. W. F. Hegel. Werke 14, edited by Eva Moldenhauer, and Karl Markus Michel. Frankfurt a. M.: Suhrkamp.

Heinßen, Johannes. 2003. *Historismus und Kulturkritik. Studien zur deutschen Geschichtskultur im späten 19. Jahrhundert*. Göttingen: Vandenhoeck & Ruprecht.

Heintschel von Heinegg, Wolf. 1996. Rechtsstaatlichkeit in Deutschland. In *Rechtsstaatlichkeit in Europa*, edited by Rainer Hofmann, and Maria L. Amaral, 107–40. Heidelberg: Müller.

Heller, Hermann. 1930. *Rechtsstaat oder Diktatur?* Tübingen: Mohr.

Henkelmann, Wouter F. M., Amélie Kuhrt, Robert Rollinger, and Josef Wiesehöfer. 2011. Herodotus and Babylon Reconsidered. In *Herodot und das Persische Weltreich*, edited by Robert Rollinger, Brigitte Truschnegg, and Reinhold Bichler, 449–70. Wiesbaden: Harrassowitz.

Henshall, Nicholas. 1992. *The Myth of Absolutism. Change and Continuity in Early Modern European Monarchy*. London: Longman.

Herder, Johann G. 1994 [1774]. Auch eine Philosophie der Geschichte zur Bildung der Menschheit. Beitrag zu vielen Beiträgen des Jahrhunderts. In *Johann Gottfried Herder. Werke in zehn Bänden. Band 4: Schriften zu Philosophie, Kunst und Altertum*, edited by Jürgen Brummack, and Martin Bollacher, 9–109. Frankfurt a. M.: Klassiker-Verlag.

Herder, Johann G. 2002 [1774]. This Too a Philosophy of History for the Formation of Humanity. In *Johann Gottfried Herder. Philosophical Writings*, translated and edited by Michael N. Forster, 272–358. Cambridge: Cambridge University Press.

Heschel, Susannah. 2005. Theology as a Vision for Colonialism. From Supersessionism to Dejudaization in German Protestantism. In *Germany's Colonial Pasts*, edited by Eric Ames, Maria Klotz, and Lora Wildenthal, 148–63. Lincoln: University of Nebraska Press.

Heschel, Susannah. 2008. *The Aryan Jesus. Christian Theologians and the Bible in Nazi Germany*. Princeton: Princeton University Press.
Heschel, Susannah. 2018. *Jüdischer Islam. Islam und jüdisch-deutsche Selbstbestimmung*. Berlin: Matthes & Seitz.
Hess, Jonathan M. 2000. Johann David Michaelis and the Colonial Imaginary. Orientalism and the Emergence of Racial Antisemitism in Eighteenth-Century Germany. *Jewish Social Studies* 6:56–101.
Heun, Werner. 2001. Das monarchische Prinzip und der deutsche Konstitutionalismus des 19. Jahrhunderts. In *Recht – Staat – Gemeinwohl. Festschrift für Dietrich Rauschning*, edited by Jörn Ipsen, 41–56. Cologne: Heymann.
Hintze, Otto. 1915. *Die Hohenzollern und ihr Werk. Fünfhundert Jahre vaterländischer Geschichte*. Berlin: Parey.
Hintze, Otto. 1970 [1911]. Das monarchische Prinzip und die konstitutionelle Verfassung. In Otto Hintze. *Staat und Verfassung. Gesammelte Abhandlungen zur allgemeinen Verfassungsgeschichte*, edited by Gerhard Oesterreich, 359–89. Göttingen: Vandenhoeck & Ruprecht.
Hirsch, William. 1894. *Genie und Entartung. Eine psychologische Studie*. Berlin: Oscar Coblentz.
Hoffmeister, Johannes, ed. 1970. *Briefe von und an Hegel. Band 1: 1785–1812*. Berlin: Akademie-Verlag.
Hofmann, Hasso. 1995. Geschichtlichkeit und Universalitätsanspruch des Rechtsstaats. *Der Staat* 34:1–32.
Hoheisel, Karl. 1978. *Das antike Judentum in christlicher Sicht. Ein Beitrag zur neueren Forschungsgeschichte*. Wiesbaden: Harrassowitz.
Holl, Karl, Hans Kloft, and Gerd Fesser, eds. 2001. *Caligula – Wilhelm II. und der Caesarenwahnsinn. Antikenrezeption und wilhelminische Politik am Beispiel des "Caligula" von Ludwig Quidde*. Bremen: Edition Temmen.
Holldack, Heinz. 1974. Der Physiokratismus und die absolute Monarchie. In *Der aufgeklärte Absolutismus*, edited by Karl O. F. von Aretin, 137–62. Cologne: Kiepenheuer & Witsch.
Holloway, Steven W. 2001. Biblical Assyria and Other Anxieties in the British Empire. *Journal of Religion & Society* 3:1–19.
Hölscher, Lucian. 2020. *Zeitgärten. Zeitfiguren in der Geschichte der Neuzeit*. Göttingen: Wallstein.
Holterhus, Till P. 2022. Die Idee der Rechtsstaatlichkeit. *Informationen zur politischen Bildung*. Available from https://www.bpb.de/shop/zeitschriften/izpb/rechtsstaat-351/511411/die-idee-der-rechtsstaatlichkeit, accessed 5 January 2025.
Holz, Klaus. 2001. *Nationaler Antisemitismus. Wissenssoziologie einer Weltanschauung*. Hamburg: Hamburger Edition.
Hommel, Fritz. 1885. *Geschichte Babyloniens und Assyriens*. Berlin: Grote.
Hommel, Fritz. 1897a. *Die altisraelitische Überlieferung in inschriftlicher Beleuchtung. Ein Einspruch gegen die Aufstellungen der modernen Pentateuchkritik*. Munich: Franz'sche Hofbuchhandlung.
Hommel, Fritz. 1897b. *The Ancient Hebrew Tradition as Illustrated by the Monuments. A Protest against the Modern School of Old Testament Criticism*. London: Society for Promoting Christian Knowledge.
Hommel, Fritz. 1904. *Grundriss der Geographie und Geschichte des alten Orients. Erste Hälfte: Ethnologie des Alten Orients. Babylonien und Chaldäa*. Munich: Beck.
Honneth, Axel. 2021. Recht und Sittlichkeit. Aspekte eines komplexen Wechselverhältnisses. In *Normative Ordnungen*, edited by Rainer Forst, and Klaus Günther, 42–73. Berlin: Suhrkamp.

Huber, Ernst R. 1957. *Deutsche Verfassungsgeschichte seit 1789. Band I: Reform und Restauration 1789 bis 1830.* Stuttgart: Kohlhammer.
Huber, Ernst R., ed. 1961. *Dokumente zur Deutschen Verfassungsgeschichte. Band 1: Deutsche Verfassungsdokumente 1803–1850.* Stuttgart: Kohlhammer.
Huber, Ernst R. 1970. *Deutsche Verfassungsgeschichte seit 1789. Band III: Bismarck und das Reich.* Stuttgart: Kohlhammer.
Huber, Peter M. 2019. Der Rechtsstaat nach 70 Jahren Grundgesetz. Ein gefährdetes Erfolgsmodell. In *70 Jahre Grundgesetz. In welcher Verfassung ist die Bundesrepublik?* edited by Hans M. Heinig, Frank Schorkopf, Udo Di Fabio, Dieter Grimm, and Peter M. Huber, 207–28. Göttingen: Vandenhoeck & Ruprecht.
Hull, Isabel V. 1991. "Persönliches Regiment". In *Der Ort Kaiser Wilhelms II. in der deutschen Geschichte*, edited by John C. G. Röhl, 3–24. Munich: Oldenbourg.
Hurstel, Sylvie. 1996. Der Neuhegelianismus zwischen Rechtsgeschichte und Rechtsphilosophie. In *Die Historismusdebatte in der Weimarer Republik*, edited by Wolfgang Bialas, and Gérard Raulet, 118–41. Frankfurt a. M.: Peter Lang.
Huwyler, Beat. 2013. de Wette. Wilhelm Martin Leberecht. *WiBiLex. Das wissenschaftliche Bibellexikon im Internet.* Available from https://bibelwissenschaft.de/stichwort/34804, accessed 30 May 2025.
Iggers, Georg G. 1983. *The German Conception of History. The National Tradition of Historical Thought from Herder to the Present.* Middletown: Wesleyan University Press.
Ilting, Karl-Heinz. 1983. *Naturrecht und Sittlichkeit. Begriffsgeschichtliche Studien.* Stuttgart: Klett-Cotta.
Ilting, Karl-Heinz. 1984. Sitte, Sittlichkeit, Moral. In *Geschichtliche Grundbegriffe. Historisches Lexikon zur politisch-sozialen Sprache in Deutschland.* Vol. 5, edited by Otto Brunner, Werner Conze, and Reinhart Koselleck, 863–921. Stuttgart: Klett-Cotta.
Ingrao, Charles. 1986. "Enlightened Absolutism" and the German State. *The Journal of Modern History* 58:161–80.
Ipsen, Jörn. 2017. *Macht versus Recht. Der Hannoversche Verfassungskonflikt 1837–1840.* Munich: Beck.
Jacobs, Sandra. 2014. *The Body as Property. Physical Disfigurement in Biblical Law.* London: Bloomsbury.
Jasanoff, Maya. 2006. *Edge of Empire. Conquest and Collecting in the East 1750–1850.* London: Harper Perennial.
Jeremias, Johannes. 1903. *Moses und Hammurabi.* Leipzig: Hinrichs.
Joas, Hans, and Peter Vogt, eds. 2011. *Begriffene Geschichte. Beiträge zum Werk Reinhart Kosellecks.* Berlin: Suhrkamp.
Johanning, Klaus. 1988. *Der Bibel-Babel-Streit. Eine forschungsgeschichtliche Studie.* Frankfurt a. M.: Peter Lang.
Jordan, Stefan. 2012. Die Sattelzeit. Transformation des Denkens oder revolutionärer Paradigmenwechsel? In *Frühe Neue Zeiten. Zeitwissen zwischen Reformation und Revolution*, edited by Achim Landwehr, 373–88. Bielefeld: transcript.
Jordheim, Helge. 2017. Synchronizing the World. Synchronism as Historiographical Practise, Then and Now. *History of the Present* 7:59–95.
Kain, Philip J. 2018. *Hegel and Right. A Study of the "Philosophy of Right".* New York: Suny Press.
Kaiser, Thomas. 2000. The Evil Empire? The Debate on Turkish Despotism in Eighteenth-Century French Political Culture. *The Journal of Modern History* 72:6–34.

Kant, Immanuel. 1907a [1797]. Die Metaphysik der Sitten. In *Kant's gesammelte Schriften. Erste Abtheilung: Werke*, Vol. VI, edited by Preußische Akademie der Wissenschaften, 203–492. Berlin: Reimer.

Kant, Immanuel. 1907b [1793/94]. Die Religion innerhalb der Grenzen der bloßen Vernunft. In *Kant's gesammelte Schriften. Erste Abtheilung: Werke*, Vol. VI, edited by Preußische Akademie der Wissenschaften, 1–202. Berlin: Reimer.

Kant, Immanuel. 1912 [1784]. Idee zu einer allgemeinen Geschichte in weltbürgerlicher Absicht. In *Kant's gesammelte Schriften. Erste Abtheilung: Werke*, Vol. VIII, edited by Preußische Akademie der Wissenschaften, 15–32. Berlin: Reimer.

Kant, Immanuel. 1923 [1784]. Beantwortung der Frage: Was ist Aufklärung? In *Kant's gesammelte Schriften. Erste Abtheilung: Werke*, Vol. VIII, edited by Preußische Akademie der Wissenschaften, 33–42. Berlin: Reimer.

Kant, Immanuel. 2017 [1797]. *The Metaphysics of Morals*, translated by Mary Gregor and edited by Lara Denis. Cambridge: Cambridge University Press.

Kantorowicz, Ernst. 1927. *Kaiser Wilhelm der Zweite*. Berlin: Bondi.

Käsler, Dirk. 1990. Charismatische Herrschaft und der charismatische Führer im Werk Max Webers. In *Regieren in der Bundesrepublik. Systemsteuerung und "Staatskunst"*, edited by Hans-Hermann Hartwich, Göttrik Wewer, and Lars Kastning, 275–92. Opladen: Leske + Budrich.

Kaul, Camilla G. 2007. *Friedrich Barbarossa im Kyffhäuser. Bilder eines nationalen Mythos im 19. Jahrhundert*. Cologne: Böhlau.

Kelsen, Hans. 1967 [1960]. *Pure Theory of Law*. Berkeley: University of California Press.

Kerautret, Michael. 2012. Religiöse Toleranz oder philosophische Indifferenz. In *Friedrich der Große in Europa. Geschichte einer wechselvollen Beziehung*. Vol. 2, edited by Bernd Sösemann, and Gregor Vogt-Spira, 47–66. Stuttgart: Steiner.

Kersten, Jens. 2010. Friedrich Julius Stahl (1802–1861). In *Festschrift 200 Jahre Juristische Fakultät der Humboldt-Universität zu Berlin. Geschichte, Gegenwart und Zukunft*, edited by Stefan Grundmann, Michael Kloepfer, Christoph G. Paulus, Rainer Schröder, and Gerhard Werle, 205–27. Berlin: De Gruyter.

Kimmel, Elke. 2009. Reventlow, Ernst Graf zu. In *Handbuch des Antisemitismus. Judenfeindschaft in Geschichte und Gegenwart. Band 2/2: Personen L-Z*, edited by Wolfgang Benz, 684–5. Munich: Saur.

King, Leonard W. 1898. *The Letters and Inscriptions of Hammurabi. King of Babylon about B.C. 2.200, to Which Are Added a Series of Letters of other Kings of the First Dynasty of Babylon. Vol. I: Introduction and the Babylonian Texts*. London: Luzac.

King, Leonard W. 1900a. *The Letters and Inscriptions of Hammurabi. King of Babylon about B.C. 2.200, to Which are Added a Series of Letters of other Kings of the First Dynasty of Babylon. Vol. II: Babylonian Textes, Continued*. London: Luzac.

King, Leonard W. 1900b. *The Letters and Inscriptions of Hammurabi. King of Babylon about B.C. 2.200, to Which are Added a Series of Letters of other Kings of the First Dynasty of Babylon. Vol. III: English Translations, etc.* London: Luzac.

Kipper, Rainer. 2002. *Der Germanenmythos im deutschen Kaiserreich. Formen und Funktionen historischer Selbstthematisierung*. Göttingen: Vandenhoeck & Ruprecht.

Kirsch, Martin. 1999. *Monarch und Parlament im 19. Jahrhundert. Der monarchische Konstitutionalismus als europäischer Verfassungstyp. Frankreich im Vergleich*. Göttingen: Vandenhoeck & Ruprecht.

Kirste, Stephan. 2013. Die Rule of Law in der deutschen Rechsstaatstheorie des 19. Jahrhunderts. *Jahrbuch für Recht und Ethik* 21:23–62.

Kloft, Hans. 2020 [2000]. Caligula, Ludwig Quidde und der Cäsarenwahnsinn. In Hans Kloft. *Studien zur Wirtschafts-, Sozial- und Rezeptionsgeschichte der Antike*, 138–60. Berlin: De Gruyter.

Koebner, Richard. 1951. Despot and Despotism. Vicissitudes of a Political Term. *Journal of the Warburg and Courtauld Institutes* 14:275–302.

Koetter, Matthias. 2013. "Rechtsstaat" and "Rechtstaatlichkeit" in Germany. *Wikis der Freien Universität Berlin*. Available from https://wikis.fu-berlin.de/spaces/SBprojectrol/pages/17138091/Germany, accessed 15 March 2025.

Kogge, Werner, and Lisa Wilhelmi. 2019. Despot und (orientalische) Despotie – Brüche im Konzept von Aristoteles bis Montesquieu. *Saeculum* 69:305–41.

Kohler, George Y. 2010. German Spirit and Holy Ghost – Treitschke's Call for Conversion of German Jewry. The Debate Revisited. *Modern Judaism* 30:172–95.

Kohler, Josef. 1885. Rechtsgeschichte und Kulturgeschichte. *Zeitschrift für das Privat- und Öffentliche Recht der Gegenwart* 12:583–93.

Kohler, Josef. 1903. Samuel Oettli: Das Gesetz Hammurabis und die Thora Israels [Rezension]. *Deutsche Literaturzeitung* 24:1543–9.

Kohler, Josef. 1904. *Aus Kultur und Leben. Gesammelte Essays*. Berlin: Eisner.

Kohler, Josef. 1904a [1899]. Begriff und Aufgabe der Weltgeschichte. In Josef Kohler. *Aus Kultur und Leben. Gesammelte Essays*, 15–22. Berlin: Otto Eisner.

Kohler, Josef. 1904b [1903]. Hammurabis Gesetz. In Josef Kohler. *Aus Kultur und Leben. Gesammelte Essays*, 58–64. Berlin: Otto Eisner.

Kohler, Josef. 1906. *Lehrbuch des Bürgerlichen Rechts. Erster Band: Allgemeiner Teil*. Berlin: Heymanns.

Kohler, Josef. 1907. Darstellung des talmudischen Rechts. *Zeitschrift für vergleichende Rechtswissenschaft* 20:161–264.

Kohler, Josef. 1908. *Aus vier Weltteilen. Reisebilder*. Berlin: Rothschild.

Kohler, Josef. 1914. Das Recht der orientalischen Völker. In *Allgemeine Rechtsgeschichte. Erste Hälfte: Orientalisches Recht und Recht der Griechen und Römer*, edited by Josef Kohler, and Leopold Wenger, 49–153. Leipzig: Teubner.

Kohler, Josef, and Felix E. Peiser. 1904. *Hammurabi's Gesetz. Band I: Übersetzung, Juristische Wiedergabe, Erläuterung*. Leipzig: Pfeiffer.

Kohler, Josef, and Arthur Ungnad. 1909a. *Hammurabi's Gesetz. Band II: Syllabische und zusammenhängende Umschrift nebst vollständigem Glossar*. Leipzig: Pfeiffer.

Kohler, Josef, and Arthur Ungnad. 1909b. *Hammurabi's Gesetz. Band III: Übersetzte Urkunden, Erläuterungen*. Leipzig: Pfeiffer.

Kohler, Josef, and Arthur Ungnad. 1910. *Hammurabi's Gesetz. Band IV: Übersetzte Urkunden, Erläuterungen (Fortsetzung)*. Leipzig: Pfeiffer.

Kohler, Josef, and Arthur Ungnad. 1911. *Hammurabi's Gesetz. Band V: Übersetzte Urkunden, Verwaltungsregister, Inventare, Erläuterungen*. Leipzig: Pfeiffer.

Kohler, Josef, and Leopold Wenger, eds. 1914. *Allgemeine Rechtsgeschichte. Erste Hälfte: Orientalisches Recht und Recht der Griechen und Römer*. Leipzig: Teubner.

Kohlrausch, Martin. 2005. *Der Monarch im Skandal. Die Logik der Massenmedien und die Transformation der wilhelminischen Monarchie*. Berlin: Akademie Verlag.

Köhne, Julia B. 2014. *Geniekult in Geisteswissenschaften und Literaturen um 1900 und seine filmischen Adaptionen*. Vienna: Böhlau Verlag.

König, Eduard. 1903. Hammurabis Gesetzgebung und ihre religionsgeschichtliche Tragweite. *Der Beweis des Glaubens. Monatsschrift zur Begründung und Verteidigung der christlichen Wahrheit für Gebildete* 39:169–80.

Koschaker, Paul. 1917. *Rechtsvergleichende Studien zur Gesetzgebung Hammurapis, Königs von Babylon.* Leipzig: Veit & Comp.
Koschaker, Paul, and Arthur Ungnad. 1923. *Hammurabi's Gesetz. Band VI: Übersetzte Urkunden mit Rechtserläuterungen.* Leipzig: Pfeiffer.
Koselleck, Reinhart. 1975a. Geschichte. V. Die Herausbildung des modernen Geschichtsbegriffs. In *Geschichtliche Grundbegriffe. Historisches Lexikon zur politisch-sozialen Sprache in Deutschland.* Vol. 2, edited by Otto Brunner, Werner Conze, and Reinhart Koselleck, 593–595. Stuttgart: Klett-Cotta.
Koselleck, Reinhart. 1975b Geschichte. VI. "Geschichte" als moderner Leitbegriff. In *Geschichtliche Grundbegriffe. Historisches Lexikon zur politisch-sozialen Sprache in Deutschland.* Vol. 2, edited by Otto Brunner, Werner Conze, and Reinhart Koselleck, 647–717. Stuttgart: Klett-Cotta.
Koselleck, Reinhart. 2018 [1959]. *Kritik und Krise. Eine Studie zur Pathogenese der bürgerlichen Welt.* Frankfurt a. M.: Suhrkamp.
Koser, Reinhold. 1889. Die Epochen der absoluten Monarchie in der neueren Geschichte. *Historische Zeitschrift* 61:246–87.
Koser, Reinhold. 1893. *König Friedrich der Große.* Erster Band. Stuttgart: Cotta.
Koser, Reinhold. 1903. *König Friedrich der Große.* Zweiter Band. Stuttgart: Cotta.
Kotulla, Michael. 1992. Die verfassungsrechtliche Ausprägung der Garantie der richterlichen Unabhängigkeit im 19. Jahrhundert. *Deutsche Richterzeitung* 70:285–292.
Kotulla, Michael. 2007. Machtsprüche, strafgerichtliche Bestätigungsvorbehalte und die richterliche Unabhängigkeit. In *Rechtsstaat und Grundrechte. Festschrift für Detlef Merten,* edited by Ferdinand Kirchhof, and Hans-Jürgen Papier, 199–222. Heidelberg: Müller.
Kratz, Reinhard G. 1999. Babylon im Alten Testament. In *Babylon. Focus mesopotamischer Geschichte, Wiege früher Gelehrsamkeit, Mythos in der Moderne,* edited by Johannes Renger, 477–90. Saarbrücken: SDV.
Kraus, Hans-Christof. 2004. Monarchischer Konstitutionalismus. Zu einer neuen Deutung der deutschen und europäischen Verfassungsentwicklung im 19. Jh. *Der Staat* 43:595–620.
Kraus, Hans-Joachim. 1982. *Geschichte der historisch-kritischen Erforschung des Alten Testaments.* Neukirchen-Vluyn: Neukirchener Verlag.
Krebernik, Manfred. 2006–2008. Richtergott(heiten). In *Reallexikon der Assyriologie und Vorderasiatischen Archäologie. Elfter Band,* edited by Michael P. Streck, 354–61. Berlin: De Gruyter.
Krebernik, Manfred. 2009–2011. Sonnengott. A. I. In Mesopotamien. Philologisch. In *Reallexikon der Assyriologie und Vorderasiatischen Archäologie. Zwölfter Band,* edited by Michael P. Streck, 599–611. Berlin: De Gruyter.
Kretschmer, Ernst. 1929. *Geniale Menschen.* Berlin: Springer.
Krieger, Leonard. 1975. *An Essay on the Theory of Enlightened Despotism.* Chicago: University of Chicago Press.
Kriele, Martin. 1995. *Einführung in die Staatslehre. Die geschichtlichen Legitimitätsgrundlagen des demokratischen Verfassungsstaates.* Wiesbaden: Verlag für Sozialwissenschaft.
Krone, Kerstin v. d. 2012. *Wissenschaft in Öffentlichkeit. Die Wissenschaft des Judentums und ihre Zeitschriften.* Berlin: De Gruyter.
Kuhlmann, Wolfgang, ed. 1986. *Moralität und Sittlichkeit. Das Problem Hegels und die Diskursethik.* Frankfurt a. M.: Suhrkamp.

Kuhrt, Amélie. 1995. Ancient Mesopotamia in Classical Greek and Hellenistic Thought. In *Civilizations of the Ancient Near East*. Vol. 1, edited by Jack M. Sasson, 55–66. New York: Scribner.

Kurmangaliev, Anna. 2009–2011. Sonnengott B. I. In Mesopotamien. Archäologisch. In *Reallexikon der Assyriologie und Vorderasiatischen Archäologie*. Zwölfter Band, edited by Michael P. Streck, 616–20. Berlin: De Gruyter.

Kurtz, Paul M. 2018. *Kaiser, Christ, and Canaan. The Religion of Israel in Protestant Germany 1871–1918*. Tübingen: Mohr Siebeck.

Kurtz, Paul M., ed. 2024. *Moses Among the Moderns. German Constructions of Biblical Law, 1750–1930*. Leiden: Brill.

Kusche, Ulrich. 1991. *Die unterlegene Religion. Das Judentum im Urteil deutscher Alttestamentler*. Berlin: Institut für Kirche und Judentum.

Landsberger, Benno. 1939. Die Babylonischen Termini für Gesetz und Recht. In *Symbolae ad iura orientis antiqui pertinentes. Paulo Koschaker dedicatae*, edited by Johannes Friedrich, Julius G. Lautner, and John Miles, 219–34. Leiden: Brill.

Langer, Ulrich. 1998. *Heinrich von Treitschke. Politische Biographie eines deutschen Nationalisten*. Düsseldorf: Droste.

Larsen, Mogens T. 1996. *The Conquest of Assyria. Excavations in an Antique Land, 1840–1860*. London: Routledge.

Legaspi, Michael C. 2010. *The Death of Scripture and the Rise of Biblical Studies*. New York: Oxford University Press.

Lehmann, Reinhard G. 1994. *Friedrich Delitzsch und der Babel-Bibel-Streit*. Freiburg (Schweiz): Universitätsverlag.

Lehmann, Reinhard G. 2018. "Mit Schriften keilen". Friedrich Delitzsch und der Babel-Bibel-Streit. *Zeitschrift für Ideengeschichte* 12:55–66.

Lehmann-Haupt, Carl F. 1905. *Babyloniens Kulturmission einst und jetzt. Ein Wort zur Ablenkung und Aufklärung zum Babel-Bibel-Streit*. Leipzig: Dieterich.

Lerman, Katharine A. 1982. The Decisive Relationship. Kaiser Wilhelm II and Chancellor Bernhard von Bülow, 1900–1905. In *Kaiser Wilhelm II. New Interpretations*, edited by John C. G. Röhl, and Nicolaus Sombart, 221–47. Cambridge: Cambridge University Press.

Lerman, Katharine A. 1990. *The Chancellor as Courtier. Bernhard von Bülow and the Governance of Germany, 1900–1909*. Cambridge: Cambridge University Press.

Lombroso, Cesare. 1872. *Genio e follia*. Milano: Gaetano Brigola.

Lorenz, Chris. 2019. Out of Time? Some Critical Reflections on Francois Hartog's Presentism. In *Rethinking Historical Time. New Approaches to Presentism*, edited by Marek Tamm, and Laurent Olivier, 23–42. London: Bloomsbury Academic.

Luebke, David M. 1999. Frederick the Great and the Celebrated Case of the Millers Arnold (1770–1779). A Reappraisal. *Central European History* 32:379–408.

Lux, Rüdiger. 2003. Hammurapi und Mose. Gottesrecht und Königsrecht im Alten Orient und im Alten Testament. In Rüdiger Lux. *Jenseits des Paradieses. Vorträge und Bibelarbeiten zum Alten Testament*, 112–39. Leipzig: Evangelische Verlagsanstalt.

MacCormick, Nick. 1984. Der Rechtsstaat und die Rule of Law. *JuristenZeitung* 39:65–70.

Mährlein, Christoph. 2000. *Volksgeist und Recht. Hegels Philosophie der Einheit und ihre Bedeutung in der Rechtswissenschaft*. Würzburg: Königshausen & Neumann.

Malley, Shawn. 2012. *From Archaeology to Spectacle in Victorian Britain. The Case of Assyria 1845–1854*. Farnham: Ashgate.

Mangold, Sabine. 2004. *Eine "weltbürgerliche Wissenschaft". Die deutsche Orientalistik im 19. Jahrhundert.* Stuttgart: Steiner.
Marchand, Suzanne L. 2004. Philhellenism and the "Furor Orientalis". *Modern Intellectual History* 1:331–58.
Marchand, Suzanne L. 2009. *German Orientalism in the Age of Empire. Religion, Race, and Scholarship.* Washington: German Historical Institute.
Marchand, Suzanne L. 2014. Where Does History Begin? J. G. Herder and the Problem of Near Eastern Chronology in the Age of Enlightenment. *Eighteenth-Century Studies* 47:157–75.
Marchand, Suzanne L. 2020. Herodotus as Anti-Classical Toolbox. In *Herodotus in the Long Nineteenth Century*, edited by Thomas Harrison, and Joseph Skinner, 71–99. Cambridge: Cambridge University Press.
Markschies, Christoph. 2021. Der Kaiser als Hobbywissenschaftler. Wilhelm II. – Frömmigkeit – Kommunikation – Wissenschaftspolitik. In *Der Babel-Bibel-Streit und die Wissenschaft des Judentums*, edited by Eva Cancik-Kirschbaum, and Thomas L. Gertzen, 89–105. Münster: Zaphon.
Marx, Christoph. 1988. *Völker ohne Schrift und Geschichte. Zur historischen Erfassung des vorkolonialen Schwarzafrika in der deutschen Forschung des 19. und frühen 20. Jahrhunderts.* Stuttgart: Steiner.
Matthes, Olaf. 1999. Friedrich von Hollmanns Bedeutung für die Deutsche Orient-Gesellschaft. *Mitteilungen der Deutschen Orient-Gesellschaft* 131:191–208.
Maus, Ingeborg. 1978. Entwicklung und Funktionswandel der Theorie des bürgerlichen Rechtsstaats. In *Der bürgerliche Rechtsstaat* [vol. 1], edited by Mehdi Tohidipur, 13–81. Frankfurt a. M.: Suhrkamp.
Maus, Ingeborg. 2011 [1995]. Die Transformation des Volkssouveränitätsprinzips in der Weimarer Republik. In Ingeborg Maus. *Über Volkssouveränität. Elemente einer Demokratietheorie*, 93–119. Berlin: Suhrkamp.
Mayer, Otto. 1895. *Deutsches Verwaltungsrecht. Erster Band.* Leipzig: Duncker & Humblot.
McGeough, Kevin M. 2015. *The Ancient Near East in the Nineteenth Century. Appreciations and Appropriations. Vol. I: Claiming and Conquering.* Sheffield: Phoenix Press.
Mecke, Chistoph-Eric. 2013. The "Rule of Law" and the "Rechtsstaat". A Historical and Theoretical Approach from a German Perspective. *Studia Iuridica* 79:29–47.
Meissner, Bruno. 1898. Altbabylonische Gesetze. *Beiträge zur Assyriologie und semitischen Sprachwissenschaft* 3:493–523.
Meissner, Bruno. 1926. *Könige Babyloniens und Assyriens. Charakterbilder aus der altorientalischen Geschichte.* Leipzig: Quelle & Meyer.
Messling, Markus. 2012. *Champollions Hieroglyphen. Philologie und Weltaneignung.* Berlin: Kadmos.
Meyer, Eduard. 1910. *Geschichte des Altertums. Band 1.1: Einleitung, Elemente der Anthropologie.* Stuttgart: Cotta.
Meyer, Seligmann. 1903. *Contra Delitzsch! Die Babel-Hypothesen widerlegt.* Frankfurt a. M.: Kauffmann.
Michaelis, Johann D. 1770–1775. *Mosaisches Recht [sechs Theile].* Frankfurt am Mayn: Garbe.
Mohl, Robert von. 1829. *Das Staatsrecht des Königreiches Württemberg. Erster Theil: Das Verfassungsrecht.* Tübingen: Laupp.
Mohl, Robert von. 1844. *Die Polizei-Wissenschaft nach den Grundsätzen des Rechtsstaates.* Erster Band. Tübingen: Laupp.

Mommsen, Wolfgang J. 1974 [1963]. Zum Begriff der "plebiszitären Führerdemokratie". In Wolfgang J. Mommsen. *Max Weber. Gesellschaft, Politik und Geschichte*, 44–71. Frankfurt a. M.: Suhrkamp.

Mommsen, Wolfgang J. 2002. *War der Kaiser an allem schuld? Wilhelm II. und die preußisch-deutschen Machteliten.* Munich: Propyläen.

Montesquieu, Charles L. de. 1721a. *Lettres persanes. Tome I.* Amsterdam: Brunel.

Montesquieu, Charles L. de. 1721b. *Lettres persanes. Tome II.* Amsterdam: Brunel.

Montesquieu, Charles L. de. 1748a. *De l'esprit des loix. Tome premier.* Genève: Barrilot.

Montesquieu, Charles L. de. 1748b. *De l'esprit des loix. Tome second.* Genève: Barrilot.

Muhlack, Ulrich. 1991. *Geschichtswissenschaft im Humanismus und in der Aufklärung. Die Vorgeschichte des Historismus.* Munich: Beck.

Müller, David H. 1903. *Die Gesetze Hammurabis und ihr Verhältnis zur mosaischen Gesetzgebung. Der Text in Umschrift, deutsche und hebräische Übersetzung. Erläuterung und vergleichende Analyse.* Vienna: Hölder.

Müller, Klaus E. 1993. Grundzüge des ethnologischen Historismus. In *Grundfragen der Ethnologie. Beiträge zur gegenwärtigen Theorie-Diskussion*, edited by Wolfdietrich Schmied-Kowarzik, and Justin Stagl, 197–232. Berlin: Reimer.

Münster, Reinhold. 2021. Johann Gottfried Herder und der Orient. In *"Weltpoesie allein ist Weltversöhnung". Friedrich Rückert und der Orientalismus im Europa des 19. Jahrhunderts*, edited by Ralf G. Czapla, 25–42. Baden-Baden: Ergon.

Mürdter, Friedrich. 1882. *Kurzgefasste Geschichte Babyloniens und Assyriens nach den Keilschriftdenkmälern. Mit besonderer Berücksichtigung des Alten Testaments. Mit Vorwort und Beigaben von Friedrich Delitzsch.* Stuttgart: Gundert.

Murray, Oswyn. 1990. The Idea of the Shepherd King from Cyrus to Charlemagne. In *Latin Poetry and the Classical Tradition. Essays in Medieval and Renaissance Literature*, edited by Peter Godman, and Oswyn Murray, 1–14. Oxford: Clarendon.

Naiden, Fred S. 2013. Gods, Kings, and Lawgivers. In *Law and Religion in the Eastern Mediterranean. From Antiquity to Early Islam*, edited by Anselm C. Hagedorn, and Reinhard G. Kratz, 79–104. Oxford: Oxford University Press.

Napoléon III. 1854. Extinction du paupérisme. In Napoléon III. *Oevres tome deuxième*, 107–51. Paris: Librairie D'Amyot.

Naumann, Friedrich. 1900. *Demokratie und Kaisertum. Ein Handbuch für innere Politik.* Berlin-Schöneberg: Buchverlag der "Hilfe".

Neis, Cordula. 2003. *Anthropologie im Sprachdenken des 18. Jahrhunderts. Die Berliner Preisfrage nach dem Ursprung der Sprache (1771).* Berlin: De Gruyter.

Nestor, Dermot. 2015. Merneptah's "Israel" and the Absence of Origins in Biblical Scholarship. *Currents in Biblical Research* 13:287–439.

Neumann, Hans. 2008. Göttliche Gerechtigkeit und menschliche Verantwortung im alten Mesopotamien im Spannungsfeld von Normen(durch)setzung und narrativer Formulierung. In *Recht und Religion. Menschliche und göttliche Gerechtigkeitsvorstellungen in den antiken Welten*, edited by Heinz Barta, 37–48. Wiesbaden: Harrassowitz.

Niedhart, Gottfried. 1979. Aufgeklärter Absolutismus oder Rationalisierung der Herrschaft. *Zeitschrift für historische Forschung* 6:199–211.

Nietzsche, Friedrich. 1988 [1874]. Unzeitgemäße Betrachtungen. Zweites Stück: Vom Nutzen und Nachteil der Historie für das Leben. In Friedrich Nietzsche. *Die Geburt der Tragödie.*

Unzeitgemäße Betrachtungen I–IV. Nachgelassene Schriften 1870–1873, edited by Georgio Colli, and Mazzino Montinari, 243–334. Munich: Deutscher Taschenbuch Verlag; Berlin: De Gruyter.

Nietzsche, Friedrich. 1991 [1874]. On the Uses and Disadvantages of History for Life. In Friedrich Nietzsche. *Untimely Meditations*, translated by Reginald John Hollingdale and edited by Daniel Breazeale, 57–124. Cambridge: Cambridge University Press.

Nippel, Wolfgang. 2013. Der Diskurs über die orientalische Despotie im 18. und 19. Jahrhundert. Von Montesquieu zu Marx. In *Aneignung und Abgrenzung. Wechselnde Perspektiven auf die Antithese von "Ost" und "West" in der griechischen Antike*, edited by Nicolas Zenzen, Tonio Hölscher, and Kai Trampedach, 465–84. Heidelberg: Verlag Antike.

Nipperdey, Thomas. 2013 [1990]. *Deutsche Geschichte 1866–1918. Band I: Arbeitswelt und Bürgergeist*. Munich: Beck.

Nipperdey, Thomas. 2013 [1992]. *Deutsche Geschichte 1866–1918. Band II: Machtstaat vor der Demokratie*. Munich: Beck.

Nirenberg, David. 2013. *Anti-Judaism. The Western Tradition*. New York: Norton.

Nissel, Heinz. 2006. Vom Kulturerdteil Orient zur Islamischen Welt. Eine geographische Spurensuche. In *Vom Alten Orient zum Nahen Osten*, edited by Ilja Steffelbauer, and Khaled Hakami, 11–27. Essen: Magnus.

Nougayrol, Jean. 1957. Les Fragments en pierre du code hammourabien I. *Journal Asiatique* 245:339–66.

Nougayrol, Jean. 1958. Les Fragments en pierre du code hammourabien II. *Journal Asiatique* 246:143–50.

Nowak, Kurt. 1987. Die "antihistoristische Revolution". Symptome und Folgen der Krise historischer Weltorientierung nach dem Ersten Weltkrieg in Deutschland. In *Umstrittene Moderne. Die Zukunft der Neuzeit im Urteil der Epoche Ernst Troeltschs*, edited by Horst Renz, and Friedrich W. Graf, 133–71. Gütersloh: Gütersloher Verlagshaus.

Oellig, Marie. 2023. *Die Sukzession von Weltreichen. Zu den antiken Wurzeln einer geschichtsmächtigen Idee*. Stuttgart: Steiner.

Oelsner, Joachim. 2022. *Der Kodex Hammu-rapi. Textkritische Ausgabe und Übersetzung*. Münster: Zaphon.

Oettli, Samuel. 1903. *Das Gesetz Hammurabis und die Thora Israels. Eine religions- und rechtsgeschichtliche Parallele*. Leipzig: Deichert.

Oexle, Otto G., ed. 2007a. *Krise des Historismus – Krise der Wirklichkeit. Wissenschaft, Kunst und Literatur 1880–1932*. Göttingen: Vandenhoeck & Ruprecht.

Oexle, Otto G., 2007b. Krise des Historismus – Krise der Wirklichkeit. Eine Problemgeschichte der Moderne. In *Krise des Historismus – Krise der Wirklichkeit. Wissenschaft, Kunst und Literatur 1880–1932*, edited by Otto G. Oexle, 11–116. Göttingen: Vandenhoeck & Ruprecht.

Osterhammel, Jürgen. 1994. Neue Welten in der europäischen Geschichtsschreibung (1500–1800). In *Geschichtsdiskurs. Band 2: Anfänge des modernen historischen Denkens*, edited by Wolfgang Küttler, Jörn Rüsen, and Ernst Schulin, 202–15. Frankfurt a.M.: Fischer.

Osterhammel, Jürgen. 2014. *The Transformation of the World. A Global History of the Nineteenth Century*. Princeton: Princeton University Press.

Osterhammel, Jürgen. 2018. *Unfabling the East. The Enlightenment's Encounter with Asia*. Princeton: Princeton University Press.

Otto, Eckart. 1996 [1991]. Die Geschichte der Talion im Alten Orient und Israel. In Eckart Otto. *Kontinuum und Proprium. Studien zur Sozial- und Rechtsgeschichte des Alten Orients und des Alten Testaments*, 224–45. Wiesbaden: Harrassowitz.

Otto, Eckart. 2006. Das Recht der Hebräischen Bibel im Kontext der antiken Rechtsgeschichte. Literaturbericht 1994–2004. *Theologische Rundschau* 71:389–421.

Otto, Eckart. 2010. Das Bundesbuch und der "Kodex" Hammurapi. Das biblische Recht zwischen positiver und subversiver Rezeption von Keilschriftrecht. *Zeitschrift für Altorientalische und Biblische Rechtsgeschichte* 16:1–26.

Pallis, Svend A. 1956. *The Antiquity of Iraq. A Handbook of Assyriology*. Copenhagen: Munksgaard.

Palmer, Gesine, ed. 1999. *Torah – Nomos – Ius. Abendländischer Antinomismus und der Traum vom herrschaftsfreien Raum*. Berlin: Vorwerk.

Pasto, James. 1998. When the End is the Beginning? Or When the Biblical Past Is the Political Present. Some Thoughts on Ancient Israel, "Post-Exilic Judaism," and the Politics of Biblical Scholarship. *Scandinavian Journal of the Old Testament* 12:157–202.

Pasto, James. 2003. W. M. L. de Wette and the Invention of Post-Exilic Judaism. Political Historiography and Christian Allegory in Nineteenth-Century German Biblical Scholarship. In *Jews, Antiquity, and the Nineteenth-Century Imagination*, edited by Hayim Lapin, and Dale B. Martin, 33–52. Bethesda: University Press of Maryland.

Patterson, Annabel. 1988. *Pastoral and Ideology. Virgil to Valéry*. Oxford: Clarendon.

Paul, Shalom M. 1970. *Studies in the Book of the Covenant in the Light of Cuneiform and Biblical Law*. Leiden: Brill.

Pearce, Michael. 2024. Jugend: Youth, Spring, and Love. *MutualArt*. Available from https://www.mutualart.com/Article/Jugend--Youth--Spring--and-Love/AD554F052FCB6067, accessed 30 April 2025.

Peiser, Felix E. 1890. *Jurisprudentiae Babyonicae que supersunt. Commentatio assyriologica de nonnolis quae in museis Britannico et Berolinensi extant tabulis, quam seiosit et amplissini philosophorum ordinis*. Habilitationsschrift. Breslau: Schettler's Erben.

Peleg, Yaron. 2005. *Orientalism and the Hebrew Imagination*. Ithaca: Cornell University Press.

Pezold, Dirk von. 1971. *Cäsaromanie und Byzantinismus bei Wilhelm II*. Inaugural-Dissertation. Cologne: Universität zu Köln.

Pichl, Maximilian. 2024. *Law statt Order. Der Kampf um den Rechtsstaat*. Berlin: Suhrkamp.

Pieroth, Bodo. 2011. Historische Etappen des Rechtsstaats in Deutschland. *Jura* 33:729–35.

Polaschegg, Andrea. 2005. *Der andere Orientalismus. Regeln deutsch-morgenländischer Imagination im 19. Jahrhundert*. Berlin: De Gruyter.

Polaschegg, Andrea, and Michael Weichenhan, eds. 2017. *Berlin – Babylon. Eine deutsche Faszination 1890–1930*. Berlin: Wagenbach.

Post, Albert H. 1894. *Grundriss der ethnologischen Jurisprudenz. Band 1: Allgemeiner Teil*. Oldenburg: Schulzesche Hofbuchhandlung.

Pranzl, Rudolf. 2008. Das Verhältnis von Staat und Kirche/Religion im theresianisch-josephinischen Zeitalter. In *Josephinismus als Aufgeklärter Absolutismus*, edited by Helmut Reinalter, 17–52. Vienna: Böhlau.

Prümm, Hans P. 2012. Friedrich II. von Preußen und das Recht. Das Interpretationsverbot im ALR, der Prozess des Müllers Arnold und der Überfall auf Sachsen. *Zeitschrift für das juristische Studium* 1:24–37.

Purtschert, Patricia. 2010. On the Limit of Spirit. Hegel's Racism Revisited. *Philosophy & Social Criticism* 36:1039–51.

Puschner, Uwe, and Clemens Vollnhals, eds. 2012. *Die völkisch-religiöse Bewegung im Nationalsozialismus. Eine Beziehungs- und Konfliktgeschichte*. Göttingen: Vandenhoeck & Ruprecht.

Quidde, Ludwig. 1894. *Caligula. Eine Studie über römischen Cäsarenwahnsinn.* Leipzig: Friedrich.
Quidde, Ludwig. 1926. *Caligula. Eine Studie über römischen Cäsarenwahnsinn. Ergänzt durch Erinnerungen des Verfassers im Kampf gegen Cäsarismus und Byzantinismus.* Berlin: Hensel & Co.
Ranke, Leopold v. 1881. *Weltgeschichte. Erster Theil: Die älteste historische Völkergruppe und die Griechen. Erste Abtheilung.* Leipzig: Duncker & Humblot.
Ranke, Leopold v. 1971 [1854]. *Aus Werk und Nachlass. Band II: Über die Epochen der neueren Geschichte.* Edited by Theodor Schieder, and Helmut Berding. Munich: Oldenbourg.
Ranke, Leopold v. 1975a [1833]. Die Universalgeschichte (in ihrem allgemeinen und inneren Zusammenhang). In Leopold von Ranke. *Aus Werk und Nachlass. Band IV: Vorlesungseinleitungen*, edited by Volker Dotterich, and Walther P. Fuchs, 98–100. Munich: Oldenbourg.
Ranke, Leopold v. 1975b [1831/32]. Idee der Universalhistorie. In Leopold von Ranke. *Aus Werk und Nachlass. Band IV: Vorlesungseinleitungen*, edited by Volker Dotterich, and Walther P. Fuchs, 72–89. Munich: Oldenbourg.
Ranke, Leopold v. 2011 [1854]. On Progress in History (From the First Lecture to King Maximilian II of Bavaria "On the Epochs of Modern History", 1854). In *The Theory and Practice of History*, edited by Georg G. Iggers, 20–3. Abingdon: Routledge.
Rasmussen, Stig. 1986. *Carsten Niebuhr und die Arabische Reise 1761–1767.* Heide in Holstein: Westholsteinische Verlagsanstalt.
Rauchstein, Maike. 2017. *Fremde Vergangenheit. Zur Orientalistik des Göttinger Gelehrten Johann David Michaelis (1717–1791).* Bielefeld: transcript.
Rebentisch, Jost. 2000. *Die vielen Gesichter des Kaisers. Wilhelm II. in der deutschen und britischen Karikatur (1888–1918).* Berlin: Duncker & Humblot.
Reinalter, Helmut. 2002. Der Aufgeklärte Absolutismus – Geschichte und Perspektiven der Forschung. In *Der aufgeklärte Absolutismus im europäischen Vergleich*, edited by Helmut Reinalter, and Harm Klueting, 11–20. Vienna: Böhlau.
Reinalter, Helmut, and Harm Klueting, eds. 2002. *Der aufgeklärte Absolutismus im europäischen Vergleich.* Vienna: Böhlau.
Renger, Johannes. 1994. Noch einmal: Was war der "Kodex" Hammurapi – ein erlassenes Gesetz oder ein Rechtsbuch? In *Rechtskodifizierung und soziale Normen im interkulturellen Vergleich*, edited by Hans-Joachim Gehrke, 27–60. Tübingen: Narr.
Renger, Johannes. 2001. Altorientalistik und jüdische Gelehrte in Deutschland – Deutsche und österreichische Altorientalisten im Exil. In *Jüdische Intellektuelle und die Philologien in Deutschland*, edited by Wilfried Barner, and Christoph König, 247–66. Göttingen: Wallstein.
Reventlow, Ernst Graf zu. 1906. *Kaiser Wilhelm II. und die Byzantiner.* Munich: Lehmann.
Reventlow, Henning. 2001. *Epochen der Bibelauslegung. Band IV: Von der Aufklärung bis zum 20. Jahrhundert.* Munich: Beck.
Richter, Hedwig. 2021. *Aufbruch in die Moderne. Reform und Massenpolitisierung im Kaiserreich.* Berlin: Suhrkamp.
Ritter, Joachim. 1977 [1966]. Moralität und Sittlichkeit. Hegels Auseinandersetzung mit der kantischen Ethik. In Joachim Ritter. *Metaphysik und Politik. Studien zu Aristoteles und Hegel*, 281–309. Frankfurt a. M.: Suhrkamp.
Robinson, Andrew. 2012. *Cracking the Egyptian Code. The Revolutionary Life of Jean-François Champollion.* London: Thames & Hudson.
Rogerson, John W. 1984. *Old Testament Criticism in the Nineteenth Century. England and Germany.* London: SPCK.

Rohde, Achim. 2009. The Orient Within. Orientalism, Anti-Semitism and Gender in Eighteenth to Early Twentieth Century Germany. In *Fremde, Feinde und Kurioses. Innen- und Außenansichten unseres muslimischen Nachbarn*, edited by Benjamin Jokisch, Ulrich Rebstock, and Lawrence Conrad, 147–66. Berlin: De Gruyter.
Röhl, John C. G. 1995. *The Kaiser and His Court. Wilhelm II and the Government of Germany*. Cambridge: Cambridge University Press.
Röhl, John C. G. 2004. *Wilhelm II. The Kaiser's Personal Monarchy, 1888–1900*. Cambridge: Cambridge University Press.
Rohrbach, Paul. 1914. *Die Geschichte der Menschheit*. Königsstein: Langewiesche.
Rojek, Tim. 2017. *Hegels Begriff der Weltgeschichte. Eine wissenschaftstheoretische Studie*. Berlin: De Gruyter.
Rollinger, Robert. 2008. Babylon in der antiken Tradition – Herodot, Ktesias, Semiramis und die Hängenden Gärten. In *Babylon. Mythos und Wahrheit. Band 2: Wahrheit*, edited by Joachim Marzahn, Bernd Müller-Neuhof, Günther Schauerte, and Katja Sternitzke, 487–504. Munich: Hirmer.
Roscher, Wilhelm. 1847a. Umrisse zur Naturlehre der drei Staatsformen I. *Allgemeine Zeitschrift für Geschichte* 7:79–88.
Roscher, Wilhelm. 1847b. Umrisse zur Naturlehre der drei Staatsformen II. *Allgemeine Zeitschrift für Geschichte* 7:322–65.
Roscher, Wilhelm. 1847c. Umrisse zur Naturlehre der drei Staatsformen III. *Allgemeine Zeitschrift für Geschichte* 7:436–73.
Roscher, Wilhelm. 1874. *Geschichte der National-Oekonomik in Deutschland*. Munich: Oldenbourg.
Roscher, Wilhelm. 1889. Umrisse zur Naturlehre der absoluten Monarchie. *Zeitschrift für die gesamte Staatswissenschaft* 45:1–110.
Roth, Martha T. 1995a. *Law Collections from Mesopotamia and Asia Minor*. Atlanta: Scholars.
Roth, Martha T. 1995b. Mesopotamian Legal Traditions and the Laws of Hammurabi. *Chicago-Kent Law Review* 71:13–39.
Rotteck, Carl. 1840. Monarchie; monarchisches System; monarchisches Princip; Monarchismus. In *Staats-Lexikon oder Encyklopädie der Staatswissenschaften. Zehnter Band*, edited by Carl Rotteck, and Carl Welcker, 658–77. Altona: Hammerich.
Rubiés, Joan-Pau. 2005. Oriental Despotism and European Orientalism. Botero to Montesquieu. *Journal of Early Modern History* 9:109–80.
Rüsen, Jörn. 1993. *Konfigurationen des Historismus. Studien zur deutschen Wissenschaftskultur*. Frankfurt a. M.: Suhrkamp.
Rüthers, Bernd. 1988. *Entartetes Recht. Rechtslehren und Kronjuristen im Dritten Reich*. Munich: Beck.
Sæbø, Magne, ed. 2013. *Hebrew Bible, Old Testament. The History of Its Interpretation. Vol. 3/1: From Modernism to Post-Modernism. The Nineteenth Century. A Century of Modernism and Historicism*. Göttingen: Vandenhoeck & Ruprecht.
Said, Edward W. 2003 [1978]. *Orientalism*. London: Penguin.
Samerski, Stefan, ed. 2001. *Wilhelm II. und die Religion. Facetten einer Persönlichkeit und ihres Umfeldes*. Berlin: Duncker & Humblot.
Sasson, Jack M., ed. 1995. *Civilizations of the Ancient Near East. Vol. 1*. New York: Scribner.
Sawilla, Jan M. 2004. "Geschichte": Ein Produkt der deutschen Aufklärung? Eine Kritik an Reinhart Kosellecks Begriff des "Kollektivsingulars Geschichte". *Zeitschrift für historische Forschung* 31:381–428.

Sawilla, Jan M. 2011. Geschichte und Geschichten zwischen Providenz und Machbarkeit. Überlegungen zu Reinhart Kosellecks Semantik historischer Zeiten. In *Begriffene Geschichte. Beiträge zum Werk Reinhart Kosellecks*, edited by Hans Joas, and Peter Vogt, 387–422. Berlin: Suhrkamp.

Sayce, Archibald H. 1884a. *Fresh Light from the Ancient Monuments. A Sketch from the Most Striking Confirmations of the Bible from Recent Discoveries in Egypt, Palestine, Assyria, Babylonia*. London: Religious Tract-Society.

Sayce, Archibald H. 1884b. *The Witness of Ancient Monuments to the Old Testament Scriptures*. London: Religious Tract-Society.

Sayce, Archibald H. 1894. *The "Higher Criticism" and the Verdict of the Monuments*. London: Society for Promoting Christian Knowledge.

Scheel, Benjamin. 2023. The "Babylonische Palmen" at the U-Bahnhof Klosterstraße in Berlin Mitte. *Berliner Antike-Blog*. Available from https://blogs.fu-berlin.de/knowtheancients/2023/02/21/the-babylonische-palmen-at-the-u-bahnhof-klosterstrasse-in-berlin-mitte, accessed 30 April 2025.

Scheffler, Thomas. 2003. "Fertile Crescent", "Orient", "Middle East". The Changing Mental Maps of Southwest Asia. *European Review of History* 10:253–72.

Scheil, Jean-Vincent. 1902. Code de Lois (Droit-Privé) de Hammurabi, Roi de Babylone vers l'an 2000 avant Jésus-Christ. In *Mémoires de la Mission Archéologique de Perse. Mémoires publiés sous la direction de J. de Morgan. Tome IV: Textes Élamites-Sémitiques*, edited by Jacques de Morgan, 11–162. Paris: Leroux.

Scheil, Jean-Vincent. 1904. *La Loi de Hammourabi. Vers 2000 AV. J.C.* Paris: Leroux.

Schild, Wolfgang. 2018. Napoleon und Hegel. In *Europa nach Napoleon*, edited by Christoph Enders, Michael Kahlo, and Andreas Mosbacher, 59–78. Paderborn: mentis.

Schilling, Lothar, ed. 2008. *Absolutismus – ein unersetzliches Forschungskonzept? Eine deutsch-französische Bilanz*. Paris: Deutsches Historisches Institut.

Schirrmacher, Friedrich W. 1865. *Kaiser Friedrich der Zweite. Entscheidungskampf zwischen Papstthum und Kaiserthum. Vierter Band*. Göttingen: Vandenhoeck & Ruprecht.

Schlözer, August L. v. 1785. Etwas über geheime Verbindungen. *A. L. Schlözer's Stats-Anzeigen* 31:257–93.

Schmid, Konrad. 2021. Gott als Gesetzgeber. Entstehung und Bedeutung des Gottesrechts der Tora im Rahmen der altorientalischen Rechtsgeschichte. *Zeitschrift für Theologie und Kirche* 118:267–94.

Schmidt, Christian, and Benno Zabel, eds. 2021. *Politik im Rechtsstaat*. Baden-Baden: Nomos.

Schmidt, Jochen. 1985a. *Die Geschichte des Genie-Gedankens in der deutschen Literatur, Philosophie und Politik 1770–1845. Band 1: Von der Aufklärung bis zum Idealismus*. Darmstadt: Wissenschaftliche Buchgesellschaft.

Schmidt, Jochen. 1985b. *Die Geschichte des Genie-Gedankens in der deutschen Literatur, Philosophie und Politik 1770–1845. Band 2: Von der Romantik bis zum Ende des Dritten Reiches*. Darmstadt: Wissenschaftliche Buchgesellschaft.

Schnädelbach, Herbert. 1974. *Geschichtsphilosophie nach Hegel. Die Probleme des Historismus*. Freiburg: Alber.

Schneider, Friedrich, ed. 1941. *Universalstaat oder Nationalstaat. Macht und Ende des Ersten deutschen Reiches. Die Streitschriften von Heinrich v. Sybel und Julius Ficker zur deutschen Kaiserpolitik des Mittelalters*. Innsbruck: Universitätsverlag Wagner.

Schnicke, Falko. 2014. *Die männliche Disziplin. Zur Vergeschlechtlichung der deutschen Geschichtswissenschaft 1780–1900*. Göttingen: Wallstein.

Schnurbein, Stefanie v., and Justus H. Ulbricht, eds. 2001. *Völkische Religion und Krisen der Moderne. Entwürfe "arteigener" Glaubenssysteme seit der Jahrhundertwende.* Würzburg: Königshausen & Neumann.

Schreiner, Wolfgang. 1998. "Wann kommt der Retter aus Deutschland?" Formen und Funktionen von politischem Messianismus in der Weimarer Republik. *Saeculum* 49:107–60.

Schulin, Ernst. 1958. *Die weltgeschichtliche Erfassung des Orients bei Hegel und Ranke.* Göttingen: Vandenhoeck & Ruprecht.

Scott, H. M. 1983. Whatever Happened to the Enlightened Despots? *History and Theory* 68:245–57.

Scott, Hamish M., ed. 1990a. *Enlightened Absolutism. Reform and Reformers in Later Eighteenth-Century Europe.* Basingstoke: Macmillan.

Scott, Hamish M., 1990b. Introduction: The Problem of Enlightened Absolutism. In *Enlightened Absolutism. Reform and Reformers in Later Eighteenth-Century Europe*, edited by Hamish M. Scott, 1–35. Basingstoke: Macmillan.

Seifert, Arno. 1983. "Verzeitlichung". Zur Kritik einer neueren Frühneuzeitkategorie. *Zeitschrift für historische Forschung* 10:447–77.

Sellin, Volker. 1976. Friedrich der Große und der aufgeklärte Absolutismus. Ein Beitrag zur Klärung eines umstrittenen Begriffs. In *Soziale Bewegung und politische Verfassung. Beiträge zur Geschichte der modernen Welt*, edited by Ulrich Engelhardt, Volker Sellin, and Horst Stuke, 83–112. Stuttgart: Klett.

Sellin, Volker. 2011. *Gewalt und Legitimität. Die europäische Monarchie im Zeitalter der Revolutionen.* Munich: Oldenbourg.

Seymour, Michael. 2014. *Babylon. Legend, History and the Ancient History.* London: Tauris.

Shavit, Yaacov, and Mordechai Eran. 2007. *The Hebrew Bible Reborn. From Holy Scripture to the Book of Books. A History of Biblical Culture and the Battles over the Bible in Modern Judaism.* Berlin: De Gruyter.

Sheehan, Jonathan. 2005. *The Enlightenment Bible. Translation, Scholarship, Culture.* Princeton: Princeton University Press.

Siemann, Wolfram. 1990. *Gesellschaft im Aufbruch. Deutschland 1848–1871.* Frankfurt a. M.: Suhrkamp.

Smend, Rudolf. 1989. *Deutsche Alttestamentler in drei Jahrhunderten.* Göttingen: Vandenhoeck & Ruprecht.

Smith, George. 1876. *The Chaldean Account of Genesis. Containing the Description of the Creation, the Fall of Man, the Deluge, the Tower of Babel, the Times of the Patriarchs, and Nimrod. Babylonian Fables, and Legends of the Gods. From the Cuneiform Inscriptions.* London: Sampson.

Smith, Woodruff D. 1991. *Politics and the Sciences of Culture in Germany, 1840–1920.* New York: Oxford University Press.

Sösemann, Bernd, and Gregor Vogt-Spira, eds. 2012. *Friedrich der Große in Europa. Geschichte einer wechselvollen Beziehung.* Vol. 2. Stuttgart: Steiner.

Spendel, Günter. 1983. *Josef Kohler. Bild eines Universaljuristen.* Heidelberg: Decker & Müller.

Spielmann, Heinz. 1988. *Jugend 1896–1940. Zeitschrift einer Epoche. Aspekte einer Wochenschrift "Für Kunst und Leben".* Dortmund: Harenberg.

Stahl, Friedrich J. 1845. *Das monarchische Prinzip. Eine staatsrechtlich-politische Abhandlung.* Heidelberg: Mohr.

Stahl, Friedrich J. 1846. *Die Philosophie des Rechts. Zweiter Band: Rechts- und Staatslehre auf Grundlage christlicher Weltanschauung. Zweite Abtheilung.* Heidelberg: Mohr.

Stein, Lorenz von. 1850. *Geschichte der socialen Bewegung in Frankreich von 1789 bis auf unsere Tage. Dritter Band: Das Königtum und die Souveränität der französischen Gesellschaft seit der Februarrevolution 1848*. Leipzig: Wiegand.
Stern, Fritz. 1974. *The Politics of Cultural Despair. A Study in the Rise of the Germanic Ideology*. Berkely: University of California Press.
Stockhorst, Stefanie. 2011. Novus ordo temporum. Reinhart Kosellecks These von der Verzeitlichung des Geschichtsbewusstseins durch die Aufklärungshistoriographie in methodenkritischer Perspektive. In *Begriffene Geschichte. Beiträge zum Werk Reinhart Kosellecks*, edited by Hans Joas, and Peter Vogt, 359–86. Berlin: Suhrkamp.
Stoetzler, Marcel. 2008. *The State, the Nation, & the Jews. Liberalism and the Antisemitism Dispute in Bismarck's Germany*. Lincoln: University of Nebraska Press.
Stolleis, Michael. 1990. Rechtsstaat. In *Handwörterbuch zur deutschen Rechtsgeschichte*. Vol. 4, edited by Adalbert Erler, and Ekkehard Kaufmann, 367–75. Berlin: Erich Schmidt.
Stolleis, Michael. ed. 1996. *Policey im Europa der Frühen Neuzeit*. Frankfurt a. M.: Klostermann.
Stolleis, Michael. 2014. *History of Social Law in Germany*. Berlin: Springer.
Streck, Michael P. 1999. Hammurabi oder Hammurapi? *Archiv orientální* 67:665–9.
Stuke, Horst. 1972. Aufklärung. In *Geschichtliche Grundbegriffe. Historisches Lexikon zur politisch-sozialen Sprache in Deutschland*. Vol. 1, edited by Otto Brunner, Werner Conze, and Reinhart Koselleck, 243–342. Stuttgart: Klett-Cotta.
Sweek, Joel. 1995. The Monuments, the Babel-Bibel-Streit and Responses to Historical Criticism. In *The Pitcher Is Broken. Memorial Essays for Gösta W. Ahlström*, edited by Steven W. Holloway, and Lowell K. Handy, 400–19. Sheffield: Sheffield Academy Press.
Taylor, Charles. 1975. *Hegel*. Cambridge: Cambridge University Press.
Thiele, Alexander. 2021. *Der konstituierte Staat. Eine Verfassungsgeschichte der Neuzeit*. Frankfurt a. M.: Campus.
Thompson, Robert J. 1970. *Moses and the Law in a Century of Criticism since Graf*. Leiden: Brill.
Thompson, Thomas L. 1999. *The Mythic Past. Biblical Archaeology and the Myth of Israel*. New York: Basic Books.
Thomsen, Marcus. 2005. *"Ein feuriger Herr des Anfangs ...". Kaiser Friedrich II. in der Auffassung der Nachwelt*. Ostfildern: Thorbecke.
Tibebu, Teshale. 2011. *Hegel and the Third World. The Making of Eurocentrism in World History*. Syracuse: Syracuse University Press.
Tidrick, Kathryn. 1981. *Heart-Beguiling Araby*. Cambridge: Cambridge University Press.
Tiele, Cornelis P. 1886. *Babylonisch-assyrische Geschichte. Teil 1: Von den ältesten Zeiten bis zum Tode Sargons II*. Gotha: Perthes.
Toral-Niehoff, Isabel. 2002. Der edle Beduine. In *Der Alteritätsdiskurs des Edlen Wilden. Exotismus, Anthropologie und Zivilisationskritik am Beispiel eines europäischen Topos*, edited by Monika Fludernik, 281–96. Würzburg: Ergon-Verlag.
Treitschke, Heinrich v. 1879. *Deutsche Geschichte im Neunzehnten Jahrhundert. Band 1: Bis zum zweiten Pariser Frieden*. Leipzig: Hirzel.
Troeltsch, Ernst. 2002. Die Krisis des Historismus. In *Ernst Troeltsch. Kritische Gesamtausgabe. Band 15: Schriften zur Politik und Kulturphilosophie (1918–1923)*, edited by Gangolf Hübinger, 437–55. Berlin: De Gruyter.
Ullerich, Robert. 2011. *Rechtsstaat und Rechtsgemeinschaft im Europarecht. Eine dogmatische und terminologische Untersuchung der europäischen Verträge und der Rechtsprechung des*

Europäischen Gerichtshofs. Zugleich eine Gegenüberstellung zum Bundesverfassungsrecht. Baden-Baden: Nomos.
Ungnad, Arthur. 1914. *Babylonische Briefe aus der Zeit der Hammurapi-Dynastie.* Leipzig: Hinrichs.
Ungnad, Arthur. 1919. *Briefe König Hammurapis (2123–2081 v. Chr.).* Berlin: Curtius.
Ussishkin, David. 1980. The 'Lachisch Reliefs' and the City of Lachisch. *Israel Exploration Journal* 30:174–95.
Van de Mieroop, Marc. 2005. *King Hammurabi of Babylon. A Biography.* Malden: Blackwell.
Vico, Giambattista. 1744. *Principi di Scienza Nuova d'intorno alla commune Natura delle Nazioni.* Naples: Nella Stamperia Muziana.
Voigt, Georg. 1871. Die deutsche Kaisersage. *Historische Zeitschrift* 26:131–87.
Wardenga, Ute. 1992. Orientbilder in der Deutschen Geographie im 19. und 20. Jahrhundert. In *Beziehungen zwischen Orient und Okzident. Interdisziplinäre und interregionale Forschungen,* edited by Manfred Büttner, and Wilhelm Leitner, 185–210. Bochum: Universitätsverlag Brockmeyer.
Wartke, Ralf-Bernhard. 2005. *Sam'al. Ein aramäischer Stadtstaat des 10. bis 8. Jhs. v. Chr. und die Geschichte seiner Erforschung.* Berlin: Staatliche Museen zu Berlin.
Wattenbach, Wilhelm. 1868. *Ninive und Babylon. Zwei Vorträge.* Heidelberg: Bassermann.
Weber, Max. 2019. *Economy and Society.* Translated and edited by Keith Teibe. Cambridge [MA]: Harvard University Press.
Weichenhan, Michael. 2016. *Der Panbabylonismus. Die Faszination des himmlischen Buches im Zeitalter der Zivilisation.* Berlin: Frank & Timme.
Weigend, Friedrich, Bodo M. Baumunk, and Thomas Brune. 1978. *Keine Ruhe im Kyffhäuser. Das Nachleben der Staufer. Ein Lesebuch zur deutschen Geschichte.* Stuttgart: Theiss.
Weir, Todd H. 2014. *Secularism and Religion in Nineteenth-Century Germany. The Rise of the Fourth Confession.* Cambridge: Cambridge University Press.
Weir, Todd H. 2015. Germany and the New Global History of Secularism. Questioning the Postcolonial Genealogy. *The Germanic Review* 90:6–20.
Welcker, Carl. 1813. *Die letzten Gründe von Recht, Staat und Strafe philosophische und nach den Gesetzen der merkwürdigsten Völker rechtshistorisch entwickelt.* Gießen: Heyer.
Wellhausen, Julius. 1878. *Prolegomena zur Geschichte Israels.* Berlin: Reimer.
Wellhausen, Julius. 1885. *Skizzen und Vorarbeiten. Zweites Heft: Die Composition des Hexateuchs.* Berlin: Reimer.
Wellhausen, Julius. 1894. *Israelitische und jüdische Geschichte.* Berlin: Reimer.
Westbrook, Raymond. 2009a [1989]. Cuneiform Law Codes and the Origins of Legislation. In *Law from the Tigris to the Tiber. The Writings of Raymond Westbrook. Vol. 1: The Shared Tradition,* edited by Bruce Wells, and F. R. Magdalene, 73–96. Winona Lake: Eisenbrauns.
Westbrook, Raymond. 2009b [1986]. Lex Talionis and Exodus 21:22–25. In *Law from the Tigris to the Tiber. The Writings of Raymond Westbrook. Vol. 2: Cuneiform and Biblical Sources,* edited by Bruce Wells, and F. Rachel Magdalene, 341–60. Winona Lake: Eisenbrauns.
Westbrook, Raymond. 2009c [1995]. Social Justice in the Ancient Near East. In *Law from the Tigris to the Tiber. The Writings of Raymond Westbrook. Vol. 1: The Shared Tradition,* edited by Bruce Wells, and F. Rachel Magdalene, 143–60. Winona Lake: Eisenbrauns.
Wiedemann, Felix. 2012. Zwischen Völkerflut und Heroismus. Zur Repräsentation der Beduinen in kulturhistorischen Deutungen des Vorderen Orients um 1900. In *Die Begegnung mit Fremden und das Geschichtsbewusstsein,* edited by Judith Becker, and Bettina Braun, 207–28. Göttingen: Vandenhoeck & Ruprecht.

Wiedemann, Felix. 2014. Klios Ärger mit den Söhnen Noachs. Wanderungsnarrative in den Wissenschaften vom Alten Orient und die Rolle der Völkertafel. In *Genealogie und Migrationsmythen im antiken Mittelmeerraum und auf der arabischen Halbinsel*, edited by Almut-Barbara Renger, and Isabel Toral-Niehoff, 59–84. Berlin: Edition Topoi.

Wiedemann, Felix. 2020. *Am Anfang war Migration. Wanderungsnarrative in den Wissenschaften vom Alten Orient im 19. und frühen 20. Jahrhundert*. Tübingen: Mohr Siebeck.

Wiedemann, Felix. 2021. Orientalismus. Version 2.0. *Docupedia-Zeitgeschichte*. Available from http://dx.doi.org/10.14765/zzf.dok-2185, accessed 31 May 2024.

Wiedemann, Felix. 2023. "Apologie der Semiten". Der Münchner Semitist und Assyriologe Fritz Hommel zwischen Philo- und Antisemitismus. *Zeitschrift für Religions- und Geistesgeschichte* 75:239–59.

Wiedemann, Felix. 2024a. Moses or Hammurabi? Law, Morality & Modernity in Ancient Near Eastern Studies. In *Moses Among the Moderns. German Constructions of Biblical Law, 1750–1930*, edited by Paul M. Kurtz, 90–114. Leiden: Brill.

Wiedemann, Felix. 2024b. *Rassenbilder aus der Vergangenheit. Die anthropologische Lektüre antiker Bildwerke in den Wissenschaften des 19. und 20. Jahrhunderts*. Göttingen: Wallstein.

Wienfort, Monika. 2012. Gesetzbücher, Justizreformen und der Müller-Arnold-Fall. In *Friedrich der Große in Europa. Geschichte einer wechselvollen Beziehung*. Vol. 2, edited by Bernd Sösemann, and Gregor Vogt-Spira, 33–46. Stuttgart: Steiner.

Wiese, Christian. 1999. *Wissenschaft des Judentums und protestantische Theologie im wilhelminischen Deutschland. Ein Schrei ins Leere?* Tübingen: Mohr Siebeck.

Wiesehöfer, Josef, and Stephan Conermann, eds. 2002. *Carsten Niebuhr (1733–1815) und seine Zeit*. Stuttgart: Steiner.

Wiggermann, Frans A. M. 2006–2008. Ring und Stab (Ring and Rod). In *Reallexikon der Assyriologie und Vorderasiatischen Archäologie. Elfter Band*, edited by Michael P. Streck, 414–21. Berlin: De Gruyter.

Wilhelm II. 1903. Babel und Bibel. Ein Handschreiben Seiner Majestät Kaiser Wilhelms des Zweiten an das Vorstandsmitglied der Deutschen Orientgesellschaft, Admiral Hollmann. *Die Grenzboten. Zeitschrift für Politik, Literatur und Kunst* 62:493–6.

Wilhelm II. 1938. *Das Königtum im alten Mesopotamien*. Berlin: De Gruyter.

Winckelmann, Eduard. 1863. *Geschichte Kaiser Friedrichs des Zweiten und seiner Reiche 1212–1235*. Berlin: Wittler & Sohn.

Winckler, Hugo. 1902. *Die Gesetze Hammurabis, Königs von Babylon um 2250 v. Chr. Das älteste Gesetzbuch der Welt*. Leipzig: Hinrichs.

Winckler, Hugo. 1904. *Die Gesetze Hammurabis in Umschrift und Übersetzung*. Leipzig: Hinrichs.

Winckler, Hugo. 1913. Das alte Westasien. In *Weltgeschichte. Begründet von Hans F. Helmolt. Zweiter Band: Westasien*, edited by Armin Tille, 1–240. Leipzig: Bibliographisches Institut.

Winterling, Aloys. 2011. *Caligula. A Biography*. Berkeley: University of California Press.

Wittkau, Annette. 1992. *Historismus. Zur Geschichte des Begriffs und des Problems*. Göttingen: Vandenhoeck & Ruprecht.

Wittler, Kathrin. 2019. *Morgenländischer Glanz. Eine deutsche jüdische Literaturgeschichte (1750–1850)*. Tübingen: Mohr Siebeck.

Wiwjorra, Ingo. 2002. "Ex oriente lux" – "Ex septentrione lux". Über den Widerstreit zweier Identitätsmythen. In *Prähistorie und Nationalsozialismus. Die mittel- und osteuropäische Ur- und Frühgeschichtsforschung in den Jahren 1933–1945*, edited by Achim Leube, and Morten Hegewisch, 73–106. Heidelberg: Synchron.

Wokoeck, Ursula. 2009. *German Orientalism. The Study of the Middle East and Islam from 1800 to 1945*. London: Routledge.

Wood, Allen W. 2017. Hegel's Critique of Morality. In *G. W. F. Hegel. Grundlinien der Philosophie des Rechts*, edited by Ludwig Siep, 131–48. Berlin: De Gruyter.

Wright, David P. 2009. *Inventing God's Law. How the Covenant Code of the Bible Used and Revised the Laws of Hammurabi*. New York: Oxford University Press.

Zink MacHaffie, Barbara. 1981. "Monumental Facts and Higher Critical Fancies". Archaeology and the Popularization of Old Testament Criticism in Nineteenth-Century Britain. *Church History* 50:316–28.

Zwiep, Irene. 2024. Gesetz als Gegensatz. The Modern Halachic Game. In *Moses Among the Moderns. German Constructions of Biblical Law, 1750–1930*, edited by Paul M. Kurtz, 117–45. Leiden: Brill.

Author Index

Alexander the Great   30, 31, 38
Alt, Albrecht   82
Arnold, Christian   56, 64

Bastian, Adolf   75
Bezold, Carl   15
Breasted, James Henry   71
Bülow, Bernhard von   52
Burckhardt, Jacob   28f., 31, 46

Caesar, Julius   30
Caligula   52f.
Chamberlain, Houston Stewart   1, 6f., 9, 33f., 88
Champollion, Jean-François   16
Charlemagne   6, 30, 33, 39
Cohen, Hermann   86
Cohn, Georg   75

De Wette, Wilhelm Martin Lebebrecht   73
Delitzsch, Friedrich   1, 3, 8, 24, 31f., 61, 66, 70, 73–75, 77f., 80, 95f., 98
Diderot, Dennis   41
Droysen, Johann Gustav   85

Elizabeth I (of England)   42
Ernst August I (of Hanover)   50

Feuchtwang, David   78, 86
Foucault, Michel   57f.
Frederick I (Barbarossa)   45
Frederick II (of Prussia)   6, 30, 38f., 43–46, 50, 55f., 58, 60, 64, 66, 88
Frederick II (of Sicily)   45f., 60, 89
Frederick William IV   50
Freytag, Gustav   53

Gatterer, Christoph   23
Grimme, Hubert   31, 81–83

Habermas, Jürgen   62f., 84, 93
Hampe, Karl   46f.
Harnack, Adolf von   1

Harper, Francis   4
Hart, Herbert L. A.   91
Hartung, Fritz   40
Hegel, Georg Wilhelm Friedrich   8, 12, 18, 21–23, 26–28, 30f., 37, 69, 83f.
Herder, Johann Gottfried   20–23, 26
Herodotus   20
Hintze, Otto   44f., 49, 66
Hollmann, Friedrich   32
Hommel, Fritz   24f., 73f., 86, 96

Jeremias, Johannes   81, 86

Kant, Immanuel   8, 12, 23, 33, 40–42, 62, 69, 84f., 92
Kantorowicz, Ernst   60
Kelsen, Hans   65, 91, 96
King, Leonard William   24, 54
Kittel, Rudolf   3
Koldewey, Robert   15, 34
König, Eduard   73–75
Koschaker, Paul   4, 35, 76, 96
Koselleck, Reinhart   17
Koser, Reinhold   43f.

Landsberger, Benno   96
Lhéritier, Michel   40
Lombroso, Cesare   29f.
Louis XIV (of France)   43f.

Meissner, Bruno   3, 31, 39, 66
Michaelis, Johann David   70, 82
Mohl, Robert von   63
Montesquieu, Charles de   41f.
Müller, David Heinrich   75–78, 81, 96
Mürdter, Friedrich   24, 31

Napoleon   12, 14, 30f., 38, 59f.
Naumann, Friedrich   59
Nebukadnezzar
Niebuhr, Carsten   70

Oettli, Samuel   78f., 86f., 96

Peiser, Felix   3 f., 9, 35, 39, 55, 66, 91, 96
Philip II (of Spain)   42

Ranke, Leopold von   18 f., 23 f., 26, 85
Roscher, Wilhelm   42–45, 88
Rotteck, Karl von   42

Savigny, Carl von   90
Sayce, Archibald Henry   73
Scheil, Vincent   4, 12
Schlözer, August Ludwig von   23, 42
Schmitt, Carl   65, 97
Smith, George   74 f.

Tiele, Cornelis Petrus   24

Treitschke, Heinrich von   28, 43, 50
Troeltsch, Ernst   26

Ungnad, Arthur   4, 36, 54 f., 66, 96

Vico, Giambattista   21

Weber, Max   30, 60
Welcker, Carl   63
Wilhelm II (German Emperor)   1, 6, 32–34, 39, 51 f., 55–57, 59 f., 88 f.
Winckler, Hugo   4, 25, 31, 56, 66, 69, 77 f., 88–90, 92 f., 96

The following volumes have been published in this series:

Volume 2
Detel, Wolfgang. *Subjektive und objektive Zeit: Aristoteles und die moderne Zeit-Theorie.* Berlin/Boston: De Gruyter, 2021.

Volume 3
Singer, P. N. *Time for the Ancients: Measurement, Theory, Experience.* Berlin/Boston: De Gruyter, 2022.

Volume 4
Gertzen, Thomas L. *Aber die Zeit fürchtet die Pyramiden: Die Wissenschaften vom Alten Orient und die zeitliche Dimension von Kulturgeschichte.* Berlin/Boston: De Gruyter, 2022.

Volume 6
Zachhuber, Johannes. *Time and Soul: From Aristotle to St. Augustine.* Berlin/Boston: De Gruyter, 2022.

Volume 7
Golitsis, Pantelis. *Damascius' Philosophy of Time.* Berlin/Boston: De Gruyter, 2023.

Volume 8
Defaux, Olivier. *La Table des rois: Contribution à l'histoire textuelle des ›Tables faciles‹ de Ptolémée.* Berlin/Boston: De Gruyter, 2023.

Volume 9
Fischer, Julia (ed.). *Zwiegespräche über die Zeit: Dialoge in der Berlin-Brandenburgischen Akademie der Wissenschaften aus Anlass des sechzigsten Geburtstags von Christoph Markschies.* Berlin/Boston: De Gruyter, 2024.

Volume 10
Walter, Anke (ed.). *The Temporality of Festivals: Approaches to Festive Time in Ancient Babylon, Greece, Rome, and Medieval China.* Berlin/Boston: De Gruyter, 2024.

Volume 12
Sieroka, Norman. *Zeit-Hören: Erfahrungen, Taktungen, Musik.* Berlin/Boston: De Gruyter, 2024.

Volume 13
Birk, Ralph/Coulon, Laurent (eds.). *The Thebaid in Times of Crisis: Revolt and Response in Ptolemaic Egypt.* Berlin/Boston: De Gruyter, 2025.

Volume 14
Pallavidini, Marta. *(A)synchronic (Re)actions: Crises and Their Perception in Hittite History.* Berlin/Boston: De Gruyter, 2025.

Volume 15
Nosch, Marie-Louise Bech. *Time and Textiles in Ancient Greece.* Berlin/Boston: De Gruyter, 2025.

Volume 16
Klinger, Jörg. *Das Erfassen von Zeit im Kontext der Vergangenheit.* Berlin/Boston: De Gruyter, 2026.

Volume 17
Zachhuber, Johannes. *Time and History in Denis Pétau. Philosophy, Science, and Religion in Early Modern France.* Berlin/Boston: De Gruyter, 2026.

Volume 18
Ossendrijver, Mathieu. *Conceptions of Cyclicity in Babylonian and Greco-Roman Scholarship.* Berlin/Boston: De Gruyter, 2025.

Volume 19
Schumacher, Lydia. *From Eternal to Everlasting: God and Time in Franciscan Thought.* Berlin/Boston: De Gruyter, 2026.

www.ingramcontent.com/pod-product-compliance
Lightning Source LLC
Chambersburg PA
CBHW051615230426
43668CB00013B/2120